Treating Coexisting Psychiatric And Addictive Disorders

A Practical Guide

Edited by Norman S. Miller, M.D.

HAZELDEN®

Hazelden Educational Materials
Center City, Minnesota 55012-0176

Library of Congress Cataloging-in-Publication Data:

Treating coexisting psychiatric and addictive disorders : A practical guide / edited by Norman S. Miller.

p. cm.

Includes bibliographical references and index.

ISBN: 0-89486-972-8 : $24.95

1. Dual diagnosis—Treatment. 2. Dual diagnosis—Treatment—Case studies. I. Miller, Norman S.

[DNLM: 1. Mental Disorders—therapy. 2. Substance Dependence—therapy. 3. Mental Disorders—complications. 4. Substance Dependence—complications. WM 270 T7813 1994]

RC564.68.T74 1994

616.86'06—dc20

DNLM/DLC 94-4696

for Library of Congress CIP

Editor's note:

Hazelden Educational Materials offers a variety of information on chemical dependency and related areas. Our publications do not necessarily represent Hazelden's programs, nor do they officially speak for any Twelve Step organization.

The case histories and personal stories in this book are fictional or composites of many individuals. Any resemblance to any one person, living or dead, is purely coincidental.

The Twelve Steps of A.A. are taken from *Alcoholics Anonymous,* 3d ed., published by A.A. World Services, Inc., New York, N.Y., 59-60. Reprinted with permission. Alcoholics Anonymous is for recovery from alcoholism, and Twelve Step programs patterned after A.A. address other problems.

Contents

Treatments

Delivery

Figures and Tables

Figures

Tables

Contributors

John N. Chappel, M.D., is certified in addiction medicine (1986) by the American Society of Addiction Medicine, and in addiction psychiatry (1993) by the American Board of Psychiatry and Neurology. Dr. Chappel is professor of psychiatry at the University of Nevada, Reno, and medical director for the Addictions Program at West Hills Hospital in Reno. His major focus of interest is in the education of health care professionals in the treatment of addictive disorders.

J. Calvin Chatlos, M.D., is trained as a pediatrician, child and adolescent psychiatrist, and addictionologist. He is assistant professor of clinical psychiatry at the University of Medicine and Dentistry of New Jersey in Newark, New Jersey. His major interests have been in the use of a developmental perspective to integrate research, prevention, and treatment of addiction and mental disorders.

H. Westley Clark, M.D., J.D., M.P.H., assistant clinical professor of psychiatry at the University of California, San Francisco, and chief of Associated Substance Abuse Programs at the San Francisco Veterans Administration Medical Center.

James Cocores, M.D., has eight years of experience in dual diagnosis treatment. He is senior author of fifty psychiatric articles and book chapters, editor of *The Clinical Management of Nicotine Dependence* (New York: Springer, 1991), and author of *The 800-COCAINE Book of Drug and Alcohol Recovery* (New York: Villard Books, 1990). Dr. Cocores is program director of Spruce Hill Treatment Center in Henryville, Pennsylvania.

Robert E. Drake, M.D., Ph.D., is director of the New Hampshire-Dartmouth Psychiatric Research Center and a professor of psychiatry at Dartmouth Medical School.

Robert L. DuPont, M.D., is president of the Institute for Behavior and Health, Inc., a nonprofit research organization, and vice president of Bensinger, DuPont and Associates, Inc., a national consulting firm dealing with addiction in the workplace. He has an active practice of general psychiatry and is clinical professor of psychiatry at the Georgetown University School of Medicine in Washington, D.C. Dr. DuPont was the first director of the National Institute on Drug Abuse (NIDA).

JAMES FINE, M.D., is clinical associate professor in psychiatry at Health Science Center and director at Kings County Addictive Disease Hospital in New York. He also serves as medical director of Ridge Associates in Brooklyn, New York.

MARK S. GOLD, M.D., is professor in the Departments of Neuroscience and Psychiatry at the University of Florida College of Medicine. Dr. Gold is the author of nearly seven hundred medical books, scientific papers, and chapters. In addition to his teaching and research, Dr. Gold is quite active in local, national, and international drug education and prevention and serves on the board of such organizations as DARE, PRIDE, and the American Council for Drug Education.

MICHAEL S. LEVY, PH.D., is clinical director, Center for Behavioral Medicine, at Southwood Community Hospital in Norfolk, Massachusetts. He is also a faculty member at the Center for Addiction Studies at the Cambridge Hospital and Harvard Medical School as well as a clinical instructor in psychology at Harvard Medical School. He maintains a private practice in psychotherapy in Andover, Massachusetts.

THOMAS F. MCGOVERN, ED.D., is associate professor in the Department of Psychiatry at Texas Tech University Health Sciences Center, Lubbock in Texas. He is also affiliated with the Southwest Institute for Addictive Diseases. He is director of the Bioethics Program and chairs the Bioethics Committee at the University Medical Center. His research centers on the affective components of addiction, with particular focus on loss-grief issues; further interests included health care ethics, spiritual issues in addiction, and the evolution of addiction counseling. He is editor of the *Alcoholism Treatment Quarterly*.

NORMAN S. MILLER, M.D., is associate professor of psychiatry and neurology at the University of Illinois at Chicago and the West Side Veterans Administration Medical Center. He is chief of Addiction Programs. He is board-certified in psychiatry, neurology, and clinical neurophysiology; he also has added qualifications in addiction psychiatry and certification in addiction medicine. He is editor of the *Comprehensive Handbook of Drug and Alcohol Addiction*, published by Marcel-Dekker, Inc.

DAVID MEE-LEE, M.D., is medical director of Community Systems, Behavioral Medicine Service, at Castle Medical Center in Honolulu. As Medical Director, he assists in the clinical and medical quality of outpatient and EAP programs, especially in mixed psychiatric and addiction medicine issues. Dr. Mee Lee has had a number of articles published on addiction in various publications and has developed an instrument for individualized treatment planning, the *Recovery Attitude and Treatment Evaluator* (RAATE).

KENNETH MINKOFF, M.D., is chief of psychiatry at Choate Health Systems in Woburn, Massachusetts, and assistant professor of psychiatry at Harvard Medical School. He is certified in addiction psychiatry and a nationally known expert on the chronically mentally ill, serving on the APA committee on the CMI, and on the board of directors of the American Association of Community Psychiatrists. He has written and taught extensively on the subject of dual diagnosis.

DOUGLAS L. NOORDSY, M.D., is the psychiatrist on the West Central Services Continuous Treatment Team. He is a research associate with the New Hampshire-Dartmouth Psychiatric Research Center and an assistant professor of psychiatry at Dartmouth Medical School.

MARK C. WALLEN, M.D., is the medical/clinical director of Livengrin Foundation in Bensalem, Pennsylvania. He is on the clinical faculty of Hahnemann University and Temple University Medical Schools, and is on the faculty of the summer school programs at the Rutgers University Center of Alcohol and Drug Studies. He has written a number of articles and given many presentations at the local, regional, and national levels regarding treatment of the dually diagnosed patient.

JOAN ELLEN ZWEBEN, PH.D., is a clinical psychologist with over twenty years' experience in treating addiction and training treatment practitioners. She is the founder of the 14th Street Clinic and Medical Group and the East Bay Community Recovery Project in Oakland, California, and has developed comprehensive medical and psychological services to serve a diverse patient population.

Introduction

Norman S. Miller, M.D.

WE ARE ENTERING A NEW ERA OF ADDICTION TREATMENT: namely, the integration of addiction and psychiatric treatments. Heretofore, diagnosis and treatment of addictive and psychiatric disorders have occurred in dichotomous settings. As a consequence, the patient with an addictive disorder in a psychiatric setting generally did not receive treatment for the addictive disorder, and vice versa.

This book features the patients who fall through the cracks, especially those who have a "dual diagnosis"—that is, an addictive and a psychiatric disorder. Until recently, the chronically mentally ill patient with an addictive disorder has not had access to an addiction treatment program, and these programs are not yet widespread. The approach that appears to hold the most promise integrates addiction and psychiatric treatments in the same setting or program.

Chapter 1, "The Interactions Between Coexisting Disorders," presents an overview of the principles and definitions of dual diagnosis. Further, it describes important interactions between addictive and psychiatric disorders that can confuse the best of clinicians. Chapter 2, "Initial Diagnosis and Treatment of the Dually Disordered," offers a practical and conceptual approach to sort out what is "addiction" and what is "psychiatric." The chapter focuses on how to tell when addictive disorders cause psychiatric symptoms, how long to assess the patient, and when to start what treatments for either an addictive or a psychiatric disorder.

In recent years, there have been major breakthroughs in the neurochemistry of addictive and other psychiatric disorders involving the neurotransmitters dopamine, serotonin, and norepinephrine. Specific locations in the brain have been identified as the source of these illnesses.

Chapter 3, "The Biology of Addictive and Psychiatric Disorders," is devoted to the biology of addictive and other mental disorders. It highlights similarities and differences in the chemistry of the brain where these disorders originate and are sustained.

Chapters 4 and 5, "Treating the Dually Diagnosed in Psychiatric Settings" and "Treating the Dually Diagnosed in Addiction Settings," discuss the two major settings for the treatment of dual diagnosis patients: namely, addiction or psychiatric settings. Until recently the treatment of these patients had not occurred in any setting. However, addiction programs are now adding "dual-focused" programs, and psychiatric programs are integrating addiction services with psychiatric treatments. The indicated setting is determined by the predominant milieu: psychiatric patients require a psychiatric milieu and addiction patients require an addiction milieu. A dual diagnosis patient may be treated in either, depending on the psychiatric disorder. If the psychiatric disorder is a chronic mental illness such as schizophrenia, then a psychiatric milieu is preferable; whereas anxiety, depressive, or personality disorders are better treated in an addiction milieu.

Three chapters pertain to special populations of dual diagnosis patients. Adolescents, covered in chapter 6, "Dual Diagnosis in Adolescent Populations," require programs tailored to their needs. Their mental and emotional state is different from that of an adult. Minority populations, covered in chapter 7, "Dual Diagnosis, Minority Populations, and Women," have special needs as well. Specifically, addiction treatment must be made available and usable. Addictive illnesses, covered in chapter 8, "Addictive Psychiatric Disorders," tend to bunch together, such that eating disorders—as well as a gambling disorder—are commonly associated with alcohol and drug addiction.

The book offers four chapters on specific treatments for dual diagnosis patients. There are effective treatments for both psychiatric and addictive disorders. Chapter 9, "Medications Used with the Dually

Diagnosed," discusses those medications, such as neuroleptics and antidepressants, which are frequently used for the chronically mentally ill. Whereas group and psychotherapy are effective for anxiety, depressive, and personality disorders, medications are sometimes necessary as well. The core of addiction treatment is group and individual therapy. These methods are discussed in detail in chapter 10, "Therapy with the Dually Diagnosed Person." Any approach to the treatment of addiction will require knowledge and skill in these therapies. The Twelve Step treatment approach, covered in chapter 11, "The Twelve Step Approach," is the dominant form of treatment for addictive disorders and for addiction in dual diagnosis patients. Chapters 12 and 13, "Relapse Prevention" and "Working with the Family," discuss how the treatment provider can work effectively and harmoniously with Twelve Step recovery groups for the benefit of the dual diagnosis patient.

Chapter 14, "Case Management," offers the latest methods in the treatment of the dual diagnosis patient, particularly the chronically mentally ill, using the case manager approach. A detailed description of this relatively new patient-therapist relationship is presented. The team approach that has been the mainstay of treatment for both addictive and psychiatric disorders is featured in chapter 15, "The Treatment Team." The source of reimbursement is becoming a larger determinant of who receives treatment and who does not, particularly for dual diagnosis patients. An explanation of the current mechanisms of reimbursement is provided in chapter 16, "Managed Care and Dual Diagnosis."

We have entered a time when change is the rule, and no discipline can any longer afford to take rigid positions and use inflexible approaches to the treatment of addictive disorders. It is likely that dual diagnosis is here to stay (or at least for some time). Moreover, the diagnosis and treatment of addictive disorders will occur more frequently in psychiatric settings than heretofore.

We believe that new strategies for the treatment of addictive disorders will be increasingly integrated in the education and training for counselors, social workers, psychologists, and physicians. We are working in the best of times and the worst of times. While we have the opportunity to expand our clinical approach to include addictive and other psychiatric disorders in our treatment of the dual diagnosis patient, we must also face the inevitable task of change that accompanies such major initiatives.

We dedicate this book to the pioneers in the treatment of dual diagnosis patients who are following the decades of tradition in addiction and psychiatric practice that have preceded them. We are optimistic that dual diagnosis patients will benefit from these changes as long as certain principles are maintained and active ingredients in our addiction and psychiatric treatments are preserved.

Overview

Addictive and psychiatric disorders (illnesses) are independent of each other, but they interact. Each illness requires specific treatment.

1
The Interactions Between Coexisting Disorders

Norman S. Miller, M.D.

INTRODUCTION

CURRENTLY, WE HAVE TWO PREDOMINANTLY DICHOTOMOUS SYSTEMS for the treatment of addictive and psychiatric disorders. While there has been some movement on each side toward combined treatment, progress has been limited to minor adjustments in treatment practices. As a result, many patients still do not receive adequate attention and treatment for either addictive or psychiatric disorders, depending on within which setting they seek treatment.

Because identified psychiatric patients, particularly those with a chronic mental illness, tend to utilize psychiatric services, they are underdiagnosed and do not receive comprehensive treatment for their addictive disorders. On the other hand, those with identified addictive disorders tend to be admitted to addiction programs without receiving psychiatric evaluations and treatment in addition to the addiction treatment (Ries 1993).

DEFINITION OF ADDICTIVE DISORDER

An *addictive disorder* is the preoccupation with acquiring alcohol and drugs, compulsive use of alcohol and drugs despite adverse consequences, and a pattern of relapse to alcohol and drug use despite the recurrence of adverse consequences. Central to addiction is a loss of control over alcohol and drug use which leads to consequences that are harmful to the individual and others associated with him or her. This loss of control is what makes an addiction a disease or disorder, similar to other diseases/disorders such as schizophrenia or diabetes (Miller 1991).

Definition of Psychiatric Disorder

A *psychiatric disorder* is a collection of psychiatric symptoms (pathological or abnormal psychological) which occur in a predictable pattern that is considered sufficiently unique to have its own diagnosis and course. An example is schizophrenia, where hallucinations and delusions occur with personality changes that begin in adolescence and can progress over a lifetime (Goodwin and Guze 1984).

Definition of Dual Diagnosis

The strict definition of *dual diagnosis* means that another disorder exists independent of an addictive disorder. The key words are *another* and *independent.*

Another means that any psychiatric or medical disorder coexists with or occurs in addition to the addictive disorder. In simple terms, two or more independent disorders exist in the same individual (Miller et al. 1991).

Independent means that each disorder has a life of its own and is not dependent on the other for its cause or continuation. For instance, it is a myth that anxiety or depression can cause alcohol or drug use/addiction; if this is true, then there is no dual diagnosis, because one disorder causes the other. It is true, however, that alcohol and drug use/addiction can cause anxiety and depression; likewise, there is no true dual diagnosis in this case either. Yet it is also possible that an anxiety or depressive disorder can occur *independent* of an addictive disorder. This is a bona fide dual diagnosis.

Definition of Interaction

One can see that the *interaction* between addictive and psychiatric disorders is of paramount importance. While psychiatric disorders do not cause addictive disorders, they can influence the individual's ability to accept treatment for them. At the same time, because addictive disorders can cause psychiatric symptoms that look like psychiatric disorders, addictive disorders must be distinguished from psychiatric disorders. Also, the treatment of an addictive disorder is key to the individual's ability to accept treatment for a psychiatric disorder. It is important to note that if addictive disorders are not considered independent, drinking/drug use will be attributed to other disorders or causes. If this happens, there will not be proper diagnosis and treatment of either the addictive or the psychiatric disorder. Moreover, treatment of the psychiatric disorder will be difficult and often impossible because of the uncontrolled nature of addictive disorders.

Case One

History

Doris, forty years old, had been drinking alcohol since entering college. She had begun with weekend drinking but progressed to almost daily drinking in recent years. She had noticed that most if not all of her friends and business associates were drinkers. In more recent years she had been suffering from depression of significant magnitude, such that she had felt hopeless and helpless at times, had difficulty sleeping, and had withdrawn from family and co-workers. Her pattern was to work all day, go home, and drink two to four glasses of wine almost every evening to the point of intoxication and some memory loss. Her sleep was uneven and she might wake during the night. In the morning she was depressed, gloomy, and low in energy. She derived no pleasure from ordinary activities and avoided others, except those who drank. She was in a three-year relationship with a man described as alcoholic and described the relationship as "going nowhere."

She started seeing a psychiatrist, who prescribed the antidepressant Prozac. Her mood did not change much. She began seeing another psychiatrist, who suggested she stop drinking alcohol. After not drinking for a sustained period, she experienced a dramatic improvement in her mood with total resolution of her depressive symptoms. However, about a month later she drank about four beers in an evening and reexperienced depressive symptoms. She had been taking the Prozac continuously.

She has now started attending Alcoholics Anonymous (AA) meetings and has decided to end the romantic relationship at least for now. She admits that she must now make new friends; because she no longer drinks, she does not have much in common with her old friends.

Diagnosis and Treatment

In this case, the depression was a result of the depressant effects of alcohol, and the lifestyle from addictive use of alcohol. The preoccupation and compulsive use of alcohol narrowed Doris's repertoire of life experiences. The antidepressant probably had little to do with the relief of depressive symptoms, because despite being on Prozac, she reexperienced depression when she relapsed.

This was not a dual diagnosis, because the only disorder was an addictive one; the depression was dependent on the alcohol consumption, not independent of it. Continued treatment of the alcohol addiction was sufficient to stem the alcohol-induced depression.

Case Two

History

Jim, twenty-one years old, had been coming to a mental health clinic about once every two months. He had often heard the devil telling him he was bad and should get rid of himself (hallucinations). He also had been having thoughts that others wanted to harm him, and was sometimes unable to sleep because he was certain they would come at night to get him (paranoid delusions).

Jim had always been a shy, retiring child who did not make friends easily. He had barely finished high school and had required the assistance of special education. His attendance had been inconsistent and his academic performance below average. His parents divorced when Jim was three years old, and he continued to live with his mother. His father was an alcoholic who saw his son irregularly. He had a sister six years older than he, and a grandmother who was said to have died from a "mental disorder." Jim started drinking when he was thirteen years old, then used marijuana when he was fourteen, and cocaine at nineteen. Jim started hearing voices when he was eighteen years old, his senior year of high school. It was about that time he also began thinking that laser beams were controlling him. His ability to maintain relationships became even worse, and he withdrew from family and friends, except those who used alcohol and drugs. He did not go on to college, and does not work. He lives with his mother or, periodically, on the street. He has been seeing a psychiatrist on and off at a mental health clinic for the past three years. His compliance with medications has been poor, and he has gone to the psychiatrist when his mother has brought him or when there appears to be no clear reason.

Jim continues to drink several times a week and uses marijuana and cocaine when he can get them (once or twice a week). He has never had treatment for his drug and alcohol addictions. His psychiatrist and case manager have believed Jim when he states he uses drugs/alcohol because he hears voices or feels sad. They have aimed their therapy at the voices and depression, believing that the drug use and drinking will subside. Jim often feels suicidal; he has thoughts about wanting to harm himself when he uses drugs and alcohol heavily. Thus far Jim appears to have his best periods when he is not using drugs or alcohol and is taking his prescribed medications. A not uncommon sequence is for Jim to start drinking, then to stop taking his medications, and, subsequently, to reexperience especially bad voices and paranoid thoughts. It is important to know that even when Jim is at his best (abstinent and taking medications), he is suspicious of people. In addition, making friends and being with a group of people are always difficult for him, as he becomes filled with fear and overwhelmed by others' emotions. He had never been to an AA meeting.

Diagnosis and Treatment

Jim's case is one of true dual diagnosis, in which both schizophrenia and alcohol or drug addiction occur together. Both disorders are independent of each other for causation, but do interact in the diagnosis and treatment. For instance, Jim is never totally free of hallucinations and delusions even when he is not drinking or using drugs, but he is better without the effects of drugs, which also produce psychotic symptoms and personality changes. Further, his compliance with treatment for his schizophrenia is much better when he is not using alcohol or drugs. However, because of the paranoid delusions and exaggerated sensitivity to the emotions of others, he experiences difficulties in group therapy. Consequently, he avoids addiction treatment and AA. His capacity for insight into his loss of control over alcohol and drugs is limited. He needs (a) a psychiatrist and case manager who are knowledgeable in both categories of disorders (addiction and psychiatric); (b) a treatment program designed to treat both the addictive and schizophrenic disorders.

Case Three

History

Rosalee is a forty-five-year-old woman. She comes from a family of five children—three brothers and two sisters—ranging from twenty-six to forty-five years old.

Rosalee lived with her mother until she was sixteen and then with her grandmother until she was twenty-two. She married at twenty-four. Her father left when she was a year old. Her mother worked to support the family and never had a mental illness or alcohol/drug problem. Rosalee's father lived on the streets intermittently over the years, and saw a psychiatrist at various times. Her father is alcoholic and has been known to use cocaine and marijuana.

Over the years, Rosalee has been hospitalized for "manic episodes" that were associated with heavy drinking and some drug use. She otherwise did not drink very much and was not known to use drugs except during her manic attacks. When she becomes manic her mood and affect are very euphoric. (She feels very high and good all over.) She has seemingly boundless energy and stays up most of the night without fatigue. Her insight and judgment become very poor. She frequently is in conflict with others and makes bad decisions in her work and personal life. She will sleep with strangers for no apparent reason and spend whatever money she has. She also talks fast and often makes little sense, jumping from one idea to the next in her conversations with others.

Of importance is that when Rosalee is not in a manic phase, she does not drink or use drugs and takes her lithium as prescribed. She has a tendency to stop taking her medications when she believes she no longer needs to do so. She often suffers a manic episode shortly thereafter. She also has attacks of depression with feelings of hopelessness, helplessness, and worthlessness. She withdraws from others, loses pleasure in daily activities, and becomes irritable and jumpy.

Rosalee's husband has taken her to a psychiatrist, where she has had to have ECT (electroconvulsive therapy) and has had to be placed on antidepressants. She does not drink or use drugs during those depressive times.

Rosalee's performance at work during "well" times is exemplary. She is a responsible, trustworthy, and pleasant team worker. However, others view her as a bit peculiar and as having an odd sense of humor. Rosalee is also a devoted mother and wife and values her commitments. She is very embarrassed by her manic episodes, although she believes they are out of character. She says that they are amusing to think about and will laugh when recalling her experiences while in a manic state.

Diagnosis and Treatment

In Rosalee's case, apparent addictive use of alcohol and drugs exists with a psychiatric disorder. However, on closer examination and with the knowledge of manic-depressive illness, it becomes clear that she does not suffer from alcohol or drug addiction. She drinks only when she is manic, during which time she exhibits many behaviors that indicate out-of-control behavior and poor judgment (e.g., going on spending sprees and being sexually promiscuous). She does not show a consistent pattern of addictive use of alcohol. In this case there is no dual diagnosis, and treatment of only the psychiatric disorder is indicated.

Prevalence of the Disorders

In addiction populations and settings. The prevalence of psychiatric disorders in populations of alcoholics/drug addicts and in addiction treatment settings is no greater than that for the general population. This means that most patients who enter an addiction treatment program do not have a true dual diagnosis. Among alcoholics/drug addicts, the prevalence rates for psychiatric disorders among addictive disorders are the following: 5 to 10 percent for major depression, 1 to 2 percent for schizophrenia, and 5 to 10 percent for anxiety disorders. This is in contrast to the prevalence of addictive disorders in the general population: 15 to 25 percent suffer from an alcohol and/or other drug addiction (Miller and Fine 1993).

In psychiatric populations and settings. The prevalence of addictive disorders in psychiatric populations is high; most studies show between 50 and 80 percent of those with a psychiatric diagnosis also suffer from addictive disorders. Specifically, the rates for addictive disorders in psychiatric diagnoses are as follows: 50 percent in schizophrenia, 30 percent in major depression, 30 percent in anxiety, and 50 percent in personality disorders. No wonder there is confusion about addictive and psychiatric disorders from a psychiatric point of view (Miller and Fine 1993).

Causation

The chicken-and-egg argument is sometimes used to try to clarify what causes what: for example, does anxiety cause drinking, or does drinking cause anxiety? The question of causation becomes simpler if we accept that two disorders can occur in the same individual and that they can have independent causes. For instance, clinical experience and objective scientific studies show that alcohol and drugs can frequently cause anxiety as a pharmacological effect and consequence of addictive behaviors. Once the drinking or drug use is under control, the anxiety often diminishes and resolves. Conversely, no studies show that anxiety can cause alcohol/drug use and addiction. In fact, the studies show that anxious people tend to prefer to use less alcohol and drugs when they are anxious. This is the case for depressed patients as well (Miller et al. 1991).

The reasons or motivations for drinking appear to follow no discernible pattern; that is, people use when they are sad, happy, or numb, because they were hired or fired, because somebody was born or died, because they were married or divorced, because "da Bulls" won or lost, and so on. In short, there are as many reasons why people drink as there are people.

The cause of addictive disorders is biological (neurochemical). Science has provided objective evidence for why people use alcohol and drugs. The identification of the "reinforcement" area in the brain that is activated by alcohol and drugs has provided a biochemical explanation to support the substantial genetic evidence that alcoholics/drug addicts are born, not made. "Instinctual drives" such as hunger and thirst are probably involved with the automatic and instinctive use of alcohol and drugs in the alcoholic and drug addict. The addictive use of alcohol and drugs is automatic, stereotypic, and repetitive, as are the instinctual behaviors of eating and sexual activity (Gold and Miller 1992).

Myths about Addictive Disorders

There are many destructive myths about addictive illnesses. Perhaps the most damaging one is that alcohol/drug addiction is caused by "faulty" morals. The belief is that alcoholics and drug addicts willfully use alcohol and drugs for hedonistic pleasure and for the destruction of self and others. The element of "unbridled choice" is always presumed to be present; it is also presumed that addiction is a matter of free will. There is no evidence to support these assumptions; what the evidence does support is that the addict experiences a loss of control over alcohol and drugs. Moreover, the addict continues to try to exert control in a hopeless battle of failed will against the addictive illness.

Another myth is that there is no effective treatment for alcohol/drug addiction. Studies confirm clinical and personal experiences which show that alcoholics and drug addicts can and do recover. Research shows that 90 percent of addicts can achieve abstinence if they complete a treatment program (abstinence-based Twelve Step) and attend continuing care and AA. Studies for dual diagnosis patients with major depression find similar results (Chappel 1993). Furthermore, if alcoholics/drug addicts attend AA between one and five years, they have over an 80 percent chance of staying sober another year in AA. And if they have been regular attendees in AA for five years or more, they have a greater than 90 percent chance of staying sober another year in AA. While statistics are not available for dual diagnosis patients (except for those with depression), it is certain that many with anxiety and depression, and probably those with chronic mental illness (e.g., schizophrenia), will enjoy favorable outcomes (Harrison et al. 1991). (See also Minkoff's chapter in this book.)

Myths about Psychiatric Disorders

Regarding psychiatric and addictive illnesses, the stigma is not as great for mental illness as it is for addictive illness. The acceptance of mental illness (apart from addictive illness) is greater today, although this has not always been the case. Moreover, many alcoholics/drug addicts will prefer to have a mental illness instead of an addictive illness, ostensibly because having a mental illness does not carry as much moral degradation. Nor does having a mental illness necessarily require quitting drinking and using drugs during the period when the psychiatrist and the patient search for the "reasons" for the drinking and drug use (Miller and Toft 1990).

Nevertheless, those with mental illnesses also carry "judgments" against them, such as the belief that they are inferior, weak-willed, and defective. The stigma of having both an addictive illness and a mental illness is perhaps even greater than having only one disorder and takes more understanding on the part of the family and those who work in either addictive or psychiatric settings.

Treatment of Addictive Disorders In an Integrated Approach

Currently, the treatment of dual diagnosis patients commonly occurs in stages and at different sites. But it is those with chronic mental illness who most often fall through the cracks. Almost up to the present time, we have tolerated a dichotomous approach to the diagnosis and treatment of addictive and psychiatric illness. Typically, patients with addictive illnesses enter an addiction treatment program so long as the psychiatric symptoms do not interfere with addiction treatment. The focus is on addiction. Their psychiatric symptoms tend to be viewed as secondary to the addictive illness (Ries 1993).

If patients have a severe psychiatric illness, such as schizophrenia, and cannot keep up the pace of the overall treatment program (e.g., confrontative groups), they will not be admitted to the addiction program. Rather, they will enter a psychiatric facility where the addiction will be viewed as secondary to the mental illness. The addiction will often go untreated because of the assumption that the schizophrenic is "self-medicating" with alcohol and drugs (and that alcohol and drug use is because of the mental illness). The aim to treat the schizophrenia alone is often incorrectly believed to be sufficient.

At times the patient may be stabilized on the psychiatric service and then transferred to the addiction program in what is called *serial* fashion. Or the reverse may occur; that is, the addiction is treated and then the psychiatric disorder. In either case the staff is not trained in one or the other illness, so that the patient receives a fragmented treatment approach, allowing a splitting of staff over which illness is more important and which illness should take precedence when both illnesses require equal treatment (Ries 1993).

Another approach is the *parallel* model, in which the patient is treated for one disorder and transferred daily to another setting for treatment of the other disorder. The patient lives in one setting and visits the other. Again, the staff are separated in space and time, and the patient is divided in mind and body (Ries 1993).

The *integrated* approach is a newer model that shows promise. (See Minkoff's chapter in this book.) This model requires that the patient receive treatment for both psychiatric and additive illnesses in the same setting *at the same time.* In this approach the addictive illness is seen as a disorder that is independent of and equal to the psychiatric illness. In the integrated approach, the addictive illness is another illness, or "dual diagnosis." The staff are trained and skilled in both addictive and psychiatric disorders so that the patient receives a uniform message about the importance of both disorders. There is no falling through the cracks or splitting of staff; the patient is both confronted and supported in the necessity to accept treatment for the dual disorders.

Case Four

History

Raul is an eighteen-year-old schizophrenic and alcoholic/drug addict who has had several psychiatric hospitalizations for hallucinations and delusions associated with feelings of wanting to kill himself. These hospitalizations often occur when he is drinking and/or smoking marijuana, and sometimes when he is using cocaine, PCP, or other drugs. His mood, hallucinations, and delusions often improve when he is not using alcohol and drugs, but overall the hallucinations and delusions persist. He typically spends one to two weeks in the hospital and is given medications and discharged without much mention of his alcohol and drug use by the psychiatrist or staff. He then relapses to alcohol/drugs, and the cycle repeats itself.

Diagnosis and Treatment

This time Raul is admitted to an integrated program, where he receives medications and group therapy for his alcohol/drug addictions. He is instructed on the importance of treating all his illnesses, and the staff provide him with a clear message that he cannot expect to recover from his schizophrenia or addiction if he lets one of them go untreated. He is also referred to an integrated outpatient program that has staff who are experienced in schizophrenia and addiction (Minkoff 1989). (See also Minkoff's chapter in this book.)

Prognosis and Long-Term Recovery

The prognosis for a patient with a dual diagnosis will follow that of the disorders combined or that of the predominant illness. If the anxiety and depression are a result of the addictive illness, then the course will be that of the addictive illness. If the schizophrenia and addiction are of equal importance, the course of the illness will be an approximation of both illnesses, which are typically chronic and relapsing. Also, while the goal of treatment is abstinence from alcohol and drugs, consideration of, and adjustment to, what is realistic for the dual diagnosis patient must be included. For instance, the schizophrenic may be attending AA meetings but may stop taking medications, or worsen despite taking medications, and then relapse to alcohol and drugs. The goal then becomes minimizing the relapse to alcohol and drugs and the symptoms from the schizophrenia. (See Drake's chapter in this book.)

Recovery in Twelve Step Groups

There are Twelve Step groups for many different kinds of addictive and psychiatric illnesses. These self-help groups are available to those who conform to the membership requirements; for example, in AA, having the desire not to drink. A cornerstone of recovery from any disorder—whether addictive, psychiatric, or medical—is taking personal responsibility for the treatment of the disorder(s). Without some acknowledgment of personal responsibility, it is unlikely that recovery from many disorders is possible. For example, Jim (Case 2) must be sufficiently responsible in order to visit the clinic, get the medications for schizophrenia, and also attend the AA meetings to treat the addiction (Miller and Toft, 1990).

Personal responsibility is key to recovery and appears to run counter to the "sick role" that is part of having an illness. Inherent in the "sick role" is that the patient does not cause or is not at fault for the illness; however, the patient can help himself or herself in recovery. Moreover, that a patient is able to avoid the "sick role" may or may not be true. In one sense, it is not true, because many illnesses are preventable, such as addiction, cancer, and accidents. In another sense, it is also true of these same illnesses that once they occur, they have a life of their own beyond willpower.

The individual must accept having the illness(es) and responsibility for participating in treatment. The responsibility is the same whether medication or AA is the "higher power." In this way the individual with an anxiety disorder turns his or her will over to medications (or groups) and a form of spirituality. In either case, actions must be taken to treat either illness.

Case Five

History

Ming is a thirty-two-year-old woman who has a diagnosis of panic attacks. She also suffers from alcohol and benzodiazepine addictions. Since achieving sobriety five years ago, her panic attacks have lessened, but she still has clusters of them at times.

Diagnosis and Treatment

She took antidepressants for the initial two years. Ming now attends anxiety support groups but "forgets" to do so at times. When she attends these groups regularly, her attacks are less frequent. She also notices that when she is attending her AA meetings she is less likely to have anxiety in general. She also is more likely to attend her anxiety group. She can get in trouble when she begins to believe not only that she is powerless over her anxiety but that she is also powerless to do anything about her anxiety and resigns herself to suffering from it. Her mentality then becomes that of a victim who can do nothing to help herself. On the other hand, by attending AA meetings more regularly, Ming stops feeling overwhelmed and assumes control of her recovery and her life. By attending her support group for anxiety disorders, Ming takes responsibility for treatment and is better able to maintain her focus on treatment for the addictive disorder.

Conclusions

1. Addictive and psychiatric illnesses are independent.
2. Addictive and psychiatric illnesses interact with one another.
3. Addictive and psychiatric illnesses require specific treatment for each illness.
4. Moral stigma is not therapeutic for either addictive or psychiatric illnesses.

References

Chappel, J. N. 1993. Long-term recovery from alcoholism. *Psychiatric Clinics of North America* 16 (1):177-87.

Gold, M. S., and N. S. Miller. 1992. Seeking drugs/alcohol and avoiding withdrawal: The neuroanatomy of drive states and withdrawal. *Psychiatric Annals* 22 (8):430-35.

Goodwin, D. W., and S. B. Guze. 1984. *Psychiatric Diagnoses.* New York: Oxford University Press.

Harrison, P. A., N. G. Hoffman, and S. G. Streed. 1991. Drug and alcohol addiction treatment outcome. In *Comprehensive handbook of drug and alcohol addiction,* edited by N. S. Miller. New York: Marcel Dekker, Inc. 1163-200.

Miller, N. S. 1991. *The pharmacology of alcohol and drugs of abuse and addiction.* New York: Springer-Verlag.

Miller, N. S., and J. Fine. 1993. Current epidemiology of comorbidity of psychiatric and addictive disorders. *Psychiatric Clinics of North America* 16 (1):1-10.

Miller, N. S., J. C. Mahler, B. M. Belkin, and M. S. Gold. 1991. Psychiatric diagnosis of alcohol and drug dependence. *Annals of Clinical Psychiatry* 3 (1):79-89.

Miller, N. S., and D. Toft. 1990. *The Disease Concept.* Center City, MN: Hazelden Foundation.

Minkoff, K. 1989. An integrated treatment model for dual diagnosis of psychosis and addiction. *Hospital and Community Psychiatry* 40:1031-36.

Ries, R. K. 1993. Clinical treatment matching models for dually diagnosed patients. *Psychiatric Clinics of North America* 16 (1):167-76.

Diagnosis in the dually disordered population requires that patients be evaluated over time to ensure that their psychiatric symptoms are not caused by drug use or psychoactive medications.

2
Initial Diagnosis and Treatment of The Dually Disordered

James Fine, M.D.

PEOPLE PRESENTING FOR TREATMENT who display evidence of addictive disorders and psychiatric disturbance require special evaluation techniques (Miller and Ries 1991). Their psychiatric symptoms may be due to the addiction or to an intercurrent psychiatric illness. Practical management of these patients must begin long before a final diagnosis can be established. Initial evaluation and treatment should meet the needs of the patient and support, not complicate, the process of diagnosis. We present a method to accomplish this (Fine and Miller 1993).

THE CHALLENGE TO THE CLINICIAN

Patients enter treatment settings with rapidly changing psychiatric problems. These disturbances may be dangerous and are almost always disruptive and distressing to patients and those around them (McCarrick et al. 1985). In spite of the severity or dangerousness of these psychiatric symptoms, they are not very reliable as a basis for final diagnosis (Schuckit and Montero 1980). The initial evaluation and management of these problems is a crucial and often confusing step in the treatment process.

As therapists we must first assure the safety of the patient and others. Then we need to (1) develop a strategy to manage persistent symptoms;

(2) engage the patient as an active participant in the recovery from addiction, psychiatric illness, or both; and (3) establish the foundation necessary for accurate future diagnosis.

We need to accomplish these steps relatively rapidly, both to appease funding agencies and insurers and to avoid relapse. Finally, we need to do all this with an assumption of diagnostic uncertainty. In other words, we must begin treatment with the understanding that we do not, cannot, and need not know what or how much is "wrong" with the person in our care. This requires treating presenting problems efficiently, without adding to them, while deferring final diagnosis until sufficient information is available.

Meeting the Challenge

While these demands may seem overwhelming, the good news is that much of the standard treatment of medical illness proceeds adequately with similar restrictions. Complicated medical conditions frequently require emergency management, symptom control, and a partnership with the patient before the nature and extent of illness are diagnosed. By following some simple guidelines we have found that the process of treating co-occurrent addictive and psychiatric disturbances can be simplified. Our model, or method, suggests managing presenting problems conservatively and initiating treatment, but delaying definitive diagnosis until sufficient information is available.

The model consists of two operations: (a) classification divided into one of three syndromes and (b) management, divided into six phases or steps. The model is described in detail below.

Model for Evaluating and Managing Concurrent Psychiatric And Addictive Disturbances

A. CLASSIFY BY SYNDROME

1. Affective syndrome
2. Paranoid syndrome
3. Anxious syndrome

B. MANAGE
   1. Treat life-threatening situations
   2. Identify the goal of abstinence (through confrontation)
   3. Initiate psychiatric management
   4. Stabilize
   5. Observe
   6. Diagnose

SYNDROMAL CLASSIFICATION

A *syndrome* is a clinical picture, a collection of signs and symptoms that often appear together. The common cold, appendicitis, and pneumonia all have characteristic syndromes that most people can recognize. (A syndrome is different from a disease in that diseases have a single cause and predictable course or outcome, while syndromes can have various causes; thus the same syndrome can be seen in different diseases). Most presenting psychiatric disturbances fall into one of three general categories of psychiatric disturbances—affective, paranoid, or anxious—each consisting of (containing) two syndromes.

Affective Syndromes

DEPRESSION	MANIA
sleep disturbance	insomnia
sad mood	hyperactivity
low energy	hypersociability
suicidality	expansiveness
guilt	grandiosity
hopelessness	elation
anhedonia	

Paranoid Syndromes

PSYCHOSIS	HYPERVIGILANCE
suspiciousness	irritability
delusions	suspiciousness
hallucinations	hyperarousal
clear sensorium	
hypervigilance	

Anxiety Syndromes

PANIC	ANXIETY
shortness of breath	edginess
dizziness	inability to concentrate
palpitations	obsessive symptoms
trembling	unrealistic and overwhelming fears
sense of impending destruction	

For purposes of managing symptoms, anticipating problems, and deciding on treatment modalities, classification by syndromes can be very useful.

For example, depressed patients, regardless of the cause of their depression, often have trouble self-motivating to engage in activity and may respond well to encouragement, whereas anxious patients may require a greater degree of reassurance. Markedly paranoid patients may be unable initially or, in some cases, ever, to tolerate groups.

Syndromal or "type" classification can also be useful for communicating the clinical picture to other treating personnel; and when medications are needed, the syndrome, not the "final" diagnosis, will determine whether antidepressant, antipsychotic, or antianxiety medications are appropriate (Zweben and Smith 1989).

The symptoms that make up these syndromes are the same as those found in uncomplicated psychiatric disturbances (psychiatric illness in non-drug-involved people). However, the presence of alcohol and other drug problems makes rapid definitive diagnosis impossible and limits us initially to using provisional and general diagnoses, which are actually clinical syndromes, as described earlier. *DSM-III-R* and *DSM-IV* are well suited for this approach in that they provide sufficient provisional descriptive categories (e.g. Affective, Anxiety, or Paranoid Disorder, Not Otherwise Specified) and permit the use of "rule/out" (possible) diagnoses.

Each of the syndromes, as described, will include many possible final diagnoses. They may be entirely due to addiction ("Psychoactive Substances Use Disorders," *DSM-III-R*), or to independent (non-addictive) psychiatric illnesses, or they may represent combinations of both.

Applying the Model

After mentally choosing the syndrome that most closely approximates the actual clinical picture, we then begin the management steps.

Phase 1: Treat Life-Threatening and Dangerous Complications

Physical problems, delirium, coma, significant agitation, and signs of withdrawal all require emergency medical evaluation and take precedence over psychiatric or addictive evaluation. Once such problems have been referred or determined not to be present, emergent psychiatric problems should be addressed.

Is the patient sufficiently depressed so that he or she is not eating or is suicidal? Does the patient have delusions that make him or her dangerous to others? (Psychotically depressed patients may suicide and "take others with them" in the delusional belief they are saving them from an evil or intolerable world.) Such dangerous thinking or behavior requires hospitalization.

Is the anxious patient so disabled that he or she is neglecting nutritional needs and necessary medical care? (Phobic patients may be unable to leave their homes to eat or fill prescriptions.) Is the patient dangerously impulsive? (Anxiety is a significant risk factor for suicide in clinically depressed individuals and can be the most apparent sign of depression.)

Is the paranoid individual experiencing the first onset of psychosis? Is the individual liable to act aggressively out of a belief that he or she is at risk from others? Does the individual have dangerous grandiose beliefs (e.g., he or she can fly or is impervious to harm)?

All of the foregoing are indications for hospitalization. Whether or not these dangerous, life-threatening symptoms are addiction-related does not alter the risk they pose (Brody 1990). Addicts are also at high risk for suicide and self-damage as well as for acting against others.

In short, evaluating for dangerousness is not markedly changed by the presence of addiction. The first concern is safety; when in doubt, hospitalize. At times patients are unable to communicate due to psychosis, disorganized thinking, or anxiety, while not being immediately dangerous. These situations are dangerous in that they block further treatment and thus need to be addressed immediately. We should remember (and stress to our patients) that referral to a psychiatrist is not a punishment or admission of failure. On the contrary, it may be the first step toward recovery.

Once the issue of dangerousness has been addressed, further management can proceed.

Phase 2: Identify the Goal of Abstinence (Confrontation)

Once safety and the patient's ability to communicate are assured, identifying the goal of abstinence takes precedence over other concerns. People with mixed psychiatric and addictive pictures benefit from abstinence-oriented treatment in two ways. First, initial stabilization and accurate diagnosis of their problems require that they eliminate psychoactive chemical use. Second, many, if not most, of these patients will be found to have diagnosable addictions (not just casual or coincidental chemical use), which over time will respond best to abstinence-oriented treatment.

This issue should be raised very early on for several reasons. First, in the interest of establishing an honest treatment relationship we should point out to our patients the difficulty of achieving a safe, stable lifestyle or of benefiting from further treatment while using alcohol and other drugs. Diagnosis is obscured and psychosocial interventions, medications, and behavioral treatments are all easily reversed by getting high. Second, since the process of establishing the goal of abstinence is often a long and torturous one, it should be begun as early as possible.

Establishing this goal can take many forms and should be tailored to the patient's situation, understanding, and knowledge. Confrontation, or identifying the goal of abstinence, does not mean threatening the patient with rejection, demanding agreement, or exacting promises of compliance. It means explaining to the patient the value of abstinence and offering him or her help to achieve it.

Patients in denial of addictive problems will usually identify, or admit to, many negative situations or problems in their lives. These include health, job, psychiatric, and family problems. Our patients fail, however, to see that these problems are caused by their addictive disorders. Rather, they will often see these problems as the cause of their drinking or drug use rather than the *result* of it. Distorting this cause-and-effect relationship is the essence of denial.

Confrontation refers to correcting this failure to connect cause and effect. It means exposing the contradictions in our patients' lives and helping them understand that their miseries are the result of their illness and therefore are an incentive to treatment. For example, you can explain to patients that the unpleasant situations they wish to avoid (e.g. arrest, forced hospitalization, physical problems) can only be avoided by finding a way to stop getting high. In other words, you and the patient form a team to *confront* the contradictions caused by the patient's illness.

This process is slow and gradual and often involves repeated relapses; that is, the patient reexperiences these contradictions. Our job remains to point them out and expose them, and to make the offer of helping the patient achieve abstinence.

Patients in inpatient, controlled settings do not require special strategies around abstinence. The "confrontational" explanations offered previously should be used. Patients in outpatient or nontreatment settings should be approached with the same explanation of consequences, but in addition, an agreement, plan, or contract around abstinence is necessary. The patient's level of insight, understanding, and mental clarity affects this strategy, as shown in the following examples:

1. Patients who see no reason to stop using in spite of careful explanations of consequences should be encouraged to come back and see you again. (Remember that this is a chronic, relapsing disease and that repeated interventions are the rule.)

2. Patients who think they have a problem with use but think they can limit or stop their use without help (without Twelve Step programs or treatment) should be told that "willpower" usually does not work. However, if they are still unwilling to utilize Twelve Step groups or treatment, they should be *supported in their willingness to try to stop* and advised to come back and see you. Together you can evaluate whether their plan is working. We always tell patients that while we don't expect their plan (stopping without help) will work, we'd be pleased to be wrong in this prediction and see them succeed. In any event we remain available to patients in the hope that if and when their plan of abstinence ("willpower") doesn't work, they'll be ready for our plan (referral and treatment).

3. Patients who are (or become) willing should be referred to some form of treatment. Depending on availability and the patient's degree of psychiatric tolerance, treatment includes integrated dual diagnosis programs (combined addiction and psychiatric programs); dual diagnosis groups within a psychiatric program; addiction programs with psychiatric enhancements; addiction programs in tandem with psychiatric programs; "standard" addiction programs; and lastly, outpatient individual treatment (which we see as the last resort) (Minkoff 1989; Rosenthal et al., in press). Remember that in inpatient settings, this referral step has already happened, but it must be explained in terms of the benefits of abstinence.

Along with initiating formal treatment, you should always attempt to refer the patient to a Twelve Step program, such as AA, NA, or the now-proliferating "Double Trouble" (dual diagnosis) groups. You should also always carefully prepare patients for meetings. New experiences are always difficult, and group experiences can evoke particularly frightening (however inaccurate) images of pressure and intrusion. Patients should receive explicit information about how meetings function and what behaviors are acceptable. When possible, patients should go to meetings with someone already familiar with the program.

Once the goal of abstinence has been identified (and a plan developed), the next step can be undertaken.

Phase 3: Initiate Psychiatric Management

Up to this point in the patient's management, the symptoms have been classified into a syndrome, the dangerousness evaluated, the patient's ability to communicate established, and the goal of abstinence identified. However, we are still dealing with an individual with psychiatric disturbance, varying from mild to severe. Based on the picture of symptoms (the syndrome), psychiatric management should be planned. This management, like all medical planning, should proceed from the most conservative, least intrusive, and least dangerous treatments, to the more aggressive treatments (Zweben and Smith 1989). Basically this means progressing from *simple supportive measures, to more highly structured treatments,* and to *medications.* Support, encouragement, and reassurance are the first modes of treatment for all patients.

Referring back to the syndromes, however, we generally find depressed patients respond to encouragement, anxious patients benefit from reassurance, and paranoid patients do best with nonintrusive, nonthreatening methods. If simple support seems ineffective, group or individual structured therapy sessions should be attempted. Cognitive therapy has been studied and used for both anxious and depressed patients, but any focused, issue-oriented therapy may be as effective during this early period.

The effectiveness of reassurance and talk therapies should be carefully monitored, and patients should be evaluated for functional improvement or worsening.

The patients, while not dangerous or disorganized, may be nonfunctional. They may be immobilized by depression, too anxious to concentrate and talk, or too paranoid to tolerate contact. *These people will be unable to participate in their own recovery.* If these symptoms do not rapidly clear, they should be referred for aggressive *medication treatment.* Specific psychiatric management will not be extensively discussed here but would be syndrome-dependent; that is, the depressed lethargic patient would receive antidepressants; the anxious patient, anxiolytics; and the paranoid patient, antipsychotics. *Except for emergency sedation or pain control, sedatives or narcotics should not be used in addicted patients.*

In summary, initial psychiatric management should begin conservatively but move rapidly to control persistent incapacitating symptoms. (Remember that to this point only provisional, descriptive diagnoses such as Major Depressive Episode; Anxiety Disorder, Not Otherwise Specified; Paranoid Disorder, Not Otherwise Specified; or Atypical Psychosis should be used.)

Phase 4: Stabilize

Once addiction and psychiatric management (phases 2 and 3) have begun, a period of time is needed to monitor progress in both areas and adjust and reevaluate treatments. Patients may rapidly improve psychiatrically and no longer require special supports. They may worsen and require higher levels of support or medication or hospitalization. They may rapidly achieve abstinence with counseling and meetings or they may relapse, requiring referral detoxification and inpatient structured rehabilitation.

The period of stabilization is the most variable and may last from a few weeks to indefinitely. However long it lasts, it is valuable in that we find that balancing both areas of treatment needs, addictive and psychiatric illness, in an ongoing way produces better results. Studies show that patients with treated psychiatric disturbance have better addiction recovery than those with untreated psychiatric problems (O'Brien et al. 1984). Similarly, patients who are able to achieve meaningful recovery marked by periods of abstinence show much better response to psychiatric treatment.

For those patients whose gains seem very minimal, we find that this plan (continuous reevaluation of both areas of dysfunction) reduces the amount of time spent in hospitals and improves life adjustment (Hanson et al. 1990).

Phase 5: Observation

This phase requires observing the progress of patients over significant time periods to allow the effects of stabilization to express themselves. It means seeing that patients remain abstinent for months so persisting or emerging psychiatric symptoms can be accurately evaluated and determined not to be caused by alcohol or other drug use. When psychiatric medicines have been used and symptoms eliminated, observation should usually include a medically supervised period off medicines, again to determine whether psychiatric symptoms were induced by alcohol or other drugs or due to an independent ("comorbid") disorder.

These management techniques are not simply scientific attempts to make the final job of diagnosis simpler. The suggestions for careful readjustment of treatments, an adequate observation period, and withdrawal of medications represent, in our experience, the most efficient, humane, and practical management of dual disorders. They also permit more accurate and rational diagnoses. In other words, efficient management permits efficient diagnosis. Even when diagnosis remains unclear we can continue to provide the best possible treatment (and defer diagnosis).

Phase 6: Diagnosis

Only after abstinence is achieved and psychiatric symptoms persist or recur can an accurate psychiatric diagnosis be established. After significant abstinence these symptoms can be attributed to independent, comorbid psychiatric conditions. Diagnosis of definitive and independent disorders such as Bipolar Disorder, Recurrent Depression, Generalized Anxiety Disorder, or Schizophrenia can now be made.

Similarly, accurate assessment of addictive illness can now be made. Occasionally, patients with chronic severe psychiatric disturbances have patterns of alcohol and other drug use that seem to have little effect on their psychosis. Only over time, and after the reduction or elimination of acute psychiatric disturbance, can we assess addiction and abuse and differentiate these conditions from rarely occurring, insignificant, coincidental chemical use.

Remember that while adequate management sets the stage for adequate diagnosis, it also improves the quality of our patients' health and lives. Since diagnosis may be deferred indefinitely for some, this is an important consideration in maintaining *our* motivation to continue to treat in spite of the frequent problems and relapse that some patients experience.

References

Brody, S. L. 1990. Violence associated with acute cocaine use in patients admitted to a medical emergency department. *NIDA Research Monograph Series* 103:44-59.

Fine, J., and N. S. Miller. 1993. Evaluation and acute management of psychotic symptomatology in alcohol and drug addictions. *Comorbidity of Addictive and Psychiatric Disorders:* 12 (3):59.

Hanson, M., T. H. Kramer, and W. Gross. 1990. Outpatient treatment of adults with coexisting substance use and mental disorders. *Journal of Substance Abuse Treatment* 7.

McCarrick, A. K., R. W. Manderscheid, and D. E. Bertolucci. 1985. Correlates of acting-out behaviors among young adult chronic patients. *Hospital and Community Psychiatry* 36 (8):848-53.

Miller, N. S., and R. K. Ries. 1991. Drug and alcohol dependence and psychiatric populations: The need for diagnosis, intervention, and training. *Comprehensive Psychiatry* 32 (3):268-76.

Minkoff, K. 1989. An integrated treatment model for dual diagnosis of psychosis and addiction. *Hospital and Community Psychiatry* 40 (10):1031-36.

O'Brien, C. P., G. E. Woody, and A. T. McLellan. 1984. Psychiatric disorders in opioid-dependent patients. *Journal of Clinical Psychiatry* 45:9-13.

Rosenthal, R. N., D. J. Hellerstein, and C. R. Miner. In press. *A model of integrated services for outpatient treatment of patients with comorbid schizophrenia and addictive disorders.*

Schuckit, M. A., and M. G. Montero. 1980. Alcoholism, anxiety, depression. *British Journal of Addiction* 83:1373-80.

Zweben, J. E., and D. E. Smith. 1989. Considerations in using psychotropic medication with dual diagnosis patients in recovery. *Journal of Psychoactive Drugs* 21 (2):221-28.

Understanding the biological (neurochemical) basis of addictive and psychiatric disorders can lead to improved diagnoses and treatment practices.

3
The Biology of Addictive And Psychiatric Disorders

Mark S. Gold, M.D.
Norman S. Miller, M.D.

Introduction

RECENT RESEARCH OFFERS MOUNTING EVIDENCE that disturbances in brain neurochemistry form the biological basis not only for the disease of addiction but also for psychiatric disorders such as depression, anxiety, and psychosis. Pathological neurochemical mechanisms in these disorders are similar. Such findings help explain why psychiatric and addictive illnesses often arise in the same individual and why the symptoms may overlap to create a confusing clinical picture. Before patients can receive accurate diagnoses, they must abstain from addictive drugs to determine which of their symptoms are indeed drug-related.

This chapter presents an overview of the fundamental concepts of neurochemistry and discusses their relevance to the medical and psychotherapeutic treatment of addiction and psychiatric illnesses. Understanding the common biological pathologies shared by these serious conditions—and recognizing the critical differences between them—can lead to more specific diagnosis and more effective treatment strategies.

Neurochemistry: A Brief Refresher

The brain is a complex electrochemical system composed of billions of neurons. Each neuron is separated from its neighbors by gaps, or synapses. When a neuron on one side of the gap (the presynaptic neuron) receives an electrical signal, it releases a chemical—a neurotransmitter—in greater or lesser amounts. This chemical messenger flows across the synapse to the branchlike projections, called dendrites, on the postsynaptic neuron. Molecules of neurotransmitter attach to special receptors on the dendrites and trigger the electrical signal. This impulse then flows along the elongated portion of the nerve cell, the axon, causing vesicles located at the tip of the axon to release their supply of neurotransmitter. Once the neurotransmitter molecule has completed its task, it is reabsorbed by the presynaptic neuron in a process known as reuptake.

Examples of neurotransmitters include dopamine (DA), serotonin, and norepinephrine (NE). Examples of neuropeptides are endorphins, TRH, and neuropeptide Y. While most neurons produce only one type of neurotransmitter, some are believed to produce two or more. Neurotransmitters are involved in many functions: they regulate appetite, blood pressure, heartbeat, muscle action, mood, and so on. The roles that they play are not specific to any one body function. Rather, neurotransmitters appear to be general messengers in the brain, "workhorses" that control a vast array of vital psychological and physiological activities.

Malfunctions in a neurotransmitter system, such as diminished supply of the chemical or defects in neuronal sensitivity, can result in pathological changes. When these pathological states persist over time and take on a life of their own, they are called disorders (or illnesses or diseases). Because they are mediated at least to some degree by changes or abnormalities in various neurotransmitter systems, addictive and psychiatric disorders tend to be independent, persistent, and recurring (Gold and Miller 1992; Miller and Gold 1992).

Causes of Addictive and Psychiatric Illness

Until recently, a drug was classified as addictive if a person experienced symptoms of withdrawal when long-term use of the drug was stopped. Consequently, drugs with overt physical withdrawal symptoms, such as opiates, were labeled addictive; those with more subtle withdrawal symptoms, such as cocaine, were considered (by some experts, anyway) to be less dangerous or even nonaddictive (Gold 1993a).

However, this narrow definition failed to account for many important aspects of addiction. Why, for example, do many different addictive drugs trigger similar patterns of bingeing among users? Why, too, does medical management of withdrawal symptoms so often fail to improve long-term treatment outcomes—that is, why are patients who complete withdrawal and achieve abstinence still so vulnerable to relapse?

Modern research is forcing a new definition of a drug's addictive property (Miller and Gold 1991). It now appears that drugs are addictive because they reinforce drug-taking behavior. This seemingly tautological and simple statement has profound implications. To put it another way: Addiction arises because prolonged use of the drug alters the basic neurochemistry of the brain, leading to physiological and psychological changes (Gold 1993b). These changes in turn result in continued and accelerating use of the drug. In a way, the drug can be likened to a virus that takes over a cell as a means of self-preservation—often at great danger to the host (Gold and Miller 1992).

In many cases the changes arising from use of drugs or alcohol can mimic symptoms of psychiatric illness. Marion's story illustrates the point:

> For years, Marion had been feeling more and more depressed. On some days she was barely able to drag herself out of bed. She complained of low energy, inability to concentrate, frequent tearfulness, and feelings of hopelessness that things would ever get any better. In the last few months she had been experiencing frequent thoughts of suicide.
>
> She went to a few sessions with one psychiatrist, a classical Freudian analyst who believed the cause of her problem must lie buried deep in her troubled past. When she didn't notice any improvement she switched to a different doctor, who took a more medical approach.
>
> Both doctors asked whether she drank alcohol. She told them she had consumed one or two bottles of wine a day for the past five

years. Somewhat to her surprise, both physicians told her she was a "social" drinker. The second psychiatrist prescribed a tricyclic antidepressant, but Marion never got around to filling the prescription.

One day Marion accompanied a friend to a meeting of Alcoholics Anonymous. Deeply affected by what she saw and heard, she began going to meetings on her own. She attended thirty meetings in thirty days, during which she was able to stop drinking completely. When she told her psychiatrist how much better she felt, he attributed the improvement entirely to the antidepressant medication—which in fact she had never taken.

A common theory explains addiction as a form of self-medication, in which patients use drugs or alcohol to relieve symptoms of distress such as depression or anxiety. In this model, addiction is regarded as a secondary problem, a response to an underlying psychiatric condition. The logical conclusion of this theory is that if the psychiatric disorder is treated, the addiction will vanish.

It is true that many addicts are at great risk for numerous medical and psychiatric symptoms. But to date, no well-designed rigorous scientific study has found evidence supporting the concept that addiction arises from, and is sustained by, a preexisting illness—quite the opposite. Controlled studies indicate that anxious or depressed people do not necessarily drink more than those who are not anxious or depressed (Miller et al. 1990; Miller and Gold 1991; Gold and Miller 1992). Some confusion may have arisen concerning this question because many alcoholics attribute their drinking to psychological distress. Such reports are by their nature highly subjective. Under controlled, objective laboratory conditions, however, alcoholics are found to become increasingly anxious and depressed *as* they drink—not *before.* Similar findings have been reported for cocaine use in cocaine addicts (Miller et al. 1990; Gold and Miller 1992).

Furthermore, there is little evidence supporting the claim that alcohol or drug addiction "causes" psychiatric symptoms, such as those of bipolar disorder or schizophrenia, which may persist beyond the intoxication period. No studies show that one's basic personality structure is irreparably altered by addiction, while data do exist to support the idea that one's core personality usually reemerges when the effects of drugs or alcohol subside. It is certainly true that symptoms of anxiety and depression may arise during, or be masked by, alcohol and drug use. Nevertheless, studies do not show an increased prevalence of these disorders among alcoholics and drug addicts who are abstinent. Instead, the weight of available evidence indicates that addiction is a separate disorder that can cause feelings of anxiety and depression, and that psychiatric distress, in and of itself, does not cause addiction (Miller and Gold 1991).

Reinforcement and Addiction

Neither theory of addiction—that it is defined by the presence of withdrawal symptoms or that it is a form of self-medication—bears up under strict scientific scrutiny.

However, one model that recently has gained support looks at addiction as a self-reinforcing phenomenon. According to this concept, addictive drugs act directly on the reinforcing functions of the central nervous system. In this way drug use is analogous to biologically essential behaviors, such as eating and sex, which also reinforce themselves through neurotransmitter-mediated responses of reward, pleasure, and satisfaction (Gold and Miller 1992).

The reinforcement theory thus leads to a definition of addiction as *the pursuit of drugs despite negative consequences.* Such a definition also helps explain why certain other behaviors, such as compulsive gambling, sexual activity, and eating, resemble addictive disorders, since all of these behaviors access complex neurochemical mechanisms of reward and reinforcement. This theory has profound ramifications for the understanding and treatment of a range of addictive and psychiatric disorders (Gold 1993b).

The following sections discuss in more detail the biological basis for the reinforcing properties of various drugs of addiction.

Neurochemistry of Addictive and Psychiatric Disorders

General Aspects

To date, researchers have hypothesized specific neurochemical abnormalities that would account for the symptoms seen in most of the major psychiatric state disorders, including the following (Meltzer 1987):

- mania
- major depressive disorders
- schizophrenia and related psychotic states
- specific anxiety disorders, such as panic disorder and obsessive-compulsive disorder
- aggressive and other disinhibited states
- a variety of organic mental disorders

In addition, neurochemical changes associated with states of intoxication and the syndromes of withdrawal and chronic use have been hypothesized for alcohol as well as a number of major drugs of abuse (Meltzer 1987; Jaffe 1990). Clinical studies have also identified powerful genetic factors associated with higher risk of bipolar disorder, depressive disorder, schizophrenia, alcoholism, and alcohol and drug addiction. Such findings serve to underscore the physiological origins of, and inherited vulnerability to, these conditions.

Psychiatric disorders and substance use disorders tend to recur, causing episodic acute exacerbations. Any valid explanation for these conditions would need to account not just for the onset of single episodes but for the entire course of the illness. As will be shown, the neurochemical model elegantly meets that criterion.

Neurochemistry of Addictive Disorders

One of the most important neurotransmitters is dopamine (DA), which is involved in various physiological processes, including digestion, vasodilation, and muscle function. When molecules of drugs such as amphetamine or cocaine penetrate the blood-brain barrier, they flow into the synapses and block the reuptake of DA into the presynaptic neuron (Gold and Dackis 1984; Miller and Gold 1987; Gold 1993a). As a result, greater concentrations of DA remain in the synapses, thus causing postsynaptic neurons to continue generating electrical impulses.

Numerous studies have found evidence that increased DA levels are associated with positive reinforcement. In other words, the behavior that produced the higher levels is rewarded by increased DA-related brain activity.

Several drugs are known to enhance DA levels. In addition to amphetamine and cocaine, nicotine is considered a positive reinforcer, although not as potent as other stimulants. Tetrahydrocannabinol (THC), the active ingredient in cannabis (marijuana), acts like DA in the brain and is considered a dopamine agonist that mimics the reinforcing effects of the neurotransmitter. Ethanol has also been found to stimulate the release of DA (Gold and Miller 1992).

Opiates such as heroin or methadone act at their receptors on dopamine-producing neurons. Laboratory studies show that injecting opiates directly into specific areas of the brain can activate feeding behavior. In addition, pharmacological inhibition of the dopamine system in hungry and thirsty animals reduces the reinforcing effects of food and water (Gold and Miller 1992). Such findings provide additional evidence that opiates interact with the DA system to reinforce biological drive states.

Opiate antagonist drugs such as naloxone and naltrexone have been found to block the stimulation and reward effects produced by all classes of addictive drugs, including opiates, cocaine, amphetamine, ethanol, and benzodiazepines (Gardner 1992). This fact indicates that the body's own natural opioid system is involved in producing responses, not just to opiates but to a range of substances. As of this writing studies are under way to investigate the connections between the endogenous opioid and dopamine systems in an effort to further explain the addiction process.

The Neurochemistry of Psychiatric Disorders

Since the 1950s the neurochemistry of mood disorders has been studied extensively (Meltzer 1987; Goodwin and Jamison 1990). Theories concerning the pathophysiology of depression and bipolar affective disorder have focused on neurotransmitters known as the monoamines: dopamine, serotonin (often abbreviated 5-HT), and norepinephrine (NE).

Receptors for these neurotransmitters are found in various parts of the central nervous system, such as the hypothalamus and the limbic system, which are involved in the vegetative and the cognitive symptoms of depression. Furthermore, these neurotransmitter systems are thought to be involved in regulating the brain's pleasure and reward responses (Meltzer 1987; Jaffe 1990; Wise 1988).

The neurochemical model suggests that depression is essentially a deficit state. (See table 3.1.) In other words, depressed mood is associated with lower levels of neurotransmission. These low levels may be due to decreased neurotransmitter turnover (i.e., production, release, and reuptake), decreased receptor sensitivity, or a number of other mechanisms. This hypothesis is supported by studies showing that virtually all antidepressant medications facilitate monoaminergic neurotransmission (Meltzer 1987; Goodwin and Jamison 1990). In contrast, mania is apparently related to *increased* activity in the NE and DA systems (Meltzer 1987; Goodwin and Jamison 1990).

TABLE 3.1
HYPOTHESIZED DRUG-INDUCED DEFICIENCY STATES ASSOCIATED WITH DEPRESSION

Drug	*Neurochemical Deficiency*	*Mechanism*
Opioids (Methadone)	Endogenous opiates	Feedback inhibition of synthesis; and receptor down-regulation secondary to chronic use of opioid agonists
Cocaine	Dopamine	Feedback inhibition of synthesis and depletion of neuronal dopamine secondary to blockade of reuptake of synaptic dopamine
Alcohol	Serotonin	Serotonin depletion

Studies on patients with schizophrenia, mania, and stimulant intoxication suggest that the pathophysiology of acute psychotic disorders involves excessive levels of dopamine (Meltzer 1987). All available antipsychotic agents appear to work by blocking DA receptors or by otherwise reducing the effects of this neurotransmitter. These antipsychotic medications are used to treat any hyper-DA psychosis.

At this time there is no strong evidence to demonstrate a neurochemical basis for the anxiety disorders. However, norepinephrine overactivity is a likely explanation, since this neurotransmitter is involved in the central and sympathetic arousal seen in many anxiety states (Meltzer 1987; Gold 1993c). Also, the discovery of natural (endogenous) benzodiazepine receptors in the brain suggests that anxiety disorders may also involve changes in this system.

Patients with obsessive-compulsive disorder often respond well to serotonergic antidepressants such as clomipramine and fluoxetine. It is logical, therefore, to predict that a serotonin deficit may underlie this condition.

Physiological events such as lactate infusion or carbon dioxide inhalation can trigger episodes of panic disorder in patients with a history of this disorder. Such findings support the notion that panic involves a specific neurochemical abnormality, although exactly what this defect might be is not yet known.

Aggression and other forms of behavioral disinhibition are heterogeneous both in cause and in neurochemistry (Meltzer 1987). Similarly, impulse control disorders may be related to deficits in different neurochemical inhibiting systems as well as to organic brain syndromes of various origin. However, studies have consistently found a specific association between decreased serotonin function and aggressive behavior. Violent aggression and suicide also have been associated with low levels of a certain serotonin metabolite, 5-hydroxyindoleacetic acid (5-HIAA) (Goodwin and Jamison 1990; Brown and Goodwin 1986).

The Neurochemistry of Psychiatric Symptoms Arising from Cocaine Addiction

The same neurochemical changes associated with primary addictive disorders apparently produce psychiatric syndromes. A well-researched example of this is the impact of cocaine on the dopamine, norepinephrine, and serotonin systems (Meltzer 1987; Jaffe 1990; Wise 1988; Gold 1993a).

> Seth is a thirty-six-year-old man with schizophrenia. He had been a long-time user of cocaine, but with the help of his psychiatrist, his case manager, and his Narcotics Anonymous (NA) sponsor, he had stayed clean and sober for eight months.
>
> Recently, though, the government-sponsored program that provided him with a part-time job was canceled. After living on his own for several years, he was now forced to move back to his parents' home. A few weeks later his mother died. These sudden changes made him very depressed; he began feeling paranoid and believed that no one liked him. His hallucinations became more frequent and severe. Believing the "voices" he heard were caused by his medication, he cut back on the dosage despite the advice of his physicians. What's more, he stopped going to NA meetings altogether.
>
> For the first time since he had stopped using, Seth began to believe that if he wanted to feel better he had to go back to his "old stomping grounds"—the neighborhood near his old apartment. He told himself he just wanted to see his "old buddies" in hopes of raising his spirits. But when he found himself on a familiar street, all the memories and associations of his cocaine-using days came flooding back. He spotted the storefront where he used to buy his drugs. The door was open—and he found himself walking toward it, already anticipating the rush he would get from sniffing the snowy white powder....
>
> Later, he said that he didn't know why he'd relapsed. And his depression and paranoia grew even worse.

Seth's situation is typical of many addicts with other mental illnesses who relapse. His decision to cut back on his treatment was a clear warning sign that relapse was imminent. Despite his belief to the contrary, Seth's depression and paranoid thoughts did not improve with cocaine use; they grew worse.

Cocaine produces euphoria by blocking the reuptake of DA, thus increasing the amount of DA circulating in the synapses. For cocaine to produce behavioral effects in laboratory animals, those animals must have intact dopamine systems. Furthermore, the effects of cocaine can be blocked by specific DA blockers such as haloperidol, an antipsychotic medication used in the treatment of schizophrenia. Cocaine addicts often experience symptoms of psychosis, such as paranoia. Taken as a whole, these findings support the hypothesis that cocaine addiction and psychotic disorders, specifically schizophrenia, both involve abnormalities in the dopamine system.

Cocaine addiction appears to affect other neurotransmitter systems as well.

The aggressive behavior seen among users of cocaine, especially in the form of "crack," may arise from decreased levels or function of serotonin. And elevated norepinephrine activity may underlie the panic attacks often associated with cocaine use (Gold and Slaby 1991).

Neurochemical findings suggest that chronic use of (or withdrawal from) cocaine may eventually deplete the body's stores of dopamine (Gold 1993a; Dackis and Gold 1985). In studies on cocaine-dependent rats, decreased DA levels were found to produce decreased serum levels of the DA metabolite homovanillic acid (HVA); clinical studies found elevated serum levels of prolactin as well as receptor super-

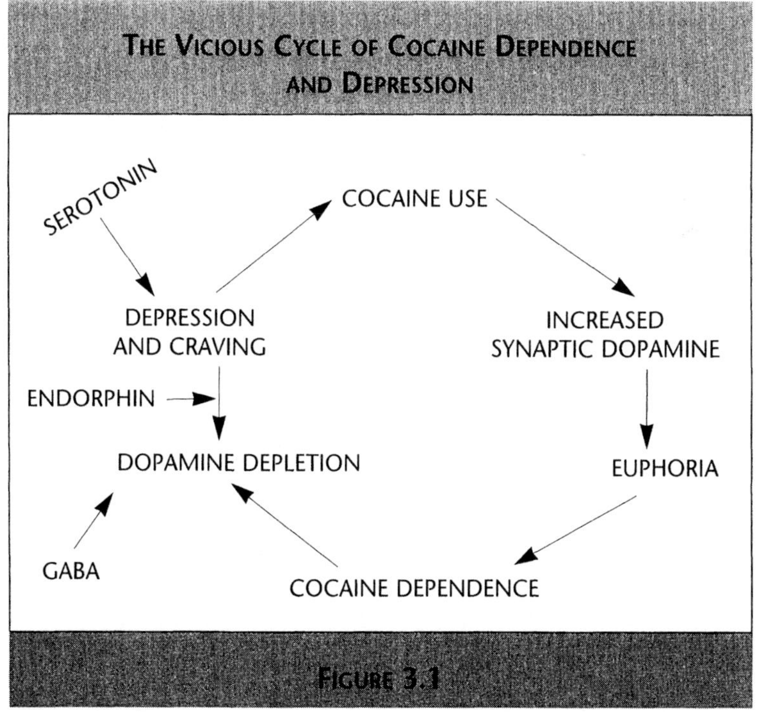

FIGURE 3.1

sensitivity in cocaine-dependent patients (Gold 1993a). Clinically, dopamine deficiency is associated with low energy, depression, and intense cocaine craving (Jaffe 1990). In sum, dopamine depletion may account for the clinical depression seen in many cocaine users (Mirin et al. 1984; Gold 1993a). The dopamine depletion hypothesis is also supported by the fact that pharmacological agents such as bromocriptine and amantadine, which possess dopamine agonist properties, effectively relieve the low energy, depression, and craving associated with cocaine withdrawal (Gold 1993a; Gold and Slaby 1991; Dackis and Gold 1985; Gold and Miller 1992).

Neurochemical Interactions Between Addictive and Psychiatric Disorders

Chronic use of cocaine and other stimulants appears to exacerbate psychosis and aggression (due to effects on the dopamine and serotonin systems) as well as depression (probably because of dopamine depletion) (Dackis and Gold 1985; Gold 1993a). This can be a lethal combination in individuals who possess suicidal tendencies. In patients with preexisting psychiatric illnesses, cocaine may trigger or worsen episodes of schizophrenic psychosis, paranoia, panic, or mania (Jaffe 1990; Goodwin and Jamison 1990).

Alcohol use initially appears to stimulate serotonin (5-HT) function; chronic alcoholism, however, is associated with decreased 5-HT function and with decreased serotonin metabolite (5-HIAA) levels in the cerebrospinal fluid (Meltzer 1987; Jaffe 1990; Goodwin and Jamison 1990). It is reasonable to assume, therefore, that by compromising 5-HT function in patients with depressive disorders, alcoholism may exacerbate depression and suicidal tendencies. Similarly, chronic abuse of alcohol or sedatives suppresses cortical function, which disinhibits behavior and which therefore may exacerbate aggressive tendencies.

Withdrawal from alcohol and sedatives arouses the sympathetic nervous system and may increase catecholamine (NE, DA) metabolism (Meltzer 1987; Jaffe 1990). Withdrawal may also lead to changes in endogenous benzodiazepine systems (Meltzer 1987). These rebound phenomena may explain why withdrawal can exacerbate anxiety states such as panic disorder (Brown and Goodwin 1986; Gold and Slaby 1991; Miller and Gold 1991). Some patients with anxiety disorders who develop alcohol or benzodiazepine dependence may have a particularly difficult time giving up these substances because of withdrawal-related changes. Often these individuals need a protracted and well-supervised detoxification to reduce anxiety and minimize the risk of further dependence on alcohol and sedatives (Jaffe 1990; Brown and Goodwin 1986; Gold and Slaby 1991; Miller and Gold 1991). Alprazolam, a benzodiazepine with an intermediate half-life, is associated with significant withdrawal effects that may mimic the initial panic symptoms for which the drug was prescribed in the first place. (Jaffe 1990).

In some patients chronic marijuana use can produce anhedonia (lack of pleasure or enthusiasm), which in turn may exacerbate depressive symptoms and the negative symptoms of schizophrenia (Gold 1989). Similarly, marijuana may induce paranoia and perceptual distortions, which may exacerbate schizophrenia or other psychotic illnesses (Jaffe 1990; Regier et al. 1990). The specific neurochemistry of these effects of marijuana is not well understood (Jaffe 1990; Miller and Gold 1994).

Hallucinogens may also exacerbate underlying psychotic disorders; LSD is thought to exert its effects at least in part by inhibiting central 5-HT functioning (Jaffe 1990). Withdrawal from opioids may trigger rebound hyperactivity in the norepinephrine system, which may explain why patients withdrawing from these drugs often experience panic or anxiety (Jaffe 1990; Gold 1993c).

Some patients in chronic pain may overuse painkillers, which may cause the body's own opioid systems to shut down or otherwise malfunction. As a result, they become dependent on these medications. If they experience recurring pain during withdrawal, they are vulnerable to relapse to opiate addiction, leading to a vicious cycle of addictive drug use (Jaffe 1990).

To summarize: Addiction and psychiatric disorders involve a range of complex pathological changes in the neurochemistry of the brain. Because neurotransmitters produce a variety of physiological effects, symptoms caused by one disorder may mask, mimic, or overlap symptoms of another. Awareness of this concept enables health care providers to better recognize the true cause(s) of their patients' distress and to offer more effective treatment.

References

Brown, G. L., and F. K. Goodwin. 1986. Cerebrospinal fluid correlates of suicide attempts and aggression. *Annals of the New York Academy of Science* 487:175-88.

Dackis, C. A., and M. S. Gold. 1985. Bromocriptine as treatment of cocaine abuse. *Lancet* 1:1151-52.

Gardner, E. L. 1992. Brain reward mechanism. Chap. 7 in *Substance abuse: A comprehensive textbook,* 2d ed., edited by J. H. Lowinson, P. Ruiz, and R. B. Millman. Baltimore: Williams & Wilkins.

Gold, M. S. 1989. *Drugs of abuse: A comprehensive series for clinicians, vol. 1. Marijuana.* New York and London: Plenum Medical Book Company.

———. 1993a. *Drugs of abuse: A comprehensive series for clinicians, vol. 3. Cocaine.* New York and London: Plenum Medical Book Company.

———. 1993b. Is there a treatment or treatments for addiction? *Contemporary Psychology* 38:1119-20.

———. 1993c. Opiate addiction and the locus coeruleus. *Psychiatric Clinics of North America* 16:61-73.

Gold, M. S., and C. A. Dackis. 1984. New insights and treatments: Opiate withdrawal and cocaine addiction. *Clinical Therapy* 7:6-21.

Gold, M. S., and N. S. Miller. 1992. Seeking drugs/alcohol and avoiding withdrawal: The neuroanatomy of drive states and withdrawal. *Psychiatric Annals* 22:430-35.

Gold, M. S., and A. E. Slaby, eds. 1991. *Dual diagnosis in substance abuse.* New York: Marcel Dekker, Inc.

Goodwin, F. K., and K. R. Jamison. 1990. *Manic-depressive illness.* New York and Oxford: Oxford University Press.

Jaffe, J. H. 1990. Drug addiction and drug abuse. In *The pharmacological basis of therapeutics,* edited by A. G. Gilman et al. New York: Pergamon Press.

Meltzer, H. Y., ed. 1987. *Psychopharmacology: The third generation of progress.* New York: Raven Press.

Miller, N. S., and M. S. Gold. 1987. The relationship of addiction, tolerance, and dependence to alcohol and drugs: A neurochemical approach. *Journal of Substance Abuse Treatment* 4:197-207.

———. 1991. *Drugs of abuse: A comprehensive series for clinicians, vol. 2. Alcohol.* New York and London: Plenum Medical Book Company.

———. 1992. The role of the psychiatrist in addiction evaluation and treatment. *Psychiatric Annals* 22:436-40.

———. 1994. LSD and Ecstasy: Pharmacology, phenonemology, and treatment. *Psychiatric Annals* 24:131-33.

Miller, N. S., J. C. Mahler, B. M. Belkin, and M. S. Gold. 1990. Psychiatric diagnosis in alcohol and drug dependence. *Annals of Clinical Psychiatry* 3 (1):79-89.

Mirin, S. M., R. D. Weiss, A. Sollogub, and J. Michael. 1984. Affective illness in substance abusers. In *Substance abuse and psychopathology,* edited by S. M. Mirin. Washington DC: American Psychiatric Press, 57-77.

Regier, D. A., M. E. Farmer, D. S. Rae, B. Z. Locke, S. J. Keith, L. L. Judd, and F. K. Goodwin. 1990. Comorbidity of mental disorders with alcohol and drug abuse. *JAMA* 264:2511-18.

Wise, R. 1988. The neurobiology of craving: Implications for the understanding and treatment of addiction. *Journal of Abnormal Psychology* 118-32.

SETTINGS

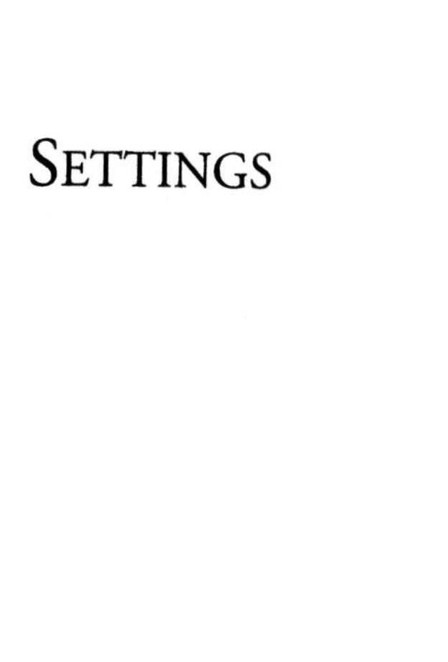

The treatment of dual diagnosis patients benefits from a unified conceptual framework using the disease and recovery models for both addictive and psychiatric disorders. Specific interventions include psychiatric medication and Twelve Step programs.

4
Treating the Dually Diagnosed In Psychiatric Settings

Kenneth Minkoff, M.D.

Introduction to the Problem

It's 3:00 a.m.—J. T., a twenty-six-year-old single man, arrives in the Psychiatric Emergency Service for the eighth time in the past three months: he's psychotic, agitated, and apparently intoxicated. Psychiatric emergency clinicians are well aware that J. T. has been noncompliant with outpatient psychiatric treatment and continually out of control with polysubstance dependence, including alcohol, marijuana, and cocaine.

The acuity of this psychosis fluctuates with the degree of his intoxication. Although currently desperate for help, he is likely to be much calmer in a few hours when sober and will probably refuse treatment. The consensus of the emergency clinicians is to postpone assessment until he is sober and then allow him to leave unless he is committable.

* * *

K. B. is a forty-one-year old woman who is separated from her husband. She was admitted to a psychiatric unit in a general hospital following an overdose of amitriptyline, alprazolam, and alcohol, precipitated by her husband's admission that he was having an affair and moving out. Ms. B. has been in outpatient treatment for "anxiety and depression" for two years, having been given multiple mood stabilizers, antidepressants, and benzodiazepines, without success. History obtained after admission from her husband and teenage children reveals a significant history of progressive alcohol dependence over the past ten years. Ms. B. refuses to acknowledge that she has an alcohol problem, maintaining that her drinking is due only to depression and anxiety caused by her failing marriage. Many of the clinicians on her treatment team agree with this assessment, and a change in antidepressant and an increase in alprazolam is recommended, particularly when the patient becomes more anxious and tremulous on the third hospital day.

* * *

C. L. is a thirty-five-year-old man with chronic schizophrenia. He lives in a supervised community residence and has irregularly attended a community clubhouse program for the past three years. Mr. L.'s progress has been limited. Although attached to staff at the residence, he regularly drinks alcohol to excess and is intermittently noncompliant with his medication. Although observed by both staff and other patients to be intoxicated, he continually denies that he has had more than one drink and refuses referral to treatment services for substance abuse. His outpatient clinic therapist, case manager, and other clinicians have attempted to control his money, limit his privileges, and confront his denial, but this has resulted only in increased anger and defensiveness on his part. Some of the program staff feel he should be terminated from the residence; others feel his psychotropic medication (trifluoperazine, 10 mg twice daily), should be withheld unless he stops drinking.

These three case examples, each in a different psychiatric setting (emergency room, inpatient unit, and outpatient program), illustrate just some of the variability and complexity of the dual diagnosis cases which present in these settings. Psychiatric clinicians working in these settings often experience powerful feelings of helplessness, confusion, and frustration when attempting to work with these patients, feelings which may readily lead to pejorative labeling ("drunk," "borderline," "manipulative," "antisocial"), lack of empathy, avoidance, and outright rejection. In other instances, such as in the second case, lack of training in recognizing and treating substance dependence may lead to misdiagnosis, inappropriate psychopharmacology and psychotherapy, and undertreatment of addiction-related pathology.

It is very striking that in much of our psychiatric service system, despite the high comorbidity of psychopathology and substance disorders, otherwise superb psychiatric treatment programs have little or no mechanisms for addressing substance disorders, and that otherwise well-trained and highly experienced clinicians feel relatively incompetent dealing with dual diagnosis patients. This situation often creates powerful barriers to effective treatment of dual diagnosis patients in psychiatric settings. Addictive disorders may be unrecognized or minimized to establish the patient's legitimacy as a "psych patient"; when addictive behavior becomes out of control, the patient may be relabeled as "really an addiction patient" and referred to a substance abuse treatment facility (which in turn may be unable to deal with the patient's psychopathology and may therefore refer the patient back). This has been termed "ping-pong therapy" (Ridgely et al. 1990).

We will briefly discuss systemic, clinical, and philosophical barriers to integrated treatment in psychiatric settings, and then propose a conceptual methodology for overcoming these barriers and facilitating the development of an integrated approach.

Systemic Barriers

In part due to chronic underattention to addictive disorders on the part of the mental health professions, a separate treatment system for alcohol and drug disorders has emerged in this country during the past fifty years, reified on the federal level (until recently) in three distinct agencies—NIMH, NIAAA, and NIDA—each with its own separate funding streams and clinical philosophies. This separation has been replicated—in total or in part—in every state (Ridgely et al. 1990), and have resulted in distinct dollars, programs, and clinicians being dedicated to substance services versus psychiatric services in each local area. No category of psychiatric illness in *DSM-III-R* other than substance abuse disorders is represented by a distinct service system.

As a consequence of this service system separation, clinicians have tended to identify themselves as either mental health or addiction specialists—rarely developing expertise in both areas.

Clinical and Philosophical Barriers

Five decades of separate service systems have contributed to the emergence of distinct clinical philosophies, which some have termed "irreconcilable" (Ridgely et al. 1986). In the perception of clinicians in psychiatric settings, traditional Twelve Step models of addiction treatment are unscientific and nonprofessional, relying on "self-help groups" and recovering counselors to deliver treatment. Psychiatric clinicians tend to minimize the importance of intensive participation in recovery programs such as AA, and overvalue the use of psychopharmacology and dynamic psychotherapy to treat the "primary" psychiatric problem that "causes" the "secondary" substance dependence. AA and related programs may be perceived as being incompatible with the need for psychotropic medication. Perhaps most important, psychiatric clinicians—and service systems—may adhere to philosophies of case management and deinstitutionalization, which conflict with the philosophies of empathic detachment and recovery that are the basis of much of addiction treatment.

As "case managers," clinicians in the mental health systems assume the responsibility for identifying client needs and providing services to meet those needs. If patients do not do well—for example, if they drink—the case manager assumes responsibility for the poor outcome, protects the patient from its negative consequences, and tries harder to meet the client's needs so he or she won't drink. In addition, because of the priority given to deinstitutionalization, hospitalization is avoided except in the most life-threatening circumstances, and clients are encouraged not to request such high levels of care.

In addiction treatment settings, by contrast, clinicians convey empathic detachment, caring for the client but requiring the client to assume responsibility to ask for the help needed to stay sober. If patients do not do well, they are expected to bear the negative consequences themselves as a stimulus to ask for more help. At the same time, the treatment system encourages patients to ask for as much help as possible—including hospitalization when indicated—to foster sobriety in the short run and promote recovery in the long run. Psychiatric clinicians often feel that having such expectations of disabled clients and offering them such resources are inappropriate, and lead clinicians to resist using typical addiction treatment interventions for such clients (Minkoff 1991).

Because these barriers create the impression that simultaneous and integrated treatments of addictive disorders and psychiatric disorders are mutually incompatible—according to standard interventions in each field—clinicians on both sides have turned away from integrated approaches. In order to change this, a unified conceptual framework is needed. Such a framework was first described by Minkoff (1989, 1991) and has begun to be applied in a range of psychiatric settings. The basic principles of this model are described below.

INTEGRATED CONCEPTUAL FRAMEWORK FOR THE TREATMENT OF DUAL DIAGNOSIS

Within psychiatric settings, dual diagnosis treatment is facilitated by emphasizing the following four principles.

1. Dual diagnosis is an expectation, not an exception, in psychiatric settings. Extensive epidemiologic literature (see Regier et al. 1990 in particular) indicates that the majority of patients with serious mental illness have coexisting substance disorders. Consequently, every clinician, and every program, must be prepared to address dual diagnosis in any patient treated and to incorporate assessment and treatment of substance abuse disorders into routine procedures.

For example, emergency assessment of dual diagnosis patients—as in the case of J. T. above—is facilitated by the use of an assessment tool that provides equal space for the detailed evaluation of both substance disorders and other psychopathology. In our setting, for instance, we use a three-page instrument. The first page describes the presenting problem; the second page provides for a psychiatric assessment (mental status, etc.) on one side and a substance assessment (signs of intoxication/withdrawal, use of recovery programs, etc.) on the other; and the final page describes diagnosis, formulation, and intervention.

2. When dual diagnosis is present, both diagnoses must be considered primary. Although psychiatric symptoms may contribute to substance abuse, and although substance abuse may cause or exacerbate psychiatric symptoms, psychiatric disorders and addictive disorders must each be treated as primary disorders when they coexist, each one requiring specific and intensive treatment. A common difficulty in psychiatric settings is that patients with serious addiction may be treated

only for psychiatric disturbance, with the expectation that if the psychiatric symptoms improve, the patient "won't have to drink." This is a consequence of the "self-medication" hypothesis of addiction.

It is important to recognize, however, that whichever emotional difficulties initially lead to the onset of heavy drinking or drug use, once the disease of addiction emerges, it becomes a primary disorder with self-sustaining substance use that persists despite negative consequences.

In the case of K. B., for example, focusing on "anxiety and depression" in the psychiatric unit leads not only to inadequate attention to her alcoholism, but to (a) inappropriate increases in medication in a patient who is actively drinking, and (b) underrecognition of impending alcohol withdrawal.

In our unit, we developed a full addiction program in addition to a full psychiatric program, without additional staffing, by prioritizing the importance of addiction treatment compared to other therapeutic activities and recognizing that at least 50 percent of our admissions had substance disorders.

All of our staff are cross-trained to work with either population, so that patients can stay with the same treatment team even if they change programs. In an integrated treatment setting such as ours, K. B. would be admitted initially to the psychiatric program because she was suicidal and not ready for addiction treatment. She would be withdrawn from alcohol, tapered from benzodiazepines, but maintained on non-addictive psychotropic medications until a clearer assessment could be made. (Note that for patients like K. B. [i.e., actively substance-abusing patients] we use phenobarbital for withdrawal from prescribed benzodiazepines, switching the patients immediately to a comparable dosage [e.g., 1 mg of clonazepam = 30 mg of phenobarbital] and then tapering. This is medically safe, and has the psychological advantage of quickly discontinuing the attachment to the medication.) During the initial withdrawal period, family assessment would determine readiness for a confrontation of the patient's need for addiction treatment. Once the patient had been initially engaged by her treatment team, she would be confronted (by staff and family) with her need to address her alcoholism and told she had to switch to the addiction program in order to remain in treatment.

3. Addiction and major mental illness are both examples of primary, chronic, biologic mental illnesses that fit into the "disease and recovery" model for conceptualizing assessment, diagnosis, and treatment.

As described by Minkoff (1989, 1991), the diseases of addiction and major mental illness have numerous parallels. They are both chronic, incurable, biologic brain diseases characterized by a lack of control of thought and behavior. Both have positive and negative symptoms. The negative symptoms of addiction are the neuropsychological and developmental deficits which remain once initial detoxification is completed and which require long-term rehabilitation to resolve. Both diseases can be stabilized with proper treatment (daily medication and various support programs for major mental illness; occasionally medication, but more commonly regular participation in a Twelve Step recovery program for addiction) and tend to progressively worsen without treatment. For both illnesses, treatment tends to be readily available, but patients are commonly noncompliant. Treatment tends to focus, therefore, on addressing the person who suffers from the illness, and dealing with his or her feelings of denial, stigma, shame, guilt, failure, and despair, which are characteristic of individuals struggling with any chronic mental illness.

Similarly, both illnesses are characterized by parallel processes of recovery, with at least four distinct phases: (1) acute stabilization, (2) engagement in initial treatment, (3) active treatment to achieve prolonged stabilization, and (4) rehabilitation.

Recovery is an internal psychological process by which an individual suffering a chronic incurable disabling condition recovers a sense of hope, purpose, and self-worth that enables him or her to make maximal use of treatment and rehabilitation and achieve the best possible level of functioning, even though the individual may remain symptomatic and disabled. Typically, the process of recovery takes many years and involves multiple treatment episodes in a variety of settings. Following are descriptions of the four phases:

- *Acute stabilization.* Involves stabilizing acute psychosis and/or detoxification, usually with medication in an inpatient setting.
- *Engagement.* Begins before or during the process of stabilization and involves (a) empathic connection with the patient "where he's

at"; (b) maintaining a relationship based on both empathic detachment and case management, in which the clinician provides what the patient needs (medication, residential supports), takes control when necessary (e.g., when the patient is committable), but remains detached from that which must be the patient's responsibility (the consequences of choosing to continue substance use or refusing voluntary psychiatric services); (c) educating the patient about the nature of his or her illnesses and the choices needed to be made to treat them; and (d) awaiting opportunities for empathic confrontation of the consequences of noncompliance, in which the patient may choose to accept treatment rather than accept those consequences.

- *Active treatment.* Begins when the patient participates in ongoing treatment (via medication compliance, AA, etc.) to maintain stability and/or sobriety. The focus on maintaining prolonged stabilization must take priority over moving too quickly to rehabilitation, or relapse will quickly occur. Ordinarily, patients must maintain stability for at least a year and work on asking for help to resist impulses to discontinue treatment prematurely before moving on to rehabilitation.
- *Rehabilitation.* Can proceed when both illnesses are stabilized. It involves learning new skills to enhance the quality of life and level of functioning while remaining cognizant of the risk of relapse and the need to maintain stabilizing treatment, but with lesser intensity (continuing AA meetings, but going less frequently, or continuing medication, but at reduced amounts).

For patients with dual diagnosis, each patient moves through these phases at his or her own pace, and generally at different rates for each disease. This leads to the next principle.

4. There is no one type of dual diagnosis treatment. Specific treatment interventions must be individualized, based on the phase of recovery; the level of acuity, severity, and disability; and the patient's motivation for treatment for each disease.

Let us consider the case of C. L. (case 3 at the beginning of this chapter):

> C. L. is psychiatrically disabled and participating in the maintenance phase of treatment for his psychiatric disorder, with ongoing residential and day support. In addition, he is clearly substance-dependent, since he meets DSM-III-R criteria by virtue of lack of control of substance use despite its ongoing harmful consequences in his living environment. However, he is just at the beginning of the engagement phase for his addictive disorder and has not even begun to consider his substance use as a problem.

This situation is extremely common in all psychiatric settings, particularly those treating the chronically mentally ill. Caregivers in these settings feel responsible for their substance-abusing clients and consequently attempt—usually unsuccessfully—to control or protect them. This leads to frustration for all concerned and results in the caregivers feeling like codependents in an alcoholic family. Inappropriate rejection from treatment or inappropriate termination of medication, as is contemplated with C. L., may result.

For engagement of psychiatrically disabled patients who are substance-abusing, the best approach involves developing specific treatment interventions and applying these interventions in any of the patient's psychiatric treatment settings (e.g., C. L.'s community residence). This can be done in individual sessions, but group is the most effective modality (Sciacca 1991; Kofoed et al., 1986).

As described by Sciacca, engagement groups are designed to be open discussions with an educational format. The overt goal is not to persuade patients to abstain, but to help group members become better informed about substances in order to make better choices. Ideally, the group leader is a clinician who is *not* identified as a substance abuse "expert" with a known agenda. The format of the group is to provide educational materials or speakers on the subject of alcohol, drugs (including caffeine and nicotine), and addiction recovery, and then to foster open discussion and critique. The influence of the peer group is more powerful than that of the clinician, and eventually members begin to (a) open up and start being honest about their substance use, (b) consider that they may have a problem, (c) try to change on their own, and finally (d) consider asking for help or getting treatment. The leader must facilitate this process by resisting the temptation to confront or preach; if a previously reticent patient opens up about the "wonderful drunk" he had the previous weekend, the proper response is to praise the patient for having the courage to share and then ask for comments from the group.

The explicit stance of the clinician in this type of group—and in any intervention for substance abuse engagement with mentally ill patients—should be the following:

> We recommend abstinence but we respect your right to make your own choices. You can drink or drug as much as you want to; how much you want to will depend on your decisions about benefits versus consequences. We will clarify consequences and offer help if you want it, but we don't want to try to run your life.

Now, let us turn to specific treatment interventions in the various phases of recovery.

Treatment Interventions for Dual Diagnosis Patients

Acute Stabilization/Psychopharmacology

There is often considerable uncertainty in psychiatric settings about how to medicate patients who may require simultaneous detoxification and stabilization of psychiatric symptoms.

We recommend the following guidelines:

1. Acute treatment of major mental illness should be conducted according to standard procedures, using standard medications, regardless of the presence of coexisting substance dependence or withdrawal. This may include acute use of parenteral or oral benzodiazepines to control acute psychosis or agitation.
2. Even if acute psychosis may be due to acute or chronic drug intoxication, proceed with neuroleptic stabilization. Discontinuation of *acute* antipsychotic medication may be considered once the psychosis has completely cleared and two weeks have elapsed since last use of drugs.
3. Patients with depression, anxiety, or panic symptoms should not have antidepressant, antipanic medication initiated during

acute detoxification unless the panic or depression is so disabling that the patient cannot participate in addiction treatment, or unless there is a clear history of posttraumatic stress disorder (PTSD). Nonaddictive medication may be initiated during a benzodiazepine or phenobarbital taper once the patient is initially stabilized.

4. Maintenance benzodiazepines are not recommended for addicted patients and should usually be discontinued early in treatment.
5. Mentally ill patients on psychotropic medication who require detoxification should be detoxed using the same protocols as for nonmentally ill patients.
6. Maintenance psychotropic medications (other than benzodiazepines) should not be discontinued during detoxification or early sobriety (up to six to twelve months). In most cases, it is better to err on the side of caution rather than risk exacerbation of mental illness in early recovery, thus jeopardizing sobriety as well.

J. T. (case 1) is admitted for simultaneous detoxification from alcohol and stabilization of schizoaffective disorder. His outpatient medication is depot fluphenazine, imipramine, and clonazepam (1 mg po QID). In the hospital, the patient is initially placed on IM fluphenazine (with oral supplementation until the psychosis clears), and imipramine. The clonazepam is switched to phenobarbital 30mg QID and tapered by 15 mg/day. Oxazepam is used for alcohol withdrawal. IM fluphenazine and imipramine are maintained indefinitely after withdrawal.

Engagement/Confrontation

The process of engagement in individual or group treatment was described earlier. Many patients will choose to "cut down" and then abstain during the course of such a process. Commonly, however, no significant change in behavior takes place unless a confrontation occurs.

In addiction settings, confrontation by employers or families frequently precipitates admission to treatment. With dual diagnosis patients in psychiatric settings, however, confrontation is often done by psychiatric clinicians.

Confrontation is not a verbal attack. Successful confrontation is always based on a caring relationship. It involves genuine, not contrived, consequences of substance abuse and requires the power to enforce all contingencies comfortably, regardless of what the patient chooses to do.

Examples of confrontations we have performed in our setting include the following:

- A stable schizophrenic patient was told that any further reduction in his antipsychotic medication was contingent upon ninety days of sobriety.
- A schizophrenic alcoholic patient in a state hospital was told by her clinician and her mother that she had to begin IM fluphenazine and enter our dual diagnosis treatment program as a condition for returning home, and that if she stopped her shots or lost sobriety she would be asked to leave home or return to the hospital.
- A case manager told a schizoaffective patient who had lost two apartments through cocaine use that she would not find him another apartment unless he successfully completed an addiction treatment program for dual diagnosis patients.
- A clinician at a day treatment program told a patient who was drunk and disruptive in the program that their policy on disruptive behavior or criminal substance use was a forty-eight-hour suspension and an offer of treatment for the first offense, a five-day suspension and an offer of treatment for the second offense, and indefinite suspension until completion of a dual diagnosis addiction program for the third offense.

After the third offense, the patient entered treatment in our unit.

As the last case illustrates, it is often helpful for psychiatric programs to develop clear, objective policies regarding substance use, defining not what is recommended, but what is *truly intolerable*, and outlining a hierarchy of enforceable consequences that culminate in a "termination versus treatment" confrontation. (Patients who are terminated from residential programs should always be offered reasonable options, including hospitalization, so that they do not have to become homeless, unless they refuse those options.)

Having such policies in place ahead of time makes dealing with dual diagnosis patients much more comfortable. In fact, the basic requirements for having a "dual diagnosis residence" for engaging actively using clients are (a) a schedule of engagement groups two to three times per week, and (b) a set of substance abuse policies and procedures.

Active Treatment/Relapse Prevention

Active treatment of the disease of addiction can occur in psychiatric settings, using the disease and recovery model discussed earlier.

The following five guidelines are recommended:

1. The content of addiction treatment in psychiatric settings should not be significantly different from that in addiction settings. Allowances may be made for patients with cognitive limitations imposed by psychiatric disability, but the skills and tasks that must be mastered are the same.
2. Similarly, the intensity of addiction treatment in psychiatric settings must be no less than that in addiction settings. If non-mentally ill addicts require a daily recovery program for addiction, so too do mentally ill addicts.
3. Reasonable stability of psychiatric illness and psychiatric medication is a precondition for successful addiction treatment. Patients usually must work from an established baseline.
4. Continued substance use in an addiction treatment program must become a condition for termination or referral to a more intensive setting.
5. There are two major educational tasks of addiction treatment: (a) teaching cognitive skills of relapse prevention, and (b) teaching utilization of Twelve Step programs of recovery. Each task is discussed below.

Relapse Prevention

Relapse prevention (Marlatt and Gordon 1985; Carroll et al. 1991) is an established cognitive-behavioral technique wherein patients are taught to identify specific thoughts and behaviors that either enhance or threaten recovery and are taught specific skills for addressing them. These techniques are applicable in both individual and group work in psychiatric settings. Specific skills include identifying relapse triggers; addressing ambivalence about abstinence; labeling high-risk situations (negative affects, peer pressure) and developing coping strategies for conditioned cues for craving; addressing and exploring apparently irrevelant decisions that lead to use ("I just went to the bar for a pack of cigarettes"); and distinguishing "lapse" ("I slipped but I can learn from my mistake") from relapse ("I slipped so I might as well keep using"). Some authors (Evans and Sullivan 1990) have recommended using index cards for each relapse trigger to list specific coping strategies. Clubhouse programs can reinforce abstinence by facilitating the development of abstinent social networks to replace ones based on substance use.

> In his day program, D. B. reported to his addiction treatment group that he drank when he felt lonely. The group leader told D. B.'s case administrator to help D. B. develop a "loneliness" index card, listing five phone numbers to call (sponsor, AA numbers, crisis hotline, etc.) when he felt this way. The case administrator then coached D. B. while he made practice calls to each number.

Programs of Recovery

Although many psychiatric clinicians believe that AA/NA, etc., are incompatible with psychiatric treatment ("They're against medication," and so on), there is increasing literature demonstrating clearly that dual diagnosis patients can be fully integrated in the Twelve Step movement (Minkoff 1989; *The Dual Disorders Recovery Book*). A major advantage of generic Twelve Step programs is that they are widely available and free of charge. Dual diagnosis patients are likely to need *daily* support to maintain abstinence; usually dual diagnosis groups in psychiatric settings will not be enough. Some psychiatric settings have established daily dual diagnosis recovery groups (with leaders) that provide abstinence support and relapse prevention training. In our setting (Minkoff 1989) we have emphasized special preparation for AA meetings. This includes (a) instruction in what to talk about and what not to talk about (e.g., "AA is not a place to get medication advice or discuss voices. If hearing voices leads to the urge to drink, you can talk about 'upsetting thoughts' in the meeting"); (b) instruction on which meetings to attend; (c) training in making phone calls, asking for rides, and asking for help (e.g., "'Asking for help' means help getting through a tough time without using; it does not mean that you will feel better, and it does not mean borrowing money or finding a place to live").

It is helpful to have meetings on-site in your setting, both to help AA members perceive that your program is serious about addiction treatment and to facilitate staff attendance (for training purposes) and patient attendance.

Our inpatient unit operates a daily "Awareness" meeting specifically as an introduction to AA for new patients. Patients in recovery come in to run the meeting and to participate in it; it functions like a regular AA meeting. Newcomers are encouraged to participate and ask questions.

For many mentally ill patients who are "trapped" in mental health service systems, participation in Twelve Step programs can represent an active step toward normalcy, as the case of F. A. indicates below.

> F. A. is in his mid-twenties and has schizophrenia. He is quite behaviorally disturbed and lives in a community residence, which makes him very ashamed and angry. He resists all efforts at psychiatric rehabilitation.
>
> He has a twelve-year history of polysubstance addiction; for the past five years he has been working on sobriety. In contrast to his avoidance of the mental health system, he is quite eager to participate in AA, and has acquired many non-mentally ill friends. His sincere desire to get sober is appreciated in AA, despite his lack of social skills. He currently has twenty-one months of sobriety and is holding a part-time job with a sober friend who owns a business.

Conclusion

In summary, utilization of an integrated model based on disease and recovery permits the development of integrated individualized interventions for dual diagnosis patients in psychiatric settings. This approach allows both illnesses to be treated simultaneously with a consistent philosophy and with individualized treatment based on the phase of recovery and the level of acuity, severity, and motivation for treatment associated with each disease.

References

Carroll, K. M., B. J. Rousanville, and D. S. Keller. 1991. Relapse prevention strategies for the treatment of cocaine abuse. *American Journal of Drug and Alcohol Abuse* 17:249-66.

Diagnostic and Statistical Manual of Mental Disorders, 3d ed., rev. (DSM-III-R) 1990. Washington, D.C.: American Psychiatric Association.

The Dual Disorders Recovery Book. 1993. Center City, Minn.: Hazelden Educational Materials.

Evans, K., and J. M. Sullivan. 1990. *Dual diagnosis: Counseling the mentally ill substance abuser.* New York: Guilford Press.

Kofoed, L., J. Kania, T. Walsh, et al. 1986. Outpatient treatment of patients with substance abuse and coexisting psychiatric disorders. *American Journal of Psychiatry* 143:867-72.

Marlatt, G. A., and J. R. Gordon, eds. 1985. Relapse prevention, maintenance strategies. In *Addictive behavior change.* New York: Guilford Press.

Minkoff, K. 1989. An integrated treatment model for dual diagnosis of psychosis and addiction. *Hospital and Community Psychiatry* 40:1031-36.

———. 1991. Program components of a comprehensive integrated care system for seriously mentally ill patients with substance abuse disorders. In *Dual diagnosis of major mental illness and substance disorder,* edited by K. Minkoff and R. E. Drake. San Francisco: Jossey-Bass.

Regier, D. A., M. E. Farmer, D. S. Rae, et al. 1990. Comorbidity of mental disorders with alcohol and other drug abuse disorders. *American Psychiatric Association* 264:2511-18.

Ridgely, M. S. 1991. Creating integrated programs for severely mentally ill persons with substance disorders. In *Dual diagnosis of major mental illness and substance disorder,* edited by K. Minkoff and R. E. Drake. San Francisco: Jossey-Bass.

Ridgely, M. S., H. H. Goldman, and M. Willenbring. 1990. Barriers to the care of persons with dual diagnosis: Organizational financing issues. *Schizophrenic Bulletin* 16:123-32.

Ridgely, M. S., F. C. Osher, and J. A. Talbott. 1986. *Chronic mentally ill young adults with substance abuse problems: Treatment and training issues.* Baltimore: Mental Health Policy Studies, University of Maryland School of Medicine.

Sciacca, K. 1991. An integrated treatment approach for severely mentally ill individuals with substance disorders. In *Dual diagnosis of major mental illness and substance disorder,* edited by K. Minkoff and R. E. Drake. San Francisco: Jossey-Bass.

Dually diagnosed patients require a comprehensive, integrated treatment approach to address both their addiction and psychiatric disorders. Addiction treatment programs can modify their treatment approaches to address these needs.

5
Treating the Dually Diagnosed In Addiction Settings

Mark C. Wallen, M.D.

Introduction

Since their inception, addiction treatment programs have unknowingly been dealing with dually diagnosed patients. Unfortunately, many of these patients, because of their psychiatric symptoms, have done poorly in addiction treatment. Many either sign themselves out of treatment programs against medical advice or are discharged because of so-called treatment resistance. Often these individuals find themselves "ping-ponged" back and forth between the mental health and addiction treatment fields, depending upon which of their symptoms predominate at any one time. They rarely receive simultaneous treatment for both of their problems, as is required for successful treatment (Wallen and Weiner 1987).

We have found that many patients admitted to our addiction treatment programs, both inpatient and outpatient, frequently present with a wide variety of psychiatric symptoms. The symptoms most frequently seen include anxiety and anxiety/panic attacks, depression and/or mood swings, paranoia and other types of psychotic symptoms (delusions, hallucinations, etc.), and a wide variety of behavioral problems suggestive of personality disorders.

The specific cause of these symptoms is highly variable and is often difficult to assess accurately early in the addiction treatment process. It has been our experience that for most patients, these symptoms are due to their substance use and resolve spontaneously with involvement in treatment and ongoing abstinence. For some patients, however, these symptoms may persist for a number of months as the result of a protracted withdrawal syndrome or post-drug-impairment syndrome. For a small but significant minority, the symptoms are due to a coexisting psychiatric disorder.

In our experience, at any one time about 5 to 10 percent of patients presenting for addiction treatment have a coexisting major psychiatric disorder such as major depression, bipolar disorder (manic-depressive illness), panic disorder, or schizophrenia. Another 20 to 25 percent of patients are probably suffering from symptoms of a personality disorder. These two groups, of course, are the dually diagnosed patient population. It is critical to identify the coexistence of a major psychiatric disorder or personality disorder, because if it is not appropriately treated, it may often result in the person's being at a higher risk for relapse to substance use. To complicate matters even more, individuals may present with various types of psychiatric symptoms as a result of their response and reaction to involvement with addiction treatment.

Now, what does all this mean for the addiction counselor? First of all, we need to be aware of the very complex relationship between psychiatric symptoms and addiction, as noted previously. We need to be on the lookout for signs and symptoms which might indicate that the patient has a coexisting psychiatric disorder. Certain elements from the clinical history can be helpful in increasing the probability of a coexisting psychiatric disorder. These include the patient presenting with significant psychiatric symptoms prior to involvement with addicting chemicals, or the presence of psychiatric symptoms during a significant period of total abstinence of at least two to three months. Also, a family history of psychiatric illness is a factor that predisposes individuals to developing similar disorders themselves. We need to be cautious, however, when eliciting family history of psychiatric disorders and treatment, keeping in mind and evaluating the possibility that these relatives may have had addiction problems that resulted in a misdiagnosis of a psychiatric illness.

The key issue for counselors is monitoring the severity of a patient's psychiatric symptoms over time. If they are extremely severe upon initial presentation, or if they persist or worsen with ongoing abstinence, then a referral to a clinical psychologist or psychiatrist who is trained in dealing with addiction is indicated. If a coexisting psychiatric disorder is identified, one that requires treatment with medication, the counselor needs to be supportive of the patient's continuing to take the medication and needs to help the patient understand why it is important for him or her to continue in treatment for both problems. The counselor should have at least some degree of familiarity with the *DSM-IV-R* (which lists all criteria for psychiatric disorders, including diagnostic criteria for substance use disorders). Patients need to meet specific criteria in order to be given a diagnosis of a psychiatric disorder.

Counseling Guidelines

The initial focus of addiction treatment is the therapeutic confrontation of patients who deny they have an addiction problem. This confrontational process commonly involves presenting the individual with all the negative consequences of the addiction with the hope that eventually the person's denial system can be broken through. This therapeutic process commonly elicits anxiety in the addicted individual, which is probably a major factor in finally breaking through the denial. Unfortunately, however, if anxiety is increased in patients with psychiatric symptoms or illnesses, one commonly sees a worsening of the psychiatric symptoms, resulting in the counselor's finding him/herself in a catch-22. Treatment approaches therefore must be modified in order to address this therapeutic dilemma.

Because of the complex relationship between psychiatric symptoms and addiction, we have found that such individuals can best be treated within a framework that provides for a multidisciplinary treatment team approach (Wallen and Weiner 1988). This requires clinicians from both the mental health and addiction fields to work together to formally integrate a treatment plan for the patient. All treatment team members need to have an understanding of the complex relationship between psychiatric symptoms and addictive disorders. We have found that the following fourteen guidelines can serve as a good basis for effective individual counseling:

1. Monitor the patient's psychiatric symptoms on an ongoing basis. If they are extremely severe initially, or if they continue to persist or worsen with ongoing abstinence, refer the patient to a clinical psychologist or psychiatrist for a more in-depth evaluation.
2. If the patient is placed on medication for the treatment of psychotic symptoms (paranoia, delusions, hallucination), provide support for the patient and try to help him or her gain an understanding as to why the medication is being used. The patient should be informed that the medication is being used to treat the psychotic symptoms and not the addiction. Once the symptoms have resolved, the medication can usually be discontinued.
3. Be cautious with intense confrontation early in the treatment process to avoid increasing anxiety, which might worsen the patient's psychiatric symptoms. Focus on "here and now," reality-oriented issues. Avoid highly charged emotional issues of the past until the individual appears capable of dealing with them. Attempt to correct perceptual distortions.
4. Present and discuss issues in a concrete and straightforward manner. Avoid highly abstract concepts. Complex metaphors and similes should be used with extreme caution.
5. Help the patient develop the coping skills necessary to deal with environmental and interpersonal stressors without having to resort to substance use. Focus initially on basic coping skills, such as getting up in the morning on time, dressing and grooming appropriately, and attending to daily activities.
6. Provide structure, guidance, and support. Some patients may be helped by formulating a daily/weekly written schedule with the counselor subsequently monitoring the patient's compliance. However, we need to avoid filling every hour of every day at the beginning, as the individual may become overwhelmed. Start out by including the most important areas the individual must address; with the passage of time, fill in additional time slots.
7. Help the individual identify cues for substance use (people, places, things, etc.) and develop plans to deal with them effec-

tively. Consider the use of role-playing. An important role-playing situation is one in which the individual learns how to turn down substances offered by others or to avoid coercion by others to use.

8. Provide verbal reinforcement for mature, responsible adult behaviors. This can include such simple things as verbally reinforcing the individual for being on time for treatment activities, being appropriately dressed, and completing any assigned tasks.
9. Be on the alert for any changes in the individual's mental status that might indicate a worsening of his or her psychiatric problem. If problems are noted, the individual should be referred to his or her psychiatrist for evaluation.
10. Promote and support involvement in constructive leisure time activities. Additional helpful adjunctive therapies include social skills training, assertiveness training, communication skills training, relaxation training, and art and music therapies.
11. Promote and support involvement in educational and vocational programs as indicated. Many individuals, as a result of their dual problems, have had extreme difficulty in either completing school or working on a regular basis. Individuals may be helped by formulating a plan to help them attain their GED and/or become involved in some kind of vocational training program.
12. Promote and support involvement in Twelve Step programs. Consider specialized Twelve Step program meetings (e.g., Double Trouble meetings, AA meetings for the psychiatrically recovering, etc.), especially for individuals on psychotropic medication (Caldwell and White 1991).

Individuals should be cautioned that if they attend regular AA, NA, or CA meetings and divulge that they are on psychotropic medication, some well-meaning but misinformed members may advise them to stop taking their medication. This happens in spite of the fact that AA has published a pamphlet entitled *A.A. Member: Medication and Other Drugs* (1984), which clearly states the official position: Individuals should take medication if appropriately prescribed for another major illness. It can be helpful to obtain some of these pamphlets through the local AA intergroup (whose phone number can be identified in the local phone directory). We commonly give individuals two copies of this pamphlet, one for themselves and one for any other person who might question the appropriateness of the person taking medication. We have also found the use of this pamphlet to be helpful for individuals who have previously attended Twelve Step meetings and have formulated the impression that they should not take any type of psychotropic medication.

13. Promote and support the taking of medication as prescribed for any medical conditions (seizures, hypertension, etc.) along with compliance with scheduled medical appointments.
14. If the individual relapses back to substance use but returns for treatment, verbally reinforce the individual for assuming a responsible role by seeking treatment. This is extremely important; individuals commonly feel quite guilty about relapsing and need to know that the important point is that they have come back for appropriate treatment.

Case Histories

The following case histories exemplify many of the issues previously discussed regarding the diagnosis and treatment of addicted individuals with coexisting psychiatric symptoms.

Case One

Carmine presented as a twenty-seven-year-old married mother of two with a five-year history of progressive alcoholism. During her childhood she was physically and emotionally abused by her alcoholic father. Her paternal grandfather and two paternal uncles also suffered from alcoholism. There was no identified history of psychiatric disorders in any biological relatives. At the age of eighteen she married her high school sweetheart to get out of the house. At age twenty they had their first child, followed two years later by their second child. Carmine began to use alcohol progressively following the birth of their second child because she had difficulty dealing with two young children and her husband had job difficulties that resulted in financial problems. Her usage progressed to the point where over the two years prior to admission she had been consuming up to a half of a fifth of vodka almost every day. She experienced numerous alcohol-related blackouts as well as physical withdrawal symptoms when she tried to stop drinking. Her marital relationship deteriorated and she began to neglect her children. About a year prior to admission she began to report a progressive problem with feelings of depression. She began to withdraw from her normal social interactions, lost interest in performing her normal daily activities, lacked interest in sexual activity, and began to experience sleep problems (difficulty falling asleep). Her appetite deteriorated; she lost fifteen pounds and began to experience fleeting suicidal thoughts (but no attempts).

Approximately two months prior to admission she began to experience increasing episodes of acute anxiety attacks and became fearful of leaving the house. She saw her primary care physician, who placed her on alprazolam (Xanax), which she began to abuse in increasing amounts. Upon admission to the detox unit she continued to display symptoms of depression. She was seen for a psychiatric consultation by the psychiatrist of the addiction treatment team. He felt that her symptoms were probably related to her alcohol use and did not prescribe any medication. Carmine's mood state slowly began to improve as she was detoxified from alcohol and Xanax. She was transferred to the rehab program, where she continued to report feeling mildly depressed but was feeling better than before admission. She still reported feeling somewhat anxious, with some sporadic anxiety attacks. The counseling staff involved her in therapeutic activities and were supportive of her symptoms, which appeared to improve steadily with ongoing abstinence. By discharge three weeks later, her mood state had reached an almost normal level. She no longer was experiencing active feelings of depression or anxiety attacks, her appetite had improved, and she was sleeping normally. She was discharged to outpatient treatment with the recommendation that she continue to monitor her mood state and that if symptoms of depression or anxiety attacks returned, she should seek out a psychiatric reevaluation. She agreed to do this.

Case Discussion

This case history is consistent with the individual who develops psychiatric symptoms as a result of progressive substance usage. If one were to look at the patient's symptoms without knowledge of her substance usage, it would appear that she would meet diagnostic criteria for major depression as well as for possible panic disorder with early symptoms of agoraphobia. Her placement on alprazolam is a common finding in patients who are misdiagnosed with panic disorder and placed on antianxiety medications—which are usually ineffective and subsequently are commonly abused. An important point here is the counseling staff's awareness of the patient's psychiatric symptoms being due to substance use and their providing support for her and helping her to deal with her symptoms as they improved with ongoing abstinence and involvement in the treatment program.

Case Two

Will is a twenty-four-year-old married father of three who presented with a five-year history of progressive alcohol dependence and a three-year history of progressive cocaine dependence. He had completed two other treatment programs in the past and following discharge on both occasions was only able to remain abstinent for several months. Prior to his relapses, Will reported that he had begun to experience episodes of increased motor activity with racing thoughts. He found that during these periods he needed very little sleep and had a very high energy level. These episodes were followed by episodes of moderate to severe depression, during which he would sleep excessively, isolate himself socially, lacked motivation and interest to work, and would even experience some fleeting suicidal thoughts without any attempts. He reported that when he felt increasingly happy, he began to think that he no longer was an addict, stopped going to outpatient counseling and Twelve Step meetings, and relapsed back to substance use.

He reported that his paternal grandfather was diagnosed as

manic depressive and that his father, although never diagnosed with any type of psychiatric disorder, frequently exhibited episodes of being "hyper" along with episodes of mild depression. Following detoxification, Will was transferred to the rehab program, where the counseling staff soon began to observe that he was becoming increasingly hyperactive and had difficulty sitting still. His speech became increasingly rapid and pressured, and he began to express some grandiose ideas about how he could deal with his addiction better than anyone else. It was also noted that he was beginning to stay up at night pacing around his room. He was seen by the psychiatrist of the addiction treatment team, who made a diagnosis of bipolar affective disorder based on the patient's clinical history, family history, and presenting symptomatology. He was placed on lithium carbonate 600 mg twice daily. Over the next seven to ten days, the clinical staff began to note a marked improvement in all of his symptoms. His activity level returned to normal, his speech became normal in rate and tone, his racing thoughts and grandiose ideas subsided, his sleep improved dramatically, and he was able to participate well in the therapeutic activities. The counseling staff worked with him to make him aware of his dual problems and of the importance of continuing treatment for both problems following discharge. He was greatly appreciative of the treatment staff for finally identifying his other problem, which appeared to have been a major impediment in his maintaining recovery.

Case Discussion

This case is a good example of a patient with a true dual diagnosis. The patient's history is consistent with cocaine and alcohol dependencies, along with a diagnosis of bipolar affective disorder. As noted from Will's case history, it is not uncommon for dually diagnosed patients to relapse to substance use if their psychiatric disorder is not identified and appropriately treated. The counselors' involvement in this case was very important in helping the patient to understand that he had a coexisting psychiatric disorder and needed to continue in treatment for that problem on an ongoing basis following discharge.

Case Three

Bonita presented as a single, unemployed twenty-one-year-old female with a four-year history of progressive cocaine and amphetamine dependence, along with polysubstance abuse. There was no family history of psychiatric disorders or addiction. Throughout her childhood Bonita reported that she had always lacked a gratifying self-image and was prone to temper tantrums. In school she exhibited some conduct problems and was evaluated for possible attention deficit disorder and learning disabilities, but no specific problem was identified. In her early teens she became involved with a number of different boyfriends and often became extremely upset when their relationships ended. On several occasions she attempted suicide by cutting her wrists and overdosing on pills. She never was involved, however, in any inpatient psychiatric treatment.

During her mid-teens she became progressively involved with multiple substances, including alcohol, cocaine, marijuana, PCP, LSD, and benzodiazepines; she even tried snorting heroin. During her late teens and early twenties she continued to exhibit problems with interpersonal relationships, angry impulsive outbursts, and problems holding down a job.

Following detoxification treatment the patient was admitted to the rehab program, where her behavior continued to be consistent with her past pattern. She went to multiple treatment team members in an effort to obtain solutions to her many life problems. She was evaluated by the addiction team psychiatrist, who diagnosed borderline personality disorder in addition to the patient's addiction problem. All members of the treatment team began to relate to her in a highly consistent manner, referring her to her primary therapist for all issues. The counseling staff verbally reinforced mature, responsible behaviors and questioned in a concerned, emotionally neutral manner immature destructive behaviors. With this treatment approach the patient was able to complete the treatment program, although it was clear that she needed ongoing therapy to address both her addiction problem and her personality disorder.

She was referred to a therapist who was experienced in dealing with personality disordered patients, with the treatment approach centering around recovery-oriented psychotherapy. The patient also attended Twelve Step meetings with a temporary sponsor (female) who was identified for her prior to her discharge.

Case Discussion

Of all the psychiatric disorders, the personality disorders have been the group most commonly associated with addiction, especially the antisocial, borderline, and dependent personality disorder types. As defined in the *DSM-III-R*, individuals are considered to be suffering from a personality disorder when their personality traits become so rigid, inflexible, and maladaptive that they result in either significant functional impairment or subjective distress. The manifestations of personality disorders are often recognizable by adolescence or earlier and continue throughout most of adult life, though they may become less obvious in middle or old age. Specific diagnostic criteria have been formulated for each of the eleven personality disorders.

We have found that there has been a tendency to overdiagnose personality disorders in addicted patients because of the behavioral problems many of them present as a result of the deterioration in their psychological and functional states, which in turn is a result of their progressive addiction. We have found that once a person becomes appropriately involved in addiction treatment, his or her personality soon begins to return to what it was prior to involvement with substances, which in most cases would not be diagnostic of a personality disorder. In this case, however, it is clear that this patient had manifestations of a borderline personality disorder prior to her involvement with substances. Her symptomatology continued following involvement in treatment. The counseling staff began to relate to her in a highly consistent manner, focusing on the development of mature, responsible behaviors while questioning immature behaviors. She was able to complete the treatment program and was then referred to a skilled therapist for follow-up upon discharge to continue to address both her addiction and personality disorder problems.

Summary

The treatment of patients presenting with psychiatric symptoms in addiction treatment settings is challenging but quite rewarding. As noted in the counseling guidelines and case histories above, modifications and treatment approaches need to be made to address both of the patient's problems appropriately. Addiction treatment programs need to staff their programs with appropriately trained and skilled counselors to be successful in meeting the many varied needs of patients with coexisting psychiatric symptoms and/or disorders. For true dual diagnosis patients, long-term simultaneous treatment of both problems is necessary in order to be successful.

References

Alcoholics Anonymous. 1984. *A.A. member: Medication and other drugs.* New York: AA World Services, Inc.

Caldwell, S., and K. K. White. 1991. Co-creating a self-help movement. *Psychosocial Rehabilitation Journal* 15 (2):91-95.

Wallen, M. C., and H. Weiner. 1987. Impediments to effective treatment of the dually diagnosed patient. *Journal of Psychoactive Drugs* 21 (2):161-68.

———. 1988. The dually diagnosed patient in an inpatient chemical dependency treatment program. *Alcoholism Treatment Quarterly* 5 (2):197-218.

Special Populations

Using a developmental model of addictive and psychiatric disorders with adolescents promotes understanding and treatment.

6
Dual Diagnosis In Adolescent Populations

J. Calvin Chatlos, M.D.

ADOLESCENCE IS THE TRANSITION INTO ADULTHOOD. It is heralded by puberty with biological changes (growth spurts, hormones, and body metamorphosis); psychological changes (new feelings and new thinking abilities); and social changes (new schools, new peer relationships, and new social and cultural opportunities and tasks).

Work with adolescents requires attention to these multiple domains in a comprehensive biopsychosocial approach, including the individual person, family members, peers, school, job, and community. This period is also composed of many transitions: junior high school, high school, geographic moves, first love, first sex, first job—and also first cigarette, first drink, or first drug use. At no other period except early childhood does a person undergo such transformation.

The adolescent period and its events are often forgotten as the initiation and early progression of disorders that continue into adulthood are later dwarfed by life events and consequences. This is particularly important when we consider that it is during adolescence and young adulthood that multiple psychiatric disorders begin—major depression, bipolar, anxiety, conduct, and substance use disorders. A rewarding part of working with adolescents is the opportunity to take a more detailed, microscopic look at the addiction and mental disorders process with an emphasis on development.

Working with multiple developmental levels, multiple domains, multiple risks, multiple substances, multiple disorders, multiple problems, and multidisciplined perspectives is like pursuing an adventure

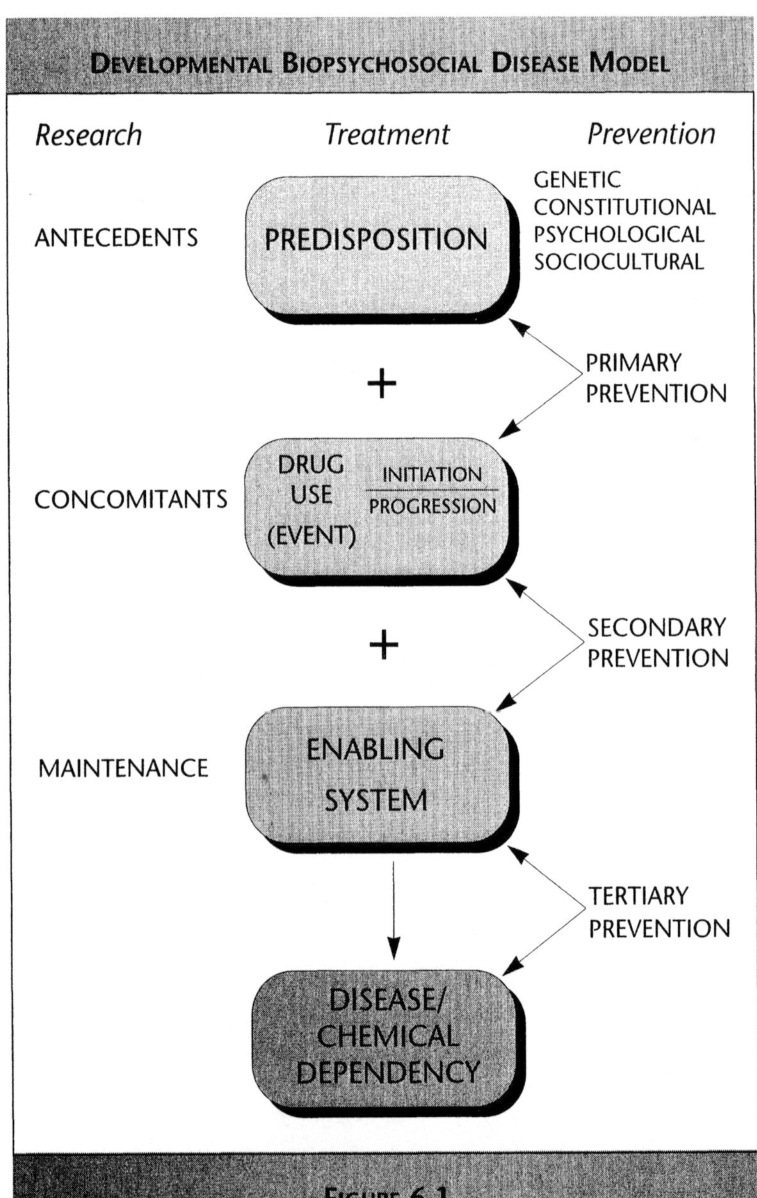

FIGURE 6.1

video game with different levels of skills—you attempt to move to new levels while at any moment you could be annihilated by a fireball, misdirected to a dead end, or held powerless by a villainous rival. Such multiplicity requires a roadmap or guide to understanding the pathological process of addiction and mental disorders as well as the recovery process.

This chapter outlines a guide for the therapist—a visual model that provides a continuum for prevention, intervention, and treatment and integrates addiction and mental disorders into a similar process—a developmental biopsychosocial disease model.

Developmental Biopsychosocial Disease Model

The developmental biopsychosocial disease model in figure 6.1 has been described previously (Chatlos 1987, 1989, 1991a). This visual model for use in treatment as well as community education and prevention settings identifies three factors at different points in time of the addiction process.

This model is based on research identifying the antecedent, concomitant, and maintenance factors of the addiction process.

The PREDISPOSITION factor is divided into genetic, constitutional, psychological, and sociocultural factors that have been described in detail elsewhere. Many formats have been developed, but Hawkins et al. (1992) have organized these "risk factors" in a systems approach in which systems are expanded from individual to family, to peer, to school/job, to community. The individual domain includes genetic, constitutional, and psychological factors. A checklist of risk factors prior to use of alcohol or drugs is useful in clinical assessment of the adolescent (table 6.1). The more risk factors a teen has, the more likely he or she is to develop substance dependence. All of these risk factors lead to an attitude toward drug use.

To this predisposing attitude a DRUG is introduced. The three major forces of INITIATION are availability of the substance, peer influence, and perceived risk of harmfulness of use. Other predictors of initiation include parental role modeling of drinking, drug use, or taking medically prescribed psychoactive substances; participation in delinquent activities; personality factors such as depression, risk taking, and low self-esteem; and parental factors, including poor quality of

TABLE 6.1
RISK FACTOR CHECKLIST

Genetic
- Children of substance abuser

Constitutional
- Early first use (before age fifteen)
- Chronic pain or disability
- Physiological factors

Psychological
- Mental health problems
- Physical, sexual, emotional abuse
- Attempted suicide

Sociocultural

Family
- Parental drug use and positive attitudes toward use
- Parental divorce/separation
- Family management problems
- Low expectations for children's success

Peer
- Friends who use drugs
- Favorable attitudes toward drug use
- Early antisocial/delinquent behavior and peer rejection

School
- Lack of enforcement of school policies
- Little commitment to school
- School failure/dropout
- Transitions to new school levels

Community
- Community laws and norms favorable toward drug use
- Lack of social bonding
- Economic and social deprivation
- Availability of drugs (including alcohol and tobacco)

relationship with parents and the extent of the teen's involvement in parental drug-taking behavior. Particularly important is the initiation of cigarette, alcohol, or drug use before age fifteen. These adolescents have a much higher risk of becoming dependent.

Once introduced, the strong reinforcement of the drug euphoria, negative reinforcement of abstinent symptoms, and genetic and biochemical effects on developing brains interact to lead to PROGRESSION. Progression goes through four stages, originally outlined by MacDonald (1984):

Stage 1.
Experimentation / Learning the Mood Swing

This stage usually begins during junior high school with peer pressure to "try it," usually involving beer drinking, marijuana smoking, or some inhalant sniffing. This usually occurs at home, at a party, or while "hanging out." There is often a desire to feel grown up. Small amounts of the drug are needed to get high, and the person usually returns quickly to a normal mood with no problems. The teenager has learned to use drugs to affect mood and affect the pleasure centers of the brain. To a young person, what feels good must be good.

Stage 2.
Regular Use / Seeking the Mood Swing

More regular use begins with the adolescent progressing to hard liquor or bouts of drinking to get drunk as use becomes more associated with dealing with stresses. Use begins to occur during the week and more of the drug is used, since the body develops tolerance. Problems occur, such as missing school because of hangovers, missing time on a job, or not performing as well on a sports team. Different drugs are tried, and the adolescent may progress to using hallucinogens and pills. Non-drug-using friends may be dropped. More money may be needed, leading to stealing from family as well as lying to hide drug use. Moods may change rapidly and without explanation. Interest in usual activities may change.

Stage 3.
Daily Preoccupation / Preoccupation with the Mood Swing

More dangerous drugs are used more often, with more problems developing in more areas of the adolescent's life. Drug use becomes a central focus of life; the teenager thinks about the last high, and where, when, and with whom the next high will occur. This often occurs without daily use. The preoccupation with drug use replaces thoughts of and activities with family, school, and community. More serious problems develop that may involve stealing, breaking of other laws, and violence. Many mood changes occur as guilt, shame, loneliness, and depression—partially covered by denial and grandiosity—are now mixed with withdrawal from or cravings for drugs. Attempts are made to cut down or quit, but are usually unsuccessful at this stage. Physical problems may develop.

Stage 4.
Harmful Dependency / Using to Feel Normal

This final stage of addiction involves "hard" or more dangerous drugs in large amounts. Since the teenager has become surrounded by drug-using friends and situations, he or she no longer knows what normal (non-drug-using) behavior is. Use has gotten out of control and life has become unmanageable in many areas: physical, psychological, social, family, school, and legal. The teenager also feels much guilt, shame, and self-hatred, which may lead to suicidal thoughts and attempts. Because of physical tolerance, the teenager no longer gets as high, and much more time is spent "trying to feel normal" and to avoid withdrawal symptoms.

A checklist is helpful in clinically assessing this progression (table 6.2, pages 91-92).

The final factor in the equation is the ENABLING SYSTEM, or the maintenance system. This includes all persons, places and things surrounding the user that knowingly or unknowingly enable the progression of the addiction, such as promoting use without knowledge of harmful effects, modeling drug use and dependence, denial of use, removal of consequences that would deter use, or economic incentives for continued use. Participants in the system may include parents, friends, teachers, employers, therapists, judges, lawyers, police officers, and the broader aspects of a political and economic system.

Table 6.2
Chemical Dependency Stages

Stage 1—Experimentation/Learning the mood swing

_____ Use of two drugs or less (not including cigarettes)
_____ Use for less than one year
_____ Use of less than one time per month during past six months
_____ No evidence of tolerance
_____ No evidence of use to cope with stress/feelings
_____ No evidence of use after significant consequences (vomiting, grounding, accidents, etc.)

Stage 2—Regular use/Seeking the mood swing

_____ Evidence of pattern to use (i.e., binge-drinking, regular weekend use, etc.)
_____ Use of more than two drugs (not including cigarettes)
_____ Use for more than one year
_____ Use of two or more times per month during past six months
_____ Use during the week
_____ Some evidence of tolerance
_____ Some evidence of use to cope with stress/feelings
_____ More than 25 percent of friends use
_____ Inability to maintain no-use contract for thirty days
_____ Rare mood swings between use
_____ Some evidence of use after significant consequences
_____ Recurrent use in physically hazardous situations
_____ No attempts to cut down or quit
_____ No evidence of withdrawal symptoms with non-use

Stage 3—Daily preoccupation/Preoccupation with the mood swing

_____ At least three signs of Stage 2
_____ Self-admission of daily preoccupation
_____ More than four significant consequences in past six months
_____ Unsuccessful attempt to cut down or quit
_____ Evidence of withdrawal symptoms with nonuse or 50 percent increase in tolerance
_____ Longest abstinence in past six months is less than one week
_____ Strong mood swings between use
_____ Important social, occupational, recreational activities reduced
_____ Dealing drugs
_____ Behaviors include stealing, lying, arguments with family
_____ Consequences include driving while intoxicated (DWI), arrest, motor vehicle accident (MVA) within past six months

Stage 4—Harmful dependency/Using to feel normal

_____ At least three signs of Stage 3
_____ Daily use
_____ Intoxication or withdrawal symptoms interfere with obligations
_____ Significant depression, suicidal thoughts
_____ Behaviors include violence, self-destructive acts, property destruction
_____ Use during morning hours

Counselor ______________________ Date ___________

In addition to rendering a diagnosis using *DSM-III-R* criteria, a clinical assessment, using this framework to understand adolescent addiction, serves as a guide to understanding addiction and treatment.

Dual Diagnosis

Another factor that plays a major role in this developmental biopsychosocial model is that of psychiatric disorder. All psychiatric disorders found in adolescence can be associated with addiction. In looking at the possible relationships, it is helpful to approach addiction and mental disorders as two parallel biopsychosocial processes. For instance, depression has a predisposition that includes specific genetic, constitutional, psychological, and sociocultural factors. However, according to the developmental biopsychosocial model, the initiation of mental disorders is triggered by an event (figure 6.1) instead of a drug. With depression, this may be specific life events that contribute to the initiation, or possibly a biological event. With the continued biological and brain maturation during adolescence, unrecognized biological factors may be contributing to the onset of various psychiatric disorders during this developmental period, as noted before. The final factor of the enabling system for depression includes the support systems or significant relationships that contribute to the progression and maintenance of the disorder. This factor may be a family member with addiction or mental disorder, denial of depression, or physical or emotional unavailability.

Interaction between these two parallel biopsychosocial processes can occur at any level—antecedent, concomitant, or maintenance. This model has been useful in the understanding and treating of affective disorder, conduct disorder, anxiety disorder, attention deficit hyperactivity disorder, posttraumatic stress disorder, and eating disorders, as well as personality disorders such as narcissistic and borderline disorders. Figure 6.2 illustrates the many possible relationships using this developmental model. For the purposes of assessment, specific distinctions as to the source (psychiatric or addictive) and the temporal sequence along the continuum (antecedent, concomitant, or maintenance) will indicate specific interventions.

Treatment

Once we have assessed the level of care, as provided by ASAM Adolescent Patient Placement Criteria (ASAM 1991), various considerations are necessary.

Relationships Between Two Disorders Using Developmental Model

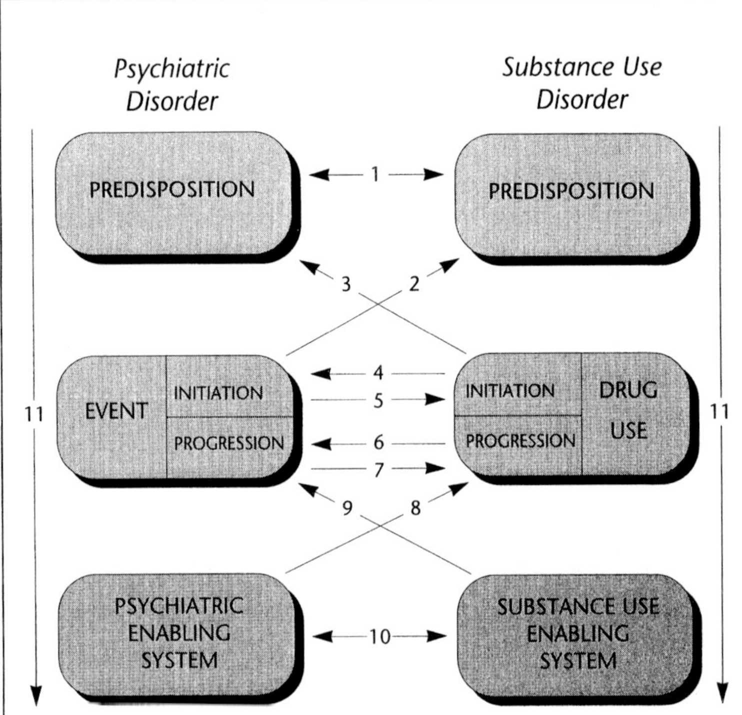

1. Risk factors may interact or overlap for two disorders (Dryfoos 1990).
2. Axis I or II psychopathology may serve as a risk factor for addictive disorders.
3. Addictive disorders may serve as a risk factor for psychopathology.
4. Psychiatric symptoms may develop as a result of acute intoxication and initiate the onset of a psychiatric disorder.
5. Psychiatric disorder may lead to initiation or acute intoxication as an attempt to self-medicate.

6. Some psychiatric disorders emerge as a consequence of use and persist into the period of remission. This may be related to withdrawal or chronic use symptoms (i.e., paranoia from cocaine; LSD flashbacks).
7. Psychopathology may modify the course of an addictive disorder in terms of rapidity of course, response to treatment, symptom picture, and long-term outcome.
8. Maintenance aspects (personal and social) of psychiatric disorder may lead to continued progression, consolidation, or relapse of substance disorder (i.e., personal and family aspects of chronic schizophrenia; or impulse disorder, such as pathological gambling; or intermittent explosive disorder).
9. Maintenance aspects of addiction disorder may lead to continued progression, consolidation, or relapse of the psychiatric disorder (i.e., codependent syndrome leading to depression; distorted thinking from use and being around users leading to increasing delusional processes).
10. Members or aspects of one enabling system interact with another (i.e., depressive family system fostering continued hopelessness of substance-using family system; violence of alcoholic family system consolidating continued manipulation of an antisocial disorder system or hopelessness of a depression-enabling system.
11. Some psychopathological conditions and addictive disorders are independent and not specifically related.

FIGURE 6.2

Abstinence/Detoxification

Teenagers rarely need detoxification with medications. Initially, assessment is done for the psychoactive substance-induced organic mental disorders of intoxication, withdrawal, withdrawal delirium, hallucinosis, delusional disorder, alcohol amnesic syndrome, posthallucinogen perception disorder, and organic mood syndrome. These are usually determined by resolution with one to two weeks of abstinence. Further accurate diagnosis of a psychiatric disorder cannot occur without abstinence.

Medication Treatment

Acute psychiatric situations such as out-of-control manic episodes, hallucinations, or psychotic depression require emergency use of medications. However, once the crisis is resolved, a trial without medication is indicated and should include psychiatric reassessment. Relegating an adolescent to six to twelve months of medication treatment may be unnecessary, since the disorder may resolve with abstinence.

If evaluation after one to two weeks of abstinence reveals a persistent psychiatric diagnosis, then medication treatment with maintenance use is indicated. Since there are no studies that have demonstrated specific efficacy of medication in teens addicted to drugs and alcohol, our medication interventions must be guided by clinical and research experience with adults or with non-substance-dependent adolescents.

In many cases, the persistence or intensity of symptoms determines treatment (rather than satisfying full *DSM-III-R* criteria), especially those that are time-related.

> Diane, a sixteen-year-old with extensive cocaine and alcohol abuse, was admitted for treatment. Initially, she was mildly depressed and guarded but cooperative and engaged in treatment. During the subsequent ten days, her affect became more depressed and tearful with psychomotor retardation, paranoid ideation developing into delusions with ideas of reference, and a morbid preoccupation with death and past deaths of relatives. These symptoms of major depression with psychotic features led to a trial of nortriptyline with increasing doses. Her mood responded. Within four days she exhibited decreased psychomotor retardation, but progressed to euphoria with giggling, inappropriate laughter, and flight of ideas. She was diagnosed as having bipolar disorder, though there was no

prior history of hypomanic or manic episodes and she did not satisfy time criteria for this disorder. She responded well to lithium and completed treatment.

Psychotherapeutic Process

Using the developmental model described, the recovery process with teenagers follows the reverse order of the addiction/mental disorders process (Enabling System ——► Progression ——► Initiation ——► Predisposition). Initial abstinence requires an intervention into the enabling system. This may involve admission to an inpatient treatment program (change of persons, places, things), leverage through school/ courts/job, or a family intervention.

A family intervention often breaks through adolescent and family denial and establishes a firm commitment to treatment. Parents are individually asked to list situations involving their child's drug/alcohol use and the effect it has had on them personally. The intervention is facilitated by the therapist while parents present their list to the teenager, who is expected to make no response or comments. A successful intervention breaks through denial and grandiosity and into awareness and expression of guilt, shame, and disappointment, which have been avoided by substance use and codependent behaviors. An important goal of the family intervention is to dispel the fantasy of being "rescued" or removed from treatment by the parents.

Adolescents entering treatment are asked to make a "commitment to abstinence." Part of this commitment is the development of an initial written contract that specifies persons with whom the teenager will/will not associate, places which will be avoided, specific hours and responsibilities for home and school, attendance at treatment and at self-help meetings (AA/NA), and agreement for ongoing urine monitoring.

The parents' commitment to treatment, together with the contract, provides a new structure to the enabling system and creates a supportive family recovery environment to fulfill the commitment to abstinence. Following this initial intervention, continued work with the family, the school, and the adolescent will strengthen other parts of the recovery environment and ultimately transform the enabling system.

Once this systems intervention has occurred, the recovery process follows the reverse order of the addiction process. The focus on drug use begins with the writing and presentation of a drug chart. This assignment reviews all alcohol and drug use from initiation and first use to current use, describing the progression and consequences in physical, emotional, social (including sexual), and spiritual domains of the adolescent's life. The *Step Workbook for Adolescent Chemical Dependency Recovery: A Guide to the First Five Steps* (Jaffe 1990) is available specifically for work with adolescent dual diagnosis patients. This workbook facilitates the process described below. When working with dual diagnosis teenagers, it is common to encounter resistance to treatment, such as with the defensive expression, "I'm not here for drug abuse, I'm here for my depression" (or the reverse). Some adolescents will attempt to use this to hide behind a diagnosis. Treating of the disorders simultaneously and using the same developmental model as described facilitate breaking through this defense and understanding their multiple problems. Educating them about the addiction process and their specific psychiatric disorder—including the risk factors, initiating events, progression, and enabling system—helps their understanding.

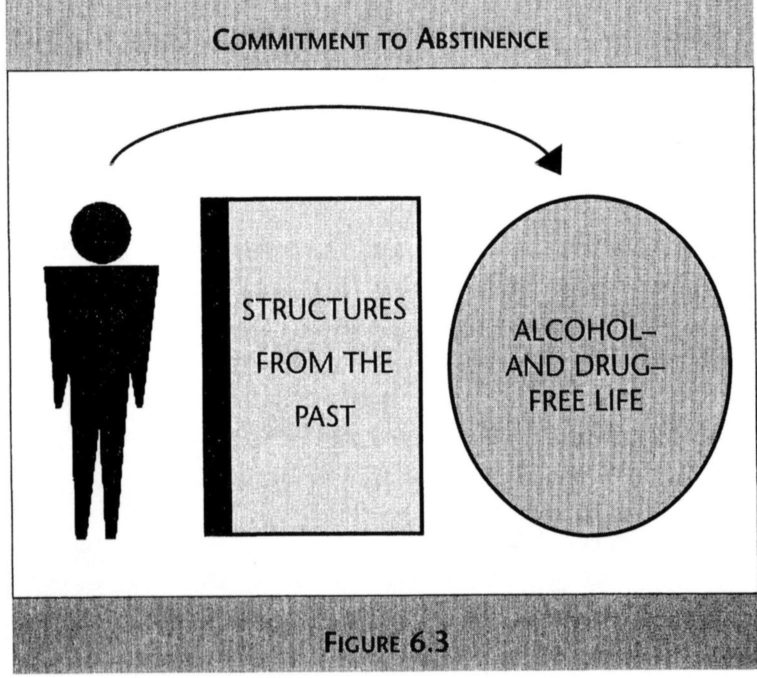

FIGURE 6.3

As teenagers pursue this effort, certain emotional and behavioral reactions occur. These reactions display patterns of behavior that demonstrate their specific psychobiological history. These patterns are referred to as "structures from the past" (figure 6.3), a neutral term that allows discussion from various therapeutic perspectives, such as psychoanalytic, psychodynamic, self-psychological, cognitive, rational-emotive, and others. These patterns, or structures, from the past are the result of the predisposing experiences and attitudes, conditioned responses, learned coping patterns (including ego defenses), and perceptual and cognitive distortions that may have occurred before or during drug use, as well as any urges or psychiatric disorders that are present. Urges are poorly differentiated feelings that are strong motivators to specific actions, such as drug urges, sex urges, binge/purge urges, violence urges, or suicidal and self-mutilation urges. Understanding and working with urges is a key to successful transformation toward recovery. Urges are the result of using mood-altering drugs to cope with emotional experiences and are psychologically linked to those feelings and memories of the experiences.

In work with dual diagnosis patients, the commitment to abstinence must be extended to include commitments to no drugs/alcohol, no depression, no panic attacks, no bingeing, purging, or compulsive dieting, and no impulsive violent or suicidal behaviors. The fulfillment of these commitments is indicated by an inner sense of peace or serenity.

Because it is unrealistic to expect teenagers to be capable of making and keeping these commitments early in recovery, the first four Steps of the Twelve Steps of AA (see p. 109) are used to provide the structure and impetus for change. We expect the adolescent to make a commitment to the completion of each Step successively. Written and behavioral assignment such as those in the workbook foster this progression. Completion occurs when a cognitive-emotional-behavioral shift is noted that is consistent with the foundation of the Steps as outlined by AA. Within the adolescent's commitment to each of the Steps, this powerful reframing reveals patterns of behavior that block recovery. What is revealed is the experience, including memories and emotions, associated with the development of this block. The therapeutic work involves (a) identifying the structures from the past, (b) recalling the events in detail, (c) reexperiencing the thoughts, feelings, and behaviors associated with the event, and then (d) acting in the present to produce a different result. At various points during the treatment, psychiatric symptoms or disorders previously unidentified may be part of the structure from the past that blocks progress. This approach allows an integrated intervention into the addiction and mental disorders with an understanding of the teenager's entire psychobiological history, as illustrated below.

> **Step One**
>
> Mike, a sixteen-year-old, was admitted for marijuana and mixed substance dependence with a diagnosis of conduct disorder. He had a history of parental separation at age two. His mother remarried when Mike was four and divorced again when Mike was seven. His medical history included several years of left-sided headaches that were associated with flashing lights and nausea. When Mike was thirteen, he was diagnosed with migraine headaches after having a normal EEG and CT scan. Initially in treatment he was generally guarded and presented a "macho" image of bravado. He revealed many issues with authority and developed mood lability with intermittent angry episodes and eventually migraine attacks. He acknowledged severe drug urges and the desire to run away at this time.
>
> During one of these attacks he stated that the therapist talking to him at that moment felt like someone beating something into his head. He recalled how his stepfather had hit him in the head and repeatedly criticized him, calling him a wimp. He recalled wishes to hit his stepfather but with fears of destructive annihilation. His headache worsened as anger was directed toward the therapist. A breakthrough occurred as he identified the disappointment in not having a father emotionally available, and he cried for the first time in treatment. He tearfully related how he wanted his father and stepfather to be proud of him and to admire him as a strong son. This occurred in the presence of a smile and the relief of the migraine attack, which did not return during the remainder of treatment.

After breaking through initial denial and grandiosity, adolescents experience guilt, shame, and disappointment as they review the consequences of their drug use. The ability to accomplish this appears partly related to their locus of control and ability for introspection. Some persons with severe conduct disorders and antisocial personality traits have a limited ability to experience guilt and shame and may be identified as having such early in treatment. Issues of authority and discipline highlight the cognitive distortions and paranoid defenses as complaints of "brainwashing" occur. As limits are set, therapists are perceived as punishing parents or law enforcement personnel with whom the teen has had bad experiences.

During Step One, severe distortion and paranoia may indicate an underlying schizophrenia or schizophreniform disorder. A therapeutic approach that confronts the defensive structures (Davanloo 1980; Davis 1989) is designed to highlight this and to distinguish it from the cognitive distortion and mistrust of the patient with borderline personality disorder. Schizophrenia or schizophrenia-like disorders begin to display primary process thinking. These patients are not appropriate for this type of treatment and must be placed in a more supportive therapeutic environment. These adolescents may have a limited ability to benefit from the Twelve Step recovery process, though their ability may be enhanced with successful medication interventions. The patients with borderline personality disorder develop more organized thought processes with confrontation. However, they also develop overwhelming urges with acting-out behaviors—to use drugs, to have sex, to binge or purge, to commit suicide or self-mutilate, to be violent, or to run away. With structure, the "abandonment depression" (Masterson 1972) breaks through. Loneliness and depression are common as teenagers begin to perceive their lives without drugs, without drug-using friends, and without behaviors that they previously used to cope with feelings of loneliness and alienation. This illustrates the degree of alienation in life that has been experienced, which is often related to increasing drug use and social withdrawal.

As in the previous example of Diane, the presence of persistent depressive symptoms must be evaluated for an underlying major depressive disorder, often evidenced by psychomotor retardation or psychotic processes. These teenagers have responded well to antidepressant medications. For some patients, the development of intense paranoid feelings without depression may be indicative of secrets regarding unexposed criminal behavior (i.e., murder or abuse); in that case, issues of confidentiality must be addressed before treatment can continue.

Our experience has shown that adolescents with attention deficit hyperactivity disorder (ADHD), learning disabilities, and prior social and school failure experience overwhelming feelings of failure accompanied by behaviors of giving up. They frequently equate treatment with school, and staff with teachers or critical parents. Reading and written assignments are especially difficult and frustrating. Our experience has shown that when addressed properly with remedial support and development of alternative coping strategies, treatment becomes one of their first successes in recovery and a very rewarding experience.

Step Two—A Case of Memory Lapse

> Tom, a motivated seventeen-year-old patient with marijuana and alcohol abuse and major depressive disorder, progressed well and completed Step One. Then his mood changed; he was not as active, was often confused, and appeared to be blocked in treatment. There was no clear explanation until he complained of pain in his leg. No physical signs of a problem were present. Soon the patient recalled an injury in which he broke a leg during a soccer game at a point in his life when he and his father dreamed of his becoming a professional athlete. He never did as well in athletics after this injury. The disappointment to his father and him were not previously resolved and had resurfaced to block his progress in treatment. The disappointment and the victimizing self-pity associated with this event were blocks to his commitment to Step Two and were part of his "insane" behaviors. Once this issue was examined, he was able to continue treatment successfully.

The emphasis during Step Two is on relationships, with particular focus on the relationship to a "Power greater than ourselves." This includes looking at life relationships with powers greater than ourselves, such as family members and significant others. Step Two begins with the reading of the comprehensive drug chart to parents, breaking through family denial and opening a family system to building new relationships. Understanding "spirituality" as the "quality of our relationships to whatever or whomever is most important in our life" (Bjorklund 1983) includes work with values and ethical rules. It requires looking at past religious experiences. Often these experiences have been emotionally and spiritually abusive or attached to cognitive distortions that often fostered magical thinking and the "Santa Claus concept" of a Higher Power.

Step Two often deals with the deepest levels of mistrust and alienation, since addicted teenagers feel betrayed by their family, by the world, and by God. There is a reexperiencing of the losses of relationships, such as by divorce or separation, disappointments in family and parents, or the loss of goals. Some of the most painful disappointments are related to the loss of trust or self-worth of the physically or sexually abused adolescent, who feels victimized by the world, including by drugs and the therapists who have been unsuccessful. Therapeutic work on unresolved grief issues and hopelessness are necessary, including work on disappointments from past unsuccessful therapeutic experiences. During this stage we must be very watchful for the recurrence of severe self-destructive behaviors, including relapse to use of drugs or alcohol, purging, depression, violence, and self-mutilation—all of which are often found during progress through this Step. These symptoms of specific psychiatric disorders will become exacerbated, or even evident for the first time, during this Step. Rather than being seen as resistance or failure, these behaviors should be interpreted as signs that the adolescent's commitment is strong. This "reframing" fosters a powerful shift from a focus on illness to empowering recovery. The appearance of these symptoms demonstrates the dynamics involved in the development of that disorder (initiating event/progression/maintenance). At this Step, these symptoms frequently indicate an undiagnosed, prolonged posttraumatic stress disorder or are related to aspects of the child of an alcoholic syndrome. Contrary to what is recommended in work with adults, it is important to treat these symptoms when they occur in treatment rather than later in recovery. Failure to address these symptoms may lead to premature termination of treatment or dangerous self-destructive behaviors.

On closer inspection, these symptoms and actions are usually preceded and motivated by specific urges—urges to get high, to escape feelings, to punish oneself, to feel pain, etc. We work with adolescents to recognize that urges are "feelings in disguise." Once the presence of an urge has been identified, a reminder of their "commitment to abstinence" assists self-control. Attempts are made to help the teenager identify the specific feeling that is present—anger, guilt, shame, disappointment, rejection, jealousy, loneliness, etc. As this occurs, it is important to identify the presence of the feeling in the here-and-now relationship with the therapist (referred to as *transference* in psychoanalytic theory). When this occurs and is expressed, there is often a breakthrough to a new level of awareness with memories of similar situations in the past that led to the crystallization of this urge/feeling/defense/block to recovery. Once this feeling is identified and fully expressed, a reality-focused approach assists the process of acting in the present to learn a new coping strategy that will give different results. This breakthrough into a new level of awareness (Chatlos 1991b; Lane and Schwartz 1987) describes the transformational and developmental process of recovery. Repeated experiences of keeping the commitment to abstinence enhance the adolescent's sense of personal integrity and wholeness.

As recovery progresses, blocks to recovery are encountered from earlier and earlier stages in the progression of the disease process. Treatment often leads to reexperiences of the critical factors associated with the initiation of alcohol and drug use. As in the example of Tom, his initiation of use was immediately preceded by a sports injury. Unknown to him, this disappointment was a major factor in his initiation and early progression.

The focus on spirituality also assists identification of adolescents involved in satanism and other cult-like activities. The spiritual focus fosters experience of intense rage, hatred, and sadistic revenge that is often associated with issues of power and humiliation and used to cover feelings of inadequacy and mortifying shame. Often these teenagers have an underlying schizotypal or schizoid personality disorder requiring treatment, or they may have dissociative states suggestive of posttraumatic stress disorder or a dissociative disorder.

Owing to the intense transference issues that arise in dealing with teenagers at this stage, emphasis on reality testing and the psychological defenses of projection and projective identification are critical for success.

Step Two—A Case of Intense Transference

Rosemary, a sixteen-year-old with a history of parental divorce at age seven followed by multiple geographic moves, was admitted with extensive cocaine, marijuana, and alcohol abuse. She was diagnosed as having conduct disorder with a history since junior high school of progressively increasing antisocial behaviors—poor school motivation, truancy, shoplifting, stealing, runaway episodes, and physical fights (including the use of knives). She was further diagnosed with major depression and borderline personality disorder, with a history of being raped at age thirteen and a suicide attempt at age fourteen from an overdose of 120 aspirin, for which she required gastric lavage. She had also been involved for two years with satanism, including daily rituals and prior animal sacrifice.

She expressed motivation in treatment, but as she dealt with Step Two and her involvement in satanism, she developed extreme anxiety with sweating, restlessness, and palpitations. During some group sessions this would occur, and panic attacks would necessitate her removal from group. Since this appeared to have a separation anxiety component, she was started on imipramine, which was increased to 100 mg/day. During the next five days, her mood fluctuated, and she had increasingly frightening dreams and thoughts about attacking a patient with a knife. Because she was less overwhelmed by her panic while on medications, therapy continued so she could deal with these issues. As she was recognizing her need to have power and get revenge, she experienced severe loneliness and a "transference" reaction of rage toward the therapist: she wanted to put a knife through his chest and kill him. Associated with this was extreme fear of dying as well as guilt and fear that Satan would come and punish her, mixed with a desire to be taken by and married to Satan. Extreme struggles of love and hate were projected onto Satan almost in a delusional manner. Issues were worked through regarding rage at her abusive father, the desire for power and revenge associated with satanism, and the guilt and fear of dying associated with betrayal of Satan. Breakthroughs into feelings of loneliness and self-hatred were sufficient to continue treatment without further panic attacks.

Step Three

Andy was an eighteen-year-old with marijuana, cocaine, and alcohol abuse, along with separation anxiety disorder and atypical depression. His father had died of a heart attack seven months prior at age forty-two. This occurred at the height of Andy's use and several months after his hospitalization due to a drug overdose. Treatment had focused on much grief and guilt because he felt responsible for his father's death. As he progressed, he at one point began to experience "survivor's guilt" for feeling so good and attempted to leave treatment. As he worked with his commitment to Step Three, he was fearful of confronting his sister, toward whom he had sexual thoughts and had once approached sexually while drunk. He expressed this embarrassment, which led to an expression of anger and hurt for his father not being available to help him with these sexual feelings and social relationships with girls. He felt burdened by the responsibility of being the oldest child and growing up without a father and had feelings of inadequacy that were associated with depressed mood. He demonstrated Step Three by surrendering his overly responsible and perfectionistic attitude. He began to reach out more to others for support and guidance, became more carefree in his relationships with a deeper level of intimacy, and became less self-critical as his depression resolved.

We use Step Three to consolidate treatment gains. It emphasizes making choices and taking responsibility because it relates to "surrendering" the defensive patterns of the structures from the past. This Step is instrumental in facilitating character transformation. Its focus on overcoming past defensive patterns, undergoing identity changes, and adopting new behaviors is often difficult for persons with a narcissistic personality disorder. Some "images" or identity changes that are related to the narcissistic self and are mostly defensive are those of the drug or street image, macho image, rebellious/anarchist image, victim image (of the abused), distrust and perfectionism image (of the child of an alcoholic), and, recently, the drug dealer image. Surrendering these images brings up issues of "not being remembered" and "not feeling significant," issues that are reflective of past patterns of life experience.

For many kids, especially the sexually dependent, the identity is so pervasive that it is reexperienced as if they were dying, with precipitation of acute panic attacks often related to a separation anxiety disorder or posttraumatic stress disorder that has its origins in early childhood experiences.

Sexual feelings are often the last defense and the strongest attachment against feelings of abandonment, loneliness, isolation, and alienation. Helpful distinctions are made between sexuality and intimacy. Adopted teenagers often regress as "adoption" into a recovering community is experienced through past emotional experiences of loss and abandonment related to being adopted by their families. This is consistent with previous recognition of the resistance to treatment that occurs among adopted patients.

Surrendering these defensive patterns often releases a new level of vitality and self-expression that had been dominated by feelings of shame and worthlessness.

This Step often deals with issues of separation-individuation as patients gain autonomy in their recovery. Concrete experiences with family members and resolution of major family conflicts are often necessary. With families that continue their own use of alcohol or drugs or have untreated psychiatric disorders, helping the adolescent recognize the family member's illness and preventing further internalization assist the emotional separation process.

Step Four

Barbara was an eighteen-year-old with cocaine, marijuana, and alcohol dependence, with psychiatric diagnoses of major depressive disorder and bulimia nervosa treated with imipramine (200 mg/day).

Her work with Step Four involved many issues of intimacy. She was a very outgoing and outspoken girl during treatment, but then became fearful of closeness to peers in group therapy. She also became frightened that her tremendous successes in treatment would not remain. She had identified feelings of inadequacy and jealousy in relation to peers getting attention, as well as loneliness as she approached termination of treatment. An issue throughout treatment was her sexual dependency.

For her Step Four group presentation she chose a female peer

> early in recovery who was also male-dependent, and whom she felt compelled to help. She demonstrated Step One by recognizing her powerlessness over this peer and over her feelings of wanting to help this "lonely" girl. Step Two was demonstrated with recognition of her "codependent" desire to help and take care of this "helpless" girl. She was able to recognize the projection of her own insecurity and helpless feelings as she was leaving treatment. She shared how hard it was for her to feel close to girls and how she had always confused sexual feelings with intimate ones. During this process she became blocked and detached from her feelings. She used Step Two to ask for group feedback. The group helped her to look at differences between her relations with boys and girls. She became anxious, and peers identified this with withholding secrets. As her anxiety increased, she demonstrated Step Three by fully trusting the group and this process and related how she was embarrassed about some male relationships. She had engaged in acts of bondage and mild physical abuse in attempts to please her boyfriends. She admitted, "If he wasn't happy, I wasn't." With this admission she recognized a source of her male dependence, was able to express her fears that closeness with girls would be abusive, and tearfully hugged her female partner in the presentation.

Step Four fosters personal responsibility and growth for continued self-motivated recovery. This Step aims for self-acceptance and acceptance by others so that the patient can form a true partnership with another human being. The openness at this point in successful treatment allows teenagers to deal with issues of intimacy and sexuality with an emotional maturity consistent with their age. A Step Four group presentation requires a patient to choose a specific character trait that has been present in him/herself throughout treatment, such as the arrogance of the perfectionist, the self-pity of the victim, the fear of living of the suicide attempter, or the fear of loneliness of the sexually dependent. The patient chooses another patient who reactivates this character structure, and in front of the peer group he or she demonstrates how to use Steps One through Three to overcome this. When done successfully, a breakthrough and transformation occurs during the presentation that moves everyone in attendance and can be nearly overwhelming in its expression of the courage of the human spirit.

As recovery at this stage progresses, the blocks to recovery that are encountered are often related to the developmental risk factors that originally predisposed the adolescent to alcohol and drug addiction or mental disorders. Through this process we continue to demonstrate the psychobiological history of the patient. As teenagers gain experience with this process, they experience recovery as an exploration and discovery and as a life adventure that helps them maintain their commitment to abstinence.

At this point, the adolescent has demonstrated choice, responsibility, willingness, and openness, which will form a working partnership with the family, friends, and sponsors to continue recovery. The expression of experienced gratitude supports the adolescent's commitment to living with integrity, vitality, and excellence.

* * *

THE TWELVE STEPS OF ALCOHOLICS ANONYMOUS*

1. We admitted we were powerless over alcohol — that our lives had become unmanageable.
2. Came to believe that a Power greater than ourselves could restore us to sanity.
3. Made a decision to turn our will and our lives over to the care of God *as we understood Him.*
4. Made a searching and fearless moral inventory of ourselves.
5. Admitted to God, to ourselves, and to another human being the exact nature of our wrongs.
6. Were entirely ready to have God remove all these defects of character.
7. Humbly asked Him to remove our shortcomings.
8. Made a list of all persons we had harmed, and became willing to make amends to them all.
9. Made direct amends to such people wherever possible, except when to do so would injure them or others.
10. Continued to take personal inventory and when we were wrong promptly admitted it.
11. Sought through prayer and meditation to improve our conscious contact with God *as we understood Him*, praying only for knowledge of His will for us and the power to carry that out.
12. Having had a spiritual awakening as the result of these steps, we tried to carry this message to alcoholics, and to practice these principles in all our affairs.

* * *

* The Twelve Steps of A.A. are taken from Alcoholics Anonymous, 3d ed., published by A.A. World Services, Inc., New York, N.Y., 59-60. Reprinted with permission of A.A. World Services, Inc. (See editor's note on copyright page.)

References

American Society of Addiction Medicine (ASAM). 1991. *Patient placement criteria for the treatment of psychoatice substance use disorders.* Washington, D.C.: ASAM. Tel. (202) 244-8948.

Bjorklund, P. E. 1983. *What is spirituality?* Center City, Minn.: Hazelden.

Chatlos, J. C. 1987. *Crack: What you should know about the cocaine epidemic.* New York: Putnam.

———. 1989. Adolescent dual diagnosis: A 12 step transformational model. *Journal of Psychoactive Drugs* 21 (2):189-201.

———. 1991a. Adolescent drug and alcohol addiction: Diagnosis and assessment. In *Comprehensive handbook of drug and alcohol addiction,* edited by N.S. Miller. New York: Marcel-Dekker, 211-33.

———. 1991b. Adolescent drug and alcohol addiction: Intervention and treatment. In *Comprehensive handbook of drug and alcohol addiction,* edited by N.S. Miller. New York: Marcel-Dekker, 235-53.

Davanloo, H. 1980. *Short-term dynamic psychotherapy.* New York: Jason Aronson.

Davis, D. M. 1989. Intensive short-term dynamic psychotherapy in the treatment of chemical dependency. Pt. 1. *International Journal of Short-Term Dynamic Psychotherapy* 4 (1):61-88.

Dryfoos, J. 1990. *Adolescents at risk.* New York: Oxford Univ. Press.

Hawkins, J. D., R. F. Catalano, and J. Y. Miller. 1992. Risk and protective factors for alcohol and other drug problems in adolescence and early adulthood: Implications for substance abuse prevention. *Psychological Bulletin* 112 (1):64-105.

Jaffe, S. L. 1990. *Step workbook for adolescent chemical dependency recovery: A guide to the first five steps.* Washington, D.C.: American Academy of Child and Adolescent Psychiatry, APA.

Lane, R. D., and G. E. Schwartz. 1987. Levels of emotional awareness: A cognitive developmental theory and its application to psychopathology. *American Journal of Psychiatry* 144 (1):133-43.

MacDonald, D. I. 1984. Drugs, drinking and adolescence. *American Journal of Diseases of Children* 138 (2):117-25.

Masterson, J. F. 1972. *Treatment of the borderline adolescent: A developmental approach.* New York: Wiley Interscience.

Ethnicity and gender influence the diagnosis and treatment of coexisting psychiatric and addictive disorders. Clinicians must recognize this and take corrective measures when possible.

7
Dual Diagnosis, Minority Populations, And Women

H. Westley Clark, M.D., J.D., M.P.H.
Joan Ellen Zweben, Ph.D.

Introduction

THERE IS A COMMON ASSUMPTION THAT TREATMENT MODELS applying to the mythical, ideal white male patient are applicable to all individuals, despite ethnicity, culture, or gender. This assumption, of course, has fundamental flaws. Since the life experiences of patients who are either not white or male are inherently different from those of white males, treatment providers need to recognize that diversity in the patient population requires diversity in the treatment approach and even in the conceptualization of treatment. This chapter will briefly present some issues that apply to the phenomenon of ethnic, cultural, and gender diversity. We, believe, however, that a brief chapter will not capture all of the core issues associated with diversity in treating dual diagnosis patients. While we have considerable clinical experience with diverse patients (including ethnic and cultural background, gender, and sexual orientation), we want to avoid the notion that there is a simple recipe for treating them. Consequently, we don't offer a cookbook approach. Rather, we combine our experience with a more theoretical approach, so that the reader can embark on his or her own clinical journey of making diversity in dual diagnosis treatment an integral part of the treatment process.

Ethnically and Culturally Diverse Dual Diagnosis Patients

It is critical that the treatment provider recognize the issues germane to the diagnosis, treatment, and long-term care of culturally diverse dual diagnosis patients. The research base for the exploration of ethnic issues in the dual diagnosis patient is relatively sparse. Fortunately, greater recognition is being given to the issues of race, culture, and class in figuring out the importance of these factors in the treatment of ethnically diverse patients. Evidence of the importance of more research and better clinical understanding of the ethnically and culturally diverse dual diagnosis patient is found in a recent paper on the relationship of crack cocaine smoking and racial/ethnic groups (Lilli-Blanton et al. 1993). The paper points out that the 1988 National Household Survey on Drug Abuse (NHSDA) reported that crack cocaine smoking is more common among African Americans and Hispanic Americans than among Caucasian Americans. A reanalysis of the data, however, suggests that the apparent differences in prevalence may be due more to social and environmental risk factors than to ethnic and racial risk factors. Thus Lilli-Blanton points out the hazards of using mere data to draw conclusions about ethnically/culturally diverse groups.

Patterns of Substance Use

Although there are hazards associated with making generalizations about the National Household Survey on Drug Abuse, the data do show some variation in alcohol and drug use among African Americans, Hispanic Americans and Caucasians. A greater percentage of African Americans reported crack cocaine use, but less cocaine use, and more heroin use than Caucasians. A greater percentage of Hispanic Americans reported cocaine use, including crack, and more heroin use than Caucasians. Alcohol, of course, is the primary drug of abuse by African Americans, Hispanic Americans, and Caucasians. Cigarettes are the second most frequently used or experienced drug of abuse. The third most frequently used drug of abuse is marijuana (National Household Survey on Drug Abuse 1989). Consequently, the dually diagnosed patient belonging to a minority population would most likely be expected to use the same drugs as the average Caucasian substance abuser, with the exception of heroin.

TREATING ETHNICALLY AND CULTURALLY DIVERSE PATIENTS

The ethnic experience is defined by race, culture, subculture, economics, language, religion, and the relationship between the ethnic group and other ethnic groups. These factors create an interplay of forces that affect a patient who presents for treatment. Major ethnic groups with whom a therapist is likely to come in contact include, among others, African Americans, Asian Americans, Native Americans, and Hispanic Americans. The broad categories of ethnic groups are not monolithic; African Americans may be from the Caribbean, Georgia, New York, Africa, or Latin America countries. Hispanic Americans can come from Puerto Rico, Boston, Florida, Cuba, Mexico, El Salvador, or Costa Rica. Asian groups may include a broad spectrum of individuals from such countries as China, Japan, Vietnam, Cambodia, the Philippines, or Thailand.

As for drug and alcohol use within the broad categories of ethnic groups, there may be differences in consumption patterns. Ruiz and Langrod (1992) noted differences in abstinence and use between Mexican Americans, Puerto Ricans, and Cuban Americans. While some of these differences were not substantial, Ruiz's observations highlight the existence of intragroup variations. Westermeyer (1992) noted that among Native Americans the risk for substance abuse differs among the various subgroups. Westermeyer also made this observation about Asian subgroups. Recognizing that an increase in alcohol use has been noted in Japanese Americans, Filipino Americans, and Korean Americans is critical.

We believe that clinically viewing an individual from a specific ethnic group in specific terms is a mistake; that is, to assume the stereotypic experiences of the ethnic group are those of the individual. The social, cultural, and environmental experiences of each individual will, nevertheless, influence his or her predisposition for psychiatric problems and for addiction. Furthermore, how a person expresses the symptoms of disease will be influenced by those same variables.

CULTURAL VARIABLES IN DIAGNOSIS

A cultural experience embracing rites, curses, witchcraft, spirits, or other supernatural forces can complicate communication with a patient if the culture does not embrace these things. In the case of schizophrenia, for example, delusions involving phenomena that the patient's culture would regard as totally implausible is a major symptom of active psychosis (*DSM-III-R*). If a therapist used his or her view of the patient's culture as the pivotal factor, the conclusion of psychotic delusion could be reached from an otherwise normal phenomenon or, alternatively, from a drug- or alcohol-induced phenomenon.

Even in the face of a major psychiatric disorder other than substance abuse, the progress of a patient might not be appreciated if indices of that progress occur in a cultural context.

A brief example is the case of an African American patient who suffers from paranoid ideation and cocaine abuse. After six months of treatment, it became clear that the patient's symptoms were not primarily the result of his cocaine abuse. The manifestations of his symptoms included irritability, ease of anger, and distrust of institutions. As the patient progressed in treatment, which included neuroleptics and group therapy, the anger persisted; however, the patient would bring the anger-provoking situations to the attention of the group before acting on them. Hence, there was an increase in trust and a decrease in the acting-out behavior. Besides relying on the treatment process, the patient joined a church and began to quote from the Bible during group therapy. Rather than viewing the increase in religiosity as symptomatic of a deteriorating psychotic process, treatment staff was able to work with the patient using his choice of religion as a belief and a metaphor for his recovery.

Another example might include a patient's organizing his or her symptoms into metaphysical phenomena that could be interpreted as evidence of delusional or psychotic thinking. This might be considered an attempt to reconcile the symptoms with a worldview that tolerates the symptoms, but not any acting out that comes from the symptoms. Care must be exercised to figure out the implications of the psychiatric symptoms in the context of the cultural experience of the patient.

Thus we suggest a biopsychosocial formulation that includes these critical variables. Failing to address these variables early in the treatment process can produce both diagnostic and treatment errors with grave consequences for both patient and treatment provider.

Economic Issues

Substance use disorders include decay in psychosocial function criteria. Similarly, major psychiatric disorders also usually include criteria that involve psychosocial function: namely social (in terms of the interaction between significant others) or occupational. The more severe disturbances produce a decrease in the level of function, that is, a decay in premorbid function.

Consequently, when premorbid psychosocial functions are low, diagnoses are confounded. African American and Hispanic American patients are more likely than Caucasian patients to have socioeconomic problems. These socioeconomic variables predispose both these ethnic groups to suffer greater adverse consequences of substance abuse and psychiatric illness (Rouse 1989). When the experience of Native Americans is considered, these variables are equally applicable.

Lilli-Blanton suggested that social and environmental factors may play a role in the drugs of choice of African Americans and Hispanic Americans. Mueser et al. suggest that socioeconomic factors, as well as access, exposure, and availability, lead African Americans to use the most commonly available illicit drugs. (Mueser et al. 1992). Socioeconomic variables also play a role in the treatment and maintenance care of the dual diagnosis patient.

Gender factors are also major concerns in the context of ethnicity. The life experience of minority males and females certainly is not uniform. Given the paucity of research data into the provision of treatment services for women, it is difficult to make adequate generalizations about treatment issues. The clinician must be astute enough, however, to view ethnicity as having two additional axes—male and female—that can create stresses, expectations, and experiences.

Female psychiatric patients are less likely than males to abuse all substances. Mueser et al. report on data on female psychiatric patient substance use. They found that women were more likely to have a history of stimulant abuse than men; in another however, within those patients who abused stimulants, there was no difference in cocaine or amphetamine abuse. Female patients suffering from schizoaffective disorder were more likely to have a history of stimulant abuse. Male psychiatric patients were also more likely than female psychiatric patients to abuse alcohol, narcotics, cannabis, and hallucinogens.

Whatever the gender differences may be, one thing is clear: programs need to address the unique life experiences of ethnically and culturally diverse women. By recognizing that there are such differences and incorporating this recognition in treatment, clinicians can make the treatment experience of ethnic and culturally diverse patients more satisfying.

Violence

The dual diagnosis patient is particularly vulnerable to violence—if not from generic mental illness, from a drug-using culture that is conducive to violence. Ethnic dual diagnosis patients may reside in communities where drug-related violence is common. Furthermore, both male and female patients may have been victims of childhood sexual abuse and violence. Female patients, of course, are at greater risk for violence.

The chronic or episodic exposure to the culture of violence associated with substance use may present a problem for both the patient and the treatment provider. Naturally, a victim of violence with eroded coping skills, a substance abuse problem, and psychiatric problems may not present as an ideal patient. We find that patients either resign themselves to a passive-aggressive demeanor or assume a highly charged aggressive stance. It is critical for the clinician to recognize that a victim of violence, even if presenting as a perpetrator, will be adversely affected by that violence. The African American, Native American, and Hispanic American dual diagnosis patient may be particularly at risk for the violence associated with racial discrimination, including harassment by police, social agencies, and treatment providers.

Treatment Provider Perspectives

Ethnicity affects how the treatment provider views the patient. Ethnicity can also, based on incorrect assumptions, create a tension in the transference and can affect how a clinician diagnoses the problems of the patient. (*Transference* refers to two basic types of events: [1] how the patient relates to the therapists, usually based on the patient's historical and developmental patterns of relationships, and [2] how the therapist relates to the patient, usually based on what emotions the patient stirs in the therapist [also known as *countertransference*].) For example, diagnoses such as schizophrenia, schizoaffective disorder, and antisocial personality, which tend to be viewed as having poorer prognoses, are likely to be applied to African Americans. Indeed, in one recently published study of a survey in the Los Angeles County mental health system, African Americans and Asian Americans had a greater proportion of psychotic diagnoses than Caucasians and Hispanic Americans, while African Americans and Hispanic Americans received fewer diagnoses of major affective disorder than Caucasians and Asians (Flaskerud 1992). A diagnosis of a major affective disorder tends to have a more favorable prognosis and tends to be viewed differently from schizophrenia. We believe that a lack of clinical empathy for cultural differences may contribute to misdiagnosis. Furthermore, especially in public situations where resources are limited, misdiagnosis can serve as a way of apologizing for limited agency or treatment-provider resources. Finally, misdiagnosis excuses the need to be culturally sensitive because there is no need to invest greater time and energy to bridge the gap between the patient and the therapist if it is perceived that the outcome will not be affected.

Since psychiatric diagnoses—particularly of certain major disorders— are often imprecise, how the therapist experiences a patient is likely to influence how the therapist treats the patient. Substances of abuse, of course, only compound the diagnostic situation.

African American males in treatment are often regarded as angry and hostile. A non-African American therapist subscribing to this stereotype can view symptoms of anger as illogical and off-putting. Yet the experience of many African Americans in white society is generally not favorable. Indeed, the symptoms of anger can be a defense against what is perceived to be a hostile or racist institution.

When dealing with the dual diagnosis population, a therapist is often dealing with economically poor patients. These patients live in a social context that reinforces the need for caution when dealing with agents of the larger society. Unless the symptoms of the patient are grossly out of control or the patient views the symptoms as distressful, the patient's presentation is often likely to be viewed as idiosyncratic.

Trust as a Clinical Issue

Another diagnostic consideration that fits into the dual diagnosis spectrum is the associated diagnosis of posttraumatic stress disorder (PTSD). Dual diagnosis patients are often homeless or consigned to living alone in single-room hotels, making them vulnerable to periodic exploitation and physical assaults. Given the level of violence in urban areas, many African Americans or Hispanic Americans may suffer from PTSD. PTSD produces symptoms of hyperarousal, which in turn may cause anger, irritability, hypervigilance (which could be mistaken for paranoia), and insomnia. Because of a lack of general responsiveness, a patient suffering from PTSD may admit to feeling detached or estranged from others, exhibit restricted affect, and complain of a sense of foreshortened future. Add to this the discrimination and racism experienced by many minority patients, and it is not difficult to see why trust is a major issue.

As therapists, we are usually regarded as agents of society, hence the patient's caution and circumspection. We therefore must understand this adaptive caution. We must show through normal therapeutic links that trust will not be casually violated and that a therapeutic relationship is possible.

The fact that the therapist is not, for example, an African American becomes less critical to a patient who trusts the therapist. A patient angry with a society that rejects him and misunderstands his condition is likely to test the therapist's commitment to him and to the treatment process. In the absence of real threats to person or property, the non-African American therapist must be willing to make a commitment to the treatment process and not view the patient as a potential threat. This commitment requires an awareness of the experience of the patient, since, as mentioned earlier, minority patients are more likely to be misdiagnosed.

How does the clinician effect trust across cultural lines? It depends on the patient and the patient's background. An African American patient may search for disparaging remarks or disapproving comments or attitudes. A Hispanic American may find trust difficult to establish across the language barrier. An Asian patient may find it difficult to overcome shame and humiliation. Any of these patients suffering from a comorbid psychiatric condition may have had previous encounters with either a substance abuse or mental health system that discounted their unique conflicts or experiences. Thus the clinician must resist the temptation to lump the ethnic dual diagnosis patient into the amorphous mass of the average patient. On the other hand, the clinician must not defer to the idea of culture to the exclusion of the patient.

Simple "how to's" may include keeping appointments with the patient, waving hello when passing the patient in the clinic or even on the street, avoiding conflicts of trust in public settings, or being able to tolerate the patient's negative affective states, such as anger or irritability, when they are nonthreatening. With substance abuse, there is often the clinical presumption that a patient's irregular behavior and thoughts are motivated by the desire to use psychoactive substances. In traditional mental health clinics, a similar view may prevail. However, a patient may miss appointments because of more pressing demands elsewhere: public assistance, housing or shelter, food and transportation issues. A brief clinical example illustrates this point.

A dual diagnosis patient was falling asleep during a group therapy session. The therapist was concerned that the patient was either using or overmedicated. A subsequent interview with the patient revealed that he was still homeless and living in a shelter. To get a bed for the next day, the line started forming at 5 A.M. This meant that the patient had to get up by 4:30 A.M. Furthermore, life in the shelter was somewhat chaotic, with noise and fear of theft, so the patient did not get to sleep until late. Thus, the nodding patient was neither overmedicated nor using illicit drugs. The patient was simply bone tired. The approach the therapist chose was not to accuse the patient of using drugs, but simply to observe that he was falling asleep in group and to wonder aloud if anything was wrong. The patient was Latino and appeared to appreciate the therapist's approach. There were no accusations, just simple observations of the patient's behavior. The therapist offered the patient the opportunity to be excused from group if he got too tired.

The vignette above shows the trust that must develop between the clinician and the dual diagnosis patient. Even a hint of an adversarial approach may be enough to attenuate, and eventually compromise, the clinical alliance.

Patient/Clinician Matching

In most clinical settings, it may not be possible to match a patient to a therapist of his/her ethnic or cultural group. It may also not be possible to match a patient to a therapist of the same gender. Treatment providers should seek out educational and training experiences to enhance their understanding of the needs of their ethnically diverse patient population. Today, there is a wealth of material that provides insight into the medical, psychological, cultural, social, economic, political, historical, and epidemiological experiences of different ethnic groups. This information should be helpful in understanding the particular patient who presents for treatment (APA Office of Ethnic Minority Affairs 1993).

Language variables are critical for establishing a rapport with a patient. The treatment provider must bridge language differences; this may be accomplished by referring the patient to a practitioner who speaks the patient's language, employing a translator who understands dual diagnosis, and employing community workers from the patient's culture (Ruiz and Langrod 1992). Language issues are, of course, critical to the description of symptoms a patient presents. A misunderstanding or mistranslation could result in either the exaggeration or minimization of a patient's symptoms.

There may be times when such treatment matching by ethnic group, culture, or language is critical, and treatment providers should have some type of clinical indices to suggest it. One of the more important indicators of treatment matching is the desire of the patient to be seen by someone of the same ethnic group or cultural background. Such a request should be honored whenever possible; when it is not, the treatment provider should address the specific concerns the patient has regarding the treatment provider.

The addiction specialist must exercise great care in dealing with the patient who suffers from an addiction and a major psychiatric disorder. Earlier in this chapter, we stressed the importance of taking into consideration ethnic and cultural issues when assessing both addiction and mental illness. It is important not to mistreat the psychiatric symptoms of a patient or attribute symptoms of distress and pathology to culture, leaving the patient at greater risk for relapse and exacerbation of symptoms.

FAMILY ROLES

Within the context of a patient's culture, assistance for the dual diagnosis patient may come from either the nuclear or extended family. The treatment provider should enlist the assistance of family members as a means of monitoring the significance of the psychoactive substance use to the patient, enlisting additional support for the patient when support is needed, and devising treatment interventions that acknowledge the importance of family in both the pathogenesis and the treatment of substance abuse and mental illness.

Family support and involvement vary in importance and in availability. Family abandonment often occurs when families have exhausted their abilities to cope with the dual complications of mental illness and substance abuse. With family abandonment may come a shame that varies to greater or lesser degrees, depending on the patient's culture and background. Some Asian families may delay the entry of a patient into treatment because they believe that providing care for the patient is the responsibility of the family. This same view may be embraced by Hispanic Americans and by the extended families of African Americans. With the admission that the family cannot manage a member who suffers from illness comes the shame of failure.

Treatment providers who are not sensitive to the patient's family members may miss an opportunity to arrest the cycle of substance use and exacerbation of psychological symptoms. Even when patients are alienated from family members, any extended period of sobriety can be used as a mechanism to reconnect the patient with the family. The positive influence of additional social supports can make a critical difference in the treatment of a patient.

For instance, one Hispanic American patient was initially brought into the clinic by his sister, with whom he was staying. After three months of medication visits, the patient stopped coming to the clinic. Knowing that the patient had no phone, we simply wrote him a letter. We knew that his sister would see the official-looking letter from the clinic and would inquire about it. Sure enough, the patient came back to the clinic for medications. He was also encouraged to talk with other Hispanic American patients about their experiences. He found support from the other patients, which assisted him in returning to the role of patient.

Self-Medication

Dual diagnosis patients will often try to medicate themselves with more socially acceptable agents, such as alcohol or street drugs. The self-medication hypothesis of dual diagnosis is validated by a number of patients. Thus patients undermedicated or overmedicated may use substances of abuse to titrate the symptoms of their conditions. In addition, a patient may get the added benefit of increasing social acceptance. One example is that of an African American male who suffered both from schizophrenia and the isolation that tends to accompany this disease. The patient stated that the cocaine helped with the neuroleptics with which he was being treated and gave him social opportunities he wouldn't have had, that is, sexual activities that would have ordinarily been denied him. Epidemiological data do indeed suggest that patients with diagnoses of major psychoses tend to have major interpersonal problems. Consequently, the drug or alcohol experience can be a normalizing one, even with the risk of increasing the psychotic experience. For cultures that place a premium on social congress, the dual diagnosis patient may be willing to accept the risk of increasing symptoms associated with drug use.

Countertransference Issues

While it is clear that ethnicity, culture, and gender play major roles in the care and treatment of patients, substance abuse practitioners and mental health professionals must be aware of the inclination to avoid critical examination of their own ethnicity, culture, and gender issues, as well as those characteristics that influence life experiences, occupational roles and attitudes, and hierarchical views of the patient. Nor should pressing clinical demands be permitted to trivialize these factors.

We believe that when treatment providers lose the ability to reflect on their own views of the importance of ethnic, cultural, and gender variables, they also lose their ability to intervene effectively.

Gender Issues and Dual Diagnosis

Gender factors play a similarly complex role, influencing research, diagnosis, accessibility to treatment, and many facets of treatment itself. Russo (1990) underscored the theme that existing research is inadequate for understanding the large and complex gender difference in patterns of mental disorder and its treatment. He identified five research priorities: (1) diagnosis and treatment of mental disorders, (2) mental health issues for older women, (3) violence against women, (4) multiple roles, and (5) poverty. To varying degrees, these factors also play a role in addictive behavior and recovery.

The differential effects of gender can be observed in the addiction field. For a long time, the relatively low rates of heavy drinking among women compared to men led to a lack of information about women's drinking patterns and problems. Most of the early research that established our basic knowledge about the physiology and pharmacology of alcohol in humans was done on male subjects. For example, only recently has it been discovered that when "normal" men and women are given equivalent single doses under standard conditions, women will reach peak blood alcohol levels that are both higher and far more variable than those of men, and that these levels will show some correlation with the menstrual cycle. These factors make the average daily quantity of alcohol consumed an even less reliable indication of alcoholism in the female than it is in the male. For the dually diagnosed patient, then, assuming that the female patient is not excessively drinking by quantifying drinks is not sufficient.

A recent ADAMHA report noted that women make up less than 25 percent of patients in alcohol treatment settings, and 30 percent of all drug admissions. The disproportionate numbers of men in treatment settings for substance abuse have perpetuated a system that often fails to describe women's different needs clearly and respond to them effectively. Consequently, when looking at the even more unique needs of the dually diagnosed female patient, the clinician must factor in even more complicated variables. For example, unlike their male counterparts, more dually diagnosed women are partners either through legal marriages or through common-law arrangements. Women's partners play a major role in their initial decision to use drugs, seek treatment, stay in treatment, and sustain commitment to recovery-related activities. Furthermore, women of child-bearing age are subject to increased scrutiny; the possibility of pregnancy only exacerbates the hostility that many receive from the health care system, and their children are more likely to be taken from them.

Dually diagnosed women are also at increased risk for sexual abuse and violence, either domestic or environmental. However, they often have few social networks outside the culture of drinking and drug use. Those more highly functioning women with a dual diagnosis may be responsible for one or more children. Child care becomes a major barrier to treatment. Such responsibility adds an increased likelihood of stress.

Help-seeking patterns vary by gender and often work against the woman seeking help. Female problem drinkers are more likely than male problem drinkers to use mental health treatment services rather than alcohol- or drug-specific settings (Weisner and Schmidt 1992). They also report greater problem severity. Unfortunately, the mental health system has historically been unable to address addiction problems adequately; thus the woman seeking help in that setting is far less likely to have her alcoholism identified, much less appropriately addressed (Zweben and Clark 1991). In addition, studies have noted gender bias in the prescribing of psychotropic drugs in primary care settings; women are much more likely to receive prescriptions for anxiolytics and antidepressants even when presenting symptoms, diagnoses, and other factors are controlled.

Recent efforts on the part of the Center for Substance Abuse Treatment have made women's needs a high priority and have initiated a variety of projects to address them. Specific funding increases have also been mandated by Congress. Equally important are the evolution of task forces and the developing of practice guidelines for women in substance abuse treatment. Some of these guidelines should also apply to the dually diagnosed woman. In the meantime, treatment providers must recognize the complex issues inherent in diagnosing and treating the substance-abusing woman who suffers from a major psychiatric illness.

Conclusion

While necessary research on the various treatment issues of dual diagnosis patients is being conducted, the practitioner is confronted with the reality of treating the patient who is present. We believe every clinician who treats ethnically diverse or female dual diagnosis patients should permit them to articulate their concerns. For some patients anger is the critical issue; for others, shame; for others, confusion; for still others, pride and hope. The practitioner who does not share the ethnic background or gender of the patient can make significant strides in the therapeutic relationship by exhibiting a sensitivity to these concerns.

Individual practitioners, community mental health centers, public substance abuse programs, and anyone else concerned with the treatment of a diverse population of patients can aid their patients' recovery by encouraging them to join self-help groups that respond to their special concerns. Patients with psychiatric disorders are often very aware of their mental status and the need to take psychiatric medications. Self-help groups may be able to tolerate the medication issue, but if the patient is viewed as alien, or if the patient's experiences are viewed as irrelevant, the patient will suffer the consequences.

It may be necessary to aid groups of patients to form appropriate self-help groups. Treatment providers can capitalize on the existence of community resources to facilitate this activity. If language barriers exist, a Spanish-speaking group (for example) may be useful. Obviously, dual diagnosis self-help groups would be useful.* In the absence of a specific community group, a group held in the treatment center where psychiatric medications are dispensed or prescribed may prove beneficial; in this situation, the patient would at least be familiar with other patients who are similarly dually diagnosed.

Since psychiatric medications can be an issue for patients with chronic psychiatric illnesses and substance abuse problems, it is important to involve family or cultural support in the taking of medication. Some communities may regard the patient's psychiatric problems as manageable without medication, attributing the patient's symptoms to drugs or alcohol. Explaining the importance of medication to such family or community members could aid the patient's stability.

Finally, gender issues function as both background and foreground elements in the diagnosis and treatment process. The treatment specialist must keep this issue in mind when treating both the male and female dual diagnosis patient.

---

*Dual Recovery Anonymous, Central Service Office, P.O. Box 8107, Prairie Village, KS 66208. There are also self-help groups for patients who primarily identify with their psychiatric illness rather than their substance abuse problems. Examples of such groups include the following:

1. The Anxiety Disorder Association of America, 6000 Executive Boulevard, Suite 513, Rockville, MD 20852-3801.
2. The Depressive and Manic-Depressive Association, 222 South Riverside Plaza, Suite 2812, Chicago, IL 60606.
3. Emotional Health Anonymous, 2420 San Gabriel Boulevard, Rosemead, CA 91770.

References

American Psychiatric Association. 1987. *Diagnostic and statistical manual of mental disorders.* 3d ed., rev. Washington, D.C.: American Psychiatric Association.

APA Office of Ethnic Minority Affairs. 1993. Guidelines for providers of psychological services to ethnic, linguistic, and culturally diverse populations. *American Psychologist* 48:45-48.

Flaskerud, J. H., and L. T. Hu. 1992. Relationship of ethnicity to psychiatric diagnosis. *Journal of Nervous and Mental Disease* 180:296-303.

Lilli-Blanton, M., J. C. Anthony, and C. R. Schuster. 1993. Probing the meaning of racial/ethnic group comparisons in crack cocaine smoking. *JAMA* 269:993-7.

Mueser, K. T., P. R. Yarnold, and A. S. Bellack. 1992. Diagnostic and demographic correlates of substance abuse in schizophrenia and major affective disorder. *Acta Psychiatrica Scandinavica* 85:48-55.

National Household Survey on Drug Abuse. 1989. *Population estimates 1988.* DHHS Publication No. (ADM) 89-1636. Washington, D.C.: Alcohol, Drug Abuse, and Mental Health Administration.

Rouse, B. 1989. *Drug abuse among racial/ethnic minorities: A special report.* Rockville, MD: National Institute of Drug Abuse.

Ruiz, P., and J. G. Langrod. 1992. Substance abuse among Hispanic-Americans: Current issues and future perspectives. In *Substance abuse: A comprehensive textbook,* edited by J. D. Lowinson and R. B. Millman. Baltimore: Williams & Wilkins.

Russo, N. F. 1990. Overview: Forging research priorities for women's mental health. *American Psychologist* 45 (3):368-73.

Westermeyer, J. 1992. Cultural perspectives: Native Americans, Asians, and new immigrants. In *Substance abuse: A comprehensive textbook,* edited by J. D. Lowinson and R. B. Millman. Baltimore: Williams & Wilkins.

Weisner, C., and L. Schmidt. 1992. Gender disparities in treatment for alcohol problems. *JAMA* 268:1872-76.

Zweben, J. E., and H. W. Clark. 1991. Unrecognized substance misuse: Clinical hazards and legal vulnerabilities. *The International Journal of the Addictions* 25:1431-51.

When left untreated, food, gambling, spending, religion, love, or sex addictions (the addictive psychiatric disorders) foster relapse to the "primary" addiction or the emergence of a new, substitute "primary" addiction.

8
Addictive Psychiatric Disorders

James Cocores, M.D.

SEASONED THERAPISTS OFTEN GLOW WITH COMPASSION AND SERENITY —like a "heart light." We instinctively shed light as a flower sheds pollen. Our challenge begins with pollination and ends in attracting another bee. Our goal is to make dual diagnosis recovery look colorful and sweet. We know we are dealing with addiction when we encounter difficulty selling recovery. The key is to attract the addict to recovery long enough, or enough times, to plant the seed of flexibility, which in turn permits growth which is change which is recovery.

ANALGESIA AND PLEASURE CYCLE

Dr. Stuckey's term, "pleasure disorder" (Stuckey 1989, 1991), has worked for us because it is much more palatable for our patients, especially when we are trying to "sell" treatment of an addictive psychiatric disorder. What does "pleasure disorder" imply? It implies that most people indulge or overindulge in food, gambling, nicotine, alcohol or other drugs, spending, or sex, because it is fun, entertaining, and pleasurable. Even patients in deep denial do not look at us as if we were speaking a foreign language when we deliver this description of addiction. They often respond, "Yeah, who doesn't!" Yet non-addicts do not consistently and almost exclusively need or rely on one or more addictive commodities (food, gambling, nicotine, alcohol or other drugs, spending, or sex) to achieve or approach happiness.

"Addiction" is not purely defined as "How much?" or "How often?" We focus on the addict's quality of life. For example, is eating or snacking the highlight of the day more often than not? What does the gambler enjoy more, watching the Super Bowl or placing the bet on the game? Can the gambler honestly enjoy the game without betting, and how consistent is the pattern? Is nicotine the principal means of reversing boredom, cognitive blurring (the mild cognitive fog that slowly refills the sensorium after the effects of the nicotine wear off), and somatic tension (Pickworth et al. 1991)? Does the fisherman pack the cooler before the tackle box? If he has time or money for only one, does he buy the beer or the fishing license? Does the best high of the week (and most other weeks) begin by planning and end in execution of a spending binge? Does fear, shame, or guilt consistently douse the flaming high? Do masturbation, peep shows, and pornography (or a combination of these) substitute for the pleasure derived from cultivating a healthy relationship?

Use of the "pleasure disorder" terminology is only half the delivery story. The following case history illustrates the other half of the description we deliver.

> Roxanne was a twenty-six-year-old married recovering heroin addict who had attended a Twelve Step Minnesota Model treatment center. Other addictions in her history included tobacco, prescription opiates, wine, food, and sex. She could not relate to the definitions of dependence, abuse, use, addiction, or compulsive behavior; nor could she relate to "pleasure," "good time," "fun," or "rush." She could not understand what peers and staff meant by "getting high." It was not until pain relief, or *analgesia,* terminology was used, that she could relate to the patients in her group. Using this descriptive term, she was also able to establish a therapeutic alliance with her therapists.
>
> After a few months we discovered why. Roxanne's mother was a high priestess in a satanic cult. Roxanne assisted her mother in human torture, sacrifice, flesh-eating, and other rituals performed in her mother's underground place of worship. (Since the age of five, Roxanne would assist or participate in the slow torture and murder of children offered to Satan on the eve of major Christian

holidays like Christmas.) Roxanne was often hung naked by her wrists as part of rituals and raped with a dagger. Fear of being sacrificed tempered her secrecy and led to almost total repression, which blossomed into intense, unbearable physical and emotional pain. Of course, she also had a dissociative disorder. Fractional recall was accomplished after years of therapy. Total recall was close to impossible and definitely not our goal, because complete release of the defense mechanisms harnessing Roxanne would have probably been inconsistent with her functioning as a wife, mother, and therapist.

The denial associated with addictive psychiatric disorders is often greater because they are perceived as "nonalcohol" or "nondrug." Because the denial associated with addictive psychiatric disorders is stronger, traditional terminology seems even more alien to these patients. We call the terminology we deliver the "analgesia and pleasure (A&P) cycle." It works best for us when delivered to patients as the common descriptive denominator for all addictive disorders. Patients seem more able to apply new concepts and behaviors learned during drug recovery therapy toward a coexisting addictive psychiatric disorder after the common denominator of the A&P cycle is understood.

Timing

In the majority of patients, we uncover at least one addictive psychiatric disorder along with the primary drug diagnosis. We see a higher drug relapse rate among patients whose treatment focused on alcohol or drug recovery while ignoring or overlooking a coexisting addictive psychiatric disorder. When ignored or overlooked, an addictive psychiatric disorder (food, gambling, spending, religion, or sex) runs amok, substituting for alcohol or other drugs, which sustains the A&P cycle of addiction (figure 8.1).

Drug indulgence results in brief analgesia or pleasure, followed by a longer "withdrawal syndrome" characterized by emotional discomfort. Drug abstinence intensifies boredom and emotional or physical pain. Then, a substitute addictive psychiatric behavior becomes the alternate analgesic that strengthens and grows, sustaining the A&P cycle at the same time. The development of a new addiction or relapse to the initial

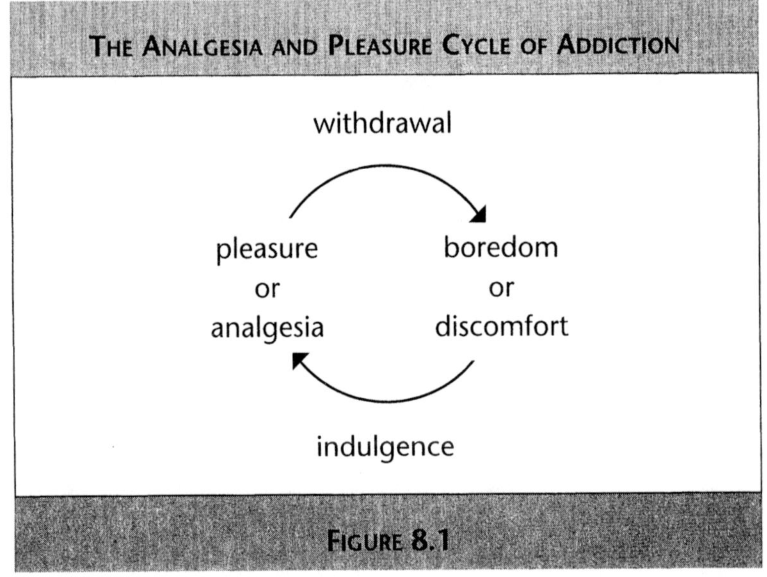

FIGURE 8.1

drug addiction is again "needed" to quiet the withdrawal pain temporarily (Cocores 1990). This is why we hunt for addictive psychiatric disorders while treating alcohol and other drug patients and their loved ones.

Delivery of the A&P cycle as it pertains to alcohol and drugs only is usually timed for after the first assessment or admission. When a patient is a relapser, we review the relapse at readmission from an A&P perspective. When a patient with a known coexisting addictive psychiatric disorder has relapsed on drugs, we review the anatomy of the relapse, focusing on the interaction between the addictions from an A&P perspective. We believe that it is a relative contraindication to talk about treatment of a coexisting addictive psychiatric disorder when it is the patient's first treatment, regardless of the delivery style. The main reason can be summed up in one word: *overwhelming.* First-time patients are usually frightened (despite the fact that they ordinarily do not frighten easily) by the idea of a Twelve Step rehabilitation and all it represents: learning, communication, sharing, honesty, change, spirituality, and love. Upon admission, first-timers think they are unwilling to stop their drug of choice. (By the Second Step they learn they were also *unable.*) In addition to asking them to abstain from their drug of choice, we require abstinence from all other mood-altering drugs, prescription medicines, and over-the-counter medicines. We also address nicotine addiction, which further terrorizes about 80 percent of our patients (Klahr 1991). We also talk about caffeine abstinence. The worst time to chat about a coexisting addictive psychiatric disorder is during the first week of rehabilitation. Patients have been known to get up and leave if "too much" is expected. The rate at which the therapist collects enough "data" to substantiate an addictive psychiatric disorder determines the timing for delivery of the A&P cycle as it relates to addictive psychiatric disorders.

Food Addictions

The most famous "foods" straddling the drug realm (caffeine) are coffee, colas, and chocolate. Putting those aside, animal fat, sugar, salt, and MSG (monosodium glutamate) are responsible for the majority of food cravings we hear about from our patients. We find it necessary to define a craving as a preoccupation that translates into a psychomotor "magnetism." Cravings are a sharp contrast to thoughts: thoughts come and go, while cravings linger and become louder and louder. The case of Dr. D. illustrates the difference between thoughts and cravings.

> Dr. D. celebrated four years of recovery from cocaine, wine, marijuana, and nicotine. She was a happily married mother of two. Her cardiology and nutrition practice was going very well. Dr. D. had a family history of heart disease. Despite her training to avoid people, places, and things associated with her using days, she unexpectedly had seen cocaine on the news or in movies and had thoughts of using. She kept the thought of using cocaine from becoming a craving by diverting her thoughts elsewhere. Although her main problem was cocaine, she thought about drinking wine at least once a month. She would quiet these thoughts with a fantasy of picking up wine in thirty-one years at the age of seventy. She missed the "philosophical" marijuana journeys she once took on weekends but had no cravings. She had no desire to smoke cigarettes or chew nicotine gum ever again. She had a history of bulimia in her teens.
>
> She reentered individual therapy fearful of what appeared to her to be very early signs of relapse. She had been coming home

from work at around 6 p.m. and had started a ritual of kneading flour, water, fast-rising yeast, salt, and sugar into pizza dough. Dr. D. would quickly put the velvet-textured dough into the oven on warm. She would then sauté herbs and spices in olive oil and let the tomato sauce simmer until 10:30 p.m. Then it was time to grind the mozzarella, romano, and parmesan cheeses at precise ratios (top secret!). She would only prepare enough for one pizza because she was "only going to do it tonight." She firmly believed that she would "not do it tomorrow." She would start flattening out the dough by 10:30; by 11:20 the crispy pizza would be devoured. She was having pizza "cravings" or more specifically, cravings for animal fat, sugar, and salt. The pizza cravings happened three days in a row and each day started with planning in the early afternoon.

We advised her to continue attending Narcotics Anonymous meetings, add an Overeaters Anonymous (OA) meeting biweekly, and continue with weekly individual therapy.

After two sessions, Dr. D. discovered where she had reentered the A&P cycle. It turned out that Dr. D. was the anonymous subject of her daughter's term paper, "The Fall and Rise of a Drug Addict." Telling her story in great detail to her daughter subconsciously triggered guilt and shame. Pizza made her feel better for a short time, and then she would feel "like a lard-ass." After therapeutic reconciliation with the First Step, Dr. D.'s pizza cravings were no more.

Gambling Addictions

About 30 percent of our drug patients have a coexisting gambling problem. Half of the A&P gambling cycle is the thought of winning, events leading to betting, and winning. The discomfort half includes losing more frequently than the gambler anticipates, and enormous emotional (and sometimes physical) pain.

Jimi G. was a forty-two-year-old divorced disbarred attorney. He had been gambling away client trust funds and was referred to us for cocaine addiction after being accused of credit card fraud in Atlantic City. He had no clue about the symbiotic cocaine-gambling tragedy he had been living. "I don't have a problem with cocaine. They found it in my urine. I'm a binge user, that's all; just sometimes on weekends to help me be a little more alert." It took us about two weeks to get him to understand at an intellectual level that he needed to abstain from cocaine, wine, beer, and all other mood-altering substances, By then we had learned that he was a typical gambling "garbage head"; a potpourri of lottery tickets, horse racing, dog racing, casinos, poker, stock options, loan sharks, and sports betting. We decided to soften him up a little by sending him to a few Gamblers Anonymous (GA) meetings to chip away a few outer denial layers before delivering the A&P cycle of addiction. He returned to our rehabilitation center after his first GA meeting: "Doc, you'd never believe those GA guys. What a bunch of fanatics! Do you believe they told me not to even play Monopoly? Besides, they all call themselves compulsive gamblers. How come you wanted me to go there?"

The worst thing we could have done at that point was to engage in defining terms with an ex-attorney. The A&P cycle helped him conceptualize his problem and worked to get him to see gambling and cocaine as equal and symbiotic dangers.

Spending Addictions

We define spending as an addiction in which spending alone or spending in conjunction with other addictions constitutes the bulk method of "feeling better or happy." The A&P is brief and is followed by anxiety, guilt, shame, or other forms of emotional discomfort. The ensuing pleasure-shame twister winds up other addictions in its path. We emphasize the A&P cycle more than the spend/income ratio.

Stevie was a twenty-four-year-old ex-call girl who had moved in with and "married" Jackie, a very successful and independently wealthy business woman. Stevie ran away from alcoholic parents and a sixty-room, fourteen-bath mansion when she was seventeen instead of going to Yale. She preferred a smelly, disgusting "hole of a room" off Forty-second street in New York City "than the sewer of a home I came from." Stevie was "kept" by Jackie for two years before moving into Jackie's penthouse. Stevie and Jackie's relation-

> ship started to hit rough waters. Jackie attempted on several occasions to encourage Stevie to sit down and work out their differences. Each time Stevie would choose not to discuss the problem and leave in an angry fit, slamming the door behind her as she had done before to her parents. Stevie would run off on a spending spree, sometimes charging over ten thousand dollars in one day. (At this point spending addicts might say, "Stevie has a problem, but I would never spend half that much in one day!") Spending large amounts of money was the only way she knew to feel better or have fun. She would feel ashamed, guilty, panicky, and depressed after binges. Stevie's emotional discomfort would in turn further strain her relationship with Jackie. This literally drove Jackie to drink. (Jackie had only had a sex addiction before Stevie moved into the penthouse.) Stevie's spending stopped and their relationship improved after Stevie learned communication skills, they attended couples therapy, Stevie attended Emotions Anonymous meetings, Jackie attended Sex and Love Addicts Anonymous meetings, and both attempted reduction of all other addictive psychiatric behaviors and abstinence from all mood-altering substances.

Recovery from a spending addiction is similar to that from all other addictions (and as such may benefit from attendance at meetings of Spender's Anonymous or Debtors Anonymous)—it means learning how to attain analgesia and pleasure in life without indulging in repetitive self-defeating behavior and the emotional discomfort or withdrawal syndrome that follows. This is why penicillin is not addicting: it has no withdrawal syndrome. Spending can be fun and normal; it is the consistent presence of a withdrawal syndrome that makes it abnormal or addictive.

Religious Addictions

Religious addictions are a doubly abstract concept. In religious addictions, religion serves almost exclusively as an analgesic and is rarely associated with pleasure. If the religious addiction is based in Satan, then a more usual balance of analgesia and pleasure is temporarily attained. The commodities most commonly abused are Scripture, religion, God, and Christ. Each can be abused when used consistently to quiet one's own emotional discomfort, avoid problems, or control others (Booth 1989).

Mrs. R. is a sixty-two-year-old retired real estate saleswoman who had tried every diet on the planet over a thirty-five-year period. She finally lost sixty-five pounds with H.O.W. (a division of OA) a few years previously. The only family history of addiction was in her father, who suffered from, and eventually died of, pathological gambling. Her codependent mother was always "sick" in bed with what sounded like depression. Mrs. R. was the oldest of five siblings. Her family was super-dysfunctional and she was most uncomfortable when she perceived herself as being "out of control." Being out of control reminded her of her "sole breadwinner" family role at the age of twelve. She used religion, Christ, the Virgin Mary, saints, and Bible quotes to control her family members, friends, and anyone else who would listen. The more she tried to control, the more out of control she felt. She would constantly critique people for not strictly adhering to fast periods. She was full of anger and could not find serenity, peace, or love. This, of course, alienated everyone she knew, including a few Christian priests, numerous monks, a monastery abbot, and an archbishop. At times she believed she was the "healing light" and when she tried to "share the good word" (i.e., attempt to control), no one would listen. Unreasonable resentments, obsessions, isolation, trances, guilt, and shame would follow.

Mrs. R. developed her second major depressive episode (the first was at the age of twenty-eight), and a member of her OA group referred her to us for an evaluation. In individual therapy we educated her about religious addictions, but we did it without using the usual addiction terminology. We firmly believed that if we put Christ and addiction in the same sentence, she would have been more difficult to engage. Food was her only source of pleasure, and she viewed lack of discipline as evil. Religion had no pleasure value for her, but was her principal analgesic. We taught her how to put the Bible in one hand and the OA Big Book in the other. Her symptoms of depression abated and she improved. She still slips monthly by getting up in her pulpit and preaching, but she is much better.

For Mrs. R., we literally did not want "spiritual perfection." We pointed her in the direction of spiritual progress along the equator between the Bible and the Big Book.

Sex and Love Addictions

Sex and Love Addiction (SLA) (Carnes 1983) developed a new low "bottom" with the AIDS epidemic. SLAs frequently kill. SLAs are an example of mistakes repeated in history. For instance, we naiveley thought that if we taught alcoholics that alcohol is poisonous and kills people, alcoholics would stop. It was only "logical." We did the same for SLAs. "Let us teach safe sex and it will help curtail the spread of AIDS." Little did we know that a condom is to the SLA what "lite" diluted cocaine is to a cocaine addiction; "safety" measures only reduce the altitude of analgesia or pleasure. The possibility of death from unsafe sex will never substitute an addict's primary objective of attaining emotional analgesia or the pleasure rush.

SLAs are often associated with incest or rape. That is, many rapists were violated as children and as adults perpetuate their horror to others in order to briefly attain analgesia or pleasure.

The SLAs more commonly reported in our clinics are what we call "soft sex addictions." These include any of the following when the behavior becomes the primary means of achieving orgasm to the exclusion of developing and nurturing healthy relationships: masturbation, exhibition, pornography, voyuerism, "cheating," multiple sex partners, or a combination of these. Another example of abuse includes the use of sex or love to control others. The following case illustrates a boundary between normal and an SLA.

Hanz was a thirty-one-year-old Ph.D. (a marital therapist). He lived in an affluent rural town with his wife Robin. They had been married for five years and had chosen to strengthen their marriage further before having children. Robin was also a psychotherapist, and they lived in a five-bedroom, center-hall colonial on a one-acre lot. Hanz and Robin had experimented with a variety of foreplay styles, sexual positions, and methods of attaining orgasm. Each was able to stop his or her partner at any point if either perceived danger or pain. (Mutual consent is the fundamental definition of normal; compromising a relationship's vitality or one's physical health marks the threshold of addiction.)

Hanz collected Batman costumes and memorabilia and decided one evening to wear the upper half of an authentic Batman costume as a new foreplay twist. Batman started kissing Robin on their bed, intermittently implying that she had been bad and needed to be disciplined. After more "threats" and some name-calling, more kisses, and all her silk garments were removed, Batman decided to handcuff each of Robin's extremities to a bed post. Batman resumed kissing Robin as she lay on her back (still normal). Batman decided to climb up on the credenza at the foot of their bed (still normal behavior) and dive onto helpless Robin. (Batman had just crossed the line into addiction.) Batman dived up into the ceiling beam and fell to the floor unconscious. There was no one else in the home. No one expected either of them for the next three days. The nearest homes were over an acre away. After hours of screaming, a neighbor called the police. The police broke in and found Batman and Robin; Batman regained consciousness shortly after he was admitted to the hospital.

This case could have had a tragic ending. Most cases of SLAs we treat appear in a blend of other addictions. Identification and treatment of SLAs coexisting with other addictive disorders are an important relapse prevention method.

Summary

The identification and treatment of addictive psychiatric disorders are a major "relapse prevention" method in the treatment of dual diagnosis patients. Alcohol and drug recovery is difficult to sell, but selling addictive psychiatric disorder treatment is often more challenging. What works best for us is precise timing and delivery of the A&P cycle concept. We believe that not treating a coexisting addictive psychiatric disorder is as dangerous as not treating coexisting alcohol abuse along with a primary cocaine addiction. With the exception of "abstinence," treatment of addictive psychiatric disorders parallels other addictions.

This chapter is dedicated to the memory
of a brilliant addictionologist,
Robert F. Stuckey, M.D.
May his soul rest in peace.
—The Author

References

Booth, Father Leo. 1989. *Breaking the Chains.* Long Beach: Emmaus Publications.

Carnes, P. 1983. *Out of the Shadows.* Minneapolis: CompCare.

Cocores, J. A. 1990. *The 800-COCAINE book of drug and alcohol recovery.* New York: Villard Books.

Klahr, A. L. 1991. Treatment of nicotine dependence in chemically dependent inpatients. In *The clinical management of nicotine dependence,* edited by J. A. Cocores. New York: Springer-Verlag.

Pickworth, W. B., E. B. Bunker, and J. E. Henningfield. 1991. Clinical laboratory testing of nicotine. In *The clinical management of nicotine dependence,* edited by J. A. Cocores. New York: Springer-Verlag.

Stuckey, R. F. 1989. Pleasure disorders. *Psychiatry News.*

———. 1991. Alcohol and drug addiction are actually disorders of pleasure. *The Psychiatric Times* (October): 42.

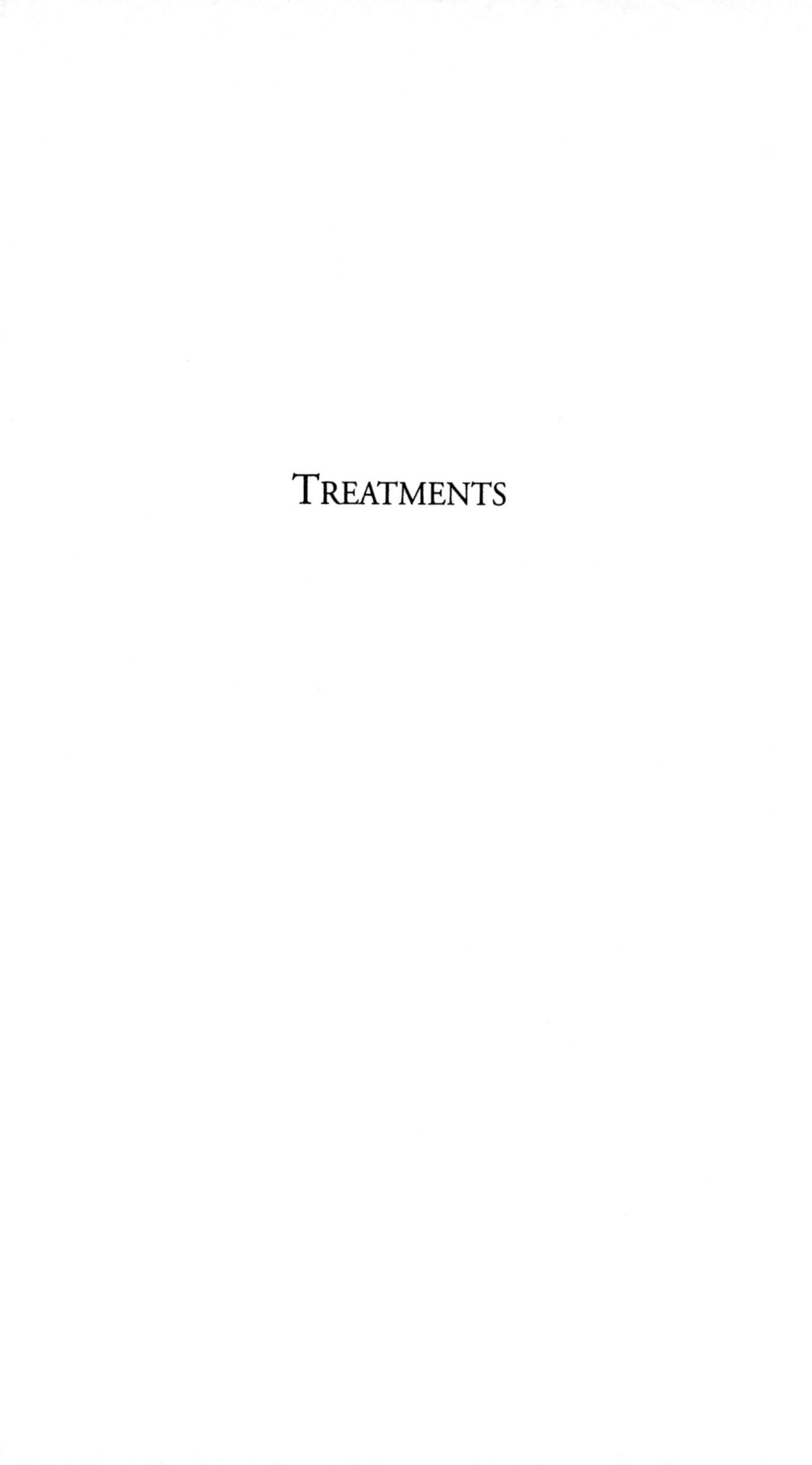

TREATMENTS

The dual disorder patient must recognize that each disorder's independent status requires specific therapies for recovery. Conservative pharmacological therapy is often indicated and must be integrated with nonpharmacological treatment.

9
Medications Used With The Dually Diagnosed

Norman S. Miller, M.D.

Integration of Pharmacological and Nonpharmacological Treatments: Addictive and Psychiatric Disorders

THE DUALLY DIAGNOSED PATIENT OFTEN NEEDS MEDICATIONS. An integrated approach, understood by both the patient and the treatment provider, will aid greatly in the acceptance of medications. Medications can be a "higher power," similar to that found in Twelve Step groups. The role of medications in the treatment of the dual diagnosis can be felt as personally as a recovery program if certain principles of integration of treatment are utilized.

The integration of pharmacological and nonpharmacological treatments for addictive disorders and attendant psychiatric comorbidity lies in securing an independent status for each disorder and utilizing the indicated therapies according to the diagnoses. Although there are relative contraindications for the use of pharmacological agents in patients with addictive disorders, the agents can be used as indicated in those patients with additional psychiatric disorders. A not well documented but clinically acknowledged observation is that the treatment of addictive disorders can be difficult without adequate treatment of the psychiatric disorder. For instance, a schizophrenic who is hallucinating and delusional and using alcohol/drugs cannot enter treatment for addiction without having adequate control over the psychotic symptoms. The same can be true of a manic who is euphoric, delusional, and alcoholic, or of a depressive or phobic who is also addicted to alcohol and/or benzodiazepines.

Nonpharmacological treatment of a comorbid addictive disorder is indicated for a patient with anxiety, depressive, schizophrenic, or manic disorder in order to allow compliance with psychiatric treatments. It is clinically self-evident and supported by data that poor control of the addictive disorder leads to an unfavorable prognosis for the psychiatric disorder. The prognosis of a combined psychiatric and addictive disorder follows that of the addictive disorders, so its treatment is mandatory to affect the course of either disorder (Miller and Gold 1992).

The Classes of Medications

There are five classes of medications: antianxiety, antidepression, antimania, antipsychotic, and antiaddiction.

Antianxiety

The medications are termed "anti" because they work against a particular disorder. The antianxiety medications work against anxiety, and the antidepressants against depression. The ideal medication works against abnormal anxiety but not normal anxiety that is needed for survival. Abnormal anxiety is arousal that is excessive for the stimulus or event. The anxiety paralyzes rather than prepares the individual for action. Physical symptoms of anxiety include sweating, tremors, palpitations, muscle tension, increased urination, etc. Psychological symptoms are nervousness, feelings of dread or impending doom (apprehension), unpleasant tenseness, and many more (Goodwin and Guze 1984).

The types of medications used in anxiety disorders are generally tranquilizers, namely, benzodiazepines and antidepressants. The benzodiazepines most commonly used are alprazolam (Xanax) and lorazepam (Ativan). Less often diazepam (Valium) and clonazepam (Clonopin) are used (Hyman and Arana 1987). The benzodiazepines can cause significant problems in the addicted patient and by themselves in nonaddicted patients. They are not generally recommended for use in alcoholics and drug addicts or for long-term use in any patients with anxiety disorders. Benzodiazepines produce addiction, tolerance, and dependence on their own, especially in those patients already exhibiting addiction to a drug or alcohol (Miller and Gold 1989).

Tranquilizers are taken daily or as needed for suppression of symptoms. They can also be used for sleep, and some are marketed only as hypnotics (sleeping pills). These are called flurazepam (Dalmane), triazolam (Halcion), or temazepam (Restoril). The hypnotics are taken at night, one-half to one hour before sleep. They are usually effective for only a few weeks before inducing insomnia themselves as pharmacological effect (tolerance dependence).

TABLE 9.1
BIOCHEMICAL ACTIVITY OF COMMONLY USED ANTIDEPRESSANTS

	Norepinephrine	Serotonin	Alpha-adrenergic
Amitriptyline	1	2	3
Doxepin	2	1	2
Desipramine	3	0	1
Nortriptyline	2	<1	1
Fluoxetine	0	3	2
Trazodone	0	1	2

Scale: <0 is no effect; 1 is mild; 2 is moderate; 3 is major

Antidepressants such as imipramine, nortryptyline, or fluoxetine (Prozac) have a low addiction potential and can be used in the addicted patient or the nonaddicted patient. They differ in their tendency to produce sedation and anxiety on their own. Imipramine, because of its anticholinergic property is more sedating, but nortriptyline and Prozac can produce anxiousness in some individuals and sedation in others. Not all individuals react the same way to a particular medication. The antidepressants have different mechanisms of action but are believed to exert their action by affecting the levels of neurotransmitters: imipramine acts on serotonin and norepinephrine; nortriptyline on norepinephrine; and Prozac on serotonin (table 9.1) (Hyman and Arana 1987).

Antidepression

The antidepressants are a mainstay in the treatment of depression. Depression is a ubiquitous symptom that is characterized by a sad mood, tearfulness, appetite and sleep disturbances, and the like. Depression is found in many conditions such as addictive, psychiatric, and medical disorders. When it exists by itself and is significant, it is referred to as major depression. Major depression is thought to have a significant biological component, namely, deficiencies in serotonin, norepinephrine, and dopamine in the central nervous system.

The antidepressants are reasonably effective in the treatment of serious depression that seems to arise for causes that are unknown, i.e., a biochemical depression. They act on the biochemical depression to alleviate the depression and enhance mood. They are not supposed to have an effect on mood in normal people. There are several different types, but they are distinguished by their action on neurotransmitters (table 9.1).

The antidepressants are not perfect drugs and work only some of the time to some extent, and mostly in moderately severe depressions. They are not as effective in either mild or very severe depression. Psychotherapy is more effective in mild depression and electroconvulsive therapy in severe depression.

TABLE 9.2
AVAILABLE PREPARATIONS

Drug	*Usual Daily Dose (mg/day)*	*Extreme Dose (mg/day)*	*Therapeutic Plasma Levels (ng/ml)*
Imipramine (Imavate, Janimine, SK Pramine, Tofranil, Presamine)	150-200	50-300	> 225[a]
Desipramine (Norpramin, Pertofrane)	150-200	50-300	> 125
Amitriptyline (Amitril, Endep, Elavil)	150-200	50-300	> 120 (?)[b]
Nortriptyline (Aventyl, Pamelor)	75-100	25-200	50-150
Doxepin (Adapin, (Sinequan, Curetin)	150-200	25-400	100-250 (?)
Trazodone (Desyrel)	200-400	100-600	
Bupropion (Wellbutrin)	200-450	unknown	
Fluoxetine (Prozac)	20-40	unknown	
Phenelzine (Nardil)	45-90	15-90	
Tranylcypromine (Parnate)	30-50	10-90	
Isocarboxazid (Marplan)	20-50	10-90	
Sertraline (Zoloft)			
Paroxetine (Paxil)			

[a]Sum of imipramine plus desipramine

[b]Sum of amitriptyline plus nortriptyline

Antidepressants are taken daily, usually one or two doses per day. Blood levels for certain antidepressants can be used to monitor how well the drug is being absorbed. For some such as nortriptyline, there is a range for what is considered therapeutic (table 9.2).

Antimania

Antimanic medications are frequently used to control the disorder called manic-depressive disease. The medications are used to control either the manic or depressed phase. The manic phase is an elevation of mood (euphoria), hyperactivity, grandiosity, and delusions. These manic states can occur cyclically and alternatively with depressed phases. The cause of manic-depressive illness is thought to be biological and to involve the neurotransmitter norepinephrine (excessive in mania and deficient in depression).

Lithium is a medication that is a natural salt, similar to sodium that is used in food. The exact way lithium works is not known, but it can be effective in either reducing or preventing the recurrence of manic attacks. Lithium must be taken daily, in doses of 600 mg to 2400 mg, two to four times per day. Lithium can also be effective in depression associated with manic-depressive illness.

Another antimanic medication is carbamazepine (Tegretol). Carbemazepine is an anticonvulsant that is also used to control seizures in epilepsy. It is effective sometimes in controlling mania when lithium is not. The theoretical explanation for why it works is that it suppresses possible mood centers in the limbic system that act as seizure foci. This theory remains to be proven (Miller and Gold 1992; Hyman and Arana 1987).

Antipsychotic

The antipsychotic medications are used principally to control hallucinations and delusions, which are manifestations of psychosis. They are taken daily, between one to three times per day. There are high potency and low potency neuroleptics. Examples of high potency neuroleptics are haloperidol (Haldol) or thiothixene (Navane). Examples of low potency neuroleptics are thioridazine (Mellaril) or chlorpromazine (Thorazine). The potency is determined by the drug's ability to block the action of the neurotransmitter dopamine on the receptor of the nerve cell (table 9.3).

TABLE 9.3

AVAILABLE PREPARATIONS OF ANTIPSYCHOTIC DRUGS

Drug	*Tablets (mg)*
Phenothiazines	
Aliphatic	
Chlorpromazine (Thorazine)	10, 25, 50, 100, 200
Piperidines	10, 25, 50, 100
Thioridazine (Mellaril)	10, 15, 25, 50, 100, 150, 200
Piperazines	
Fluphenazine (HC1) (Prolixin, Permitil)	0.25, 1, 2.5, 5, 10
Perphenazine (Trilafon)	2, 4, 8, 16
Trifluoperazine (Stelazine)	1, 2, 5, 10
Butyrophenone	
Haloperidol (Haldol)	0.5, 1, 2, 5, 10, 20
Dihydroindolone	
Molindone (Moban)	5, 10, 25

The above-named drugs have wide applications but are commonly used wherever hallucinations or delusions exist. Schizophrenia is such a condition, but other states such as dementia and delirium respond to neuroleptics. The drugs must be taken regularly to suppress or prevent psychosis (table 9.3).

Antiaddiction

Currently, there are no medications that treat the addictive disorder, i.e., help the addict regain control over the use of alcohol (or drugs, or to refrain from the preoccupation with acquiring or desiring to use alcohol or drugs). However, disulfiram (Antabuse) is an "aversive" agent that is used in patients with alcoholism. The principle is that alcohol is consumed, a chemical reaction takes place that causes the individual to become very ill, and perhaps death follows. Because the individual must take disulfiram daily in order for the reaction to occur, this medication works in only the highly motivated.

The Approach to Medications in the Dually Diagnosed: How to Use Them

Treatment of Anxiety Disorders

Anxiety is necessary for normal living, but when it becomes so excessive that it starts interfering with normal human function, it is abnormal. Normally, anxiety signals or arouses the individual to action. When the anxiety is overwhelming, it can cause the nervous system to "overreact," paralyzing the individual and inhibiting the normal responses from internal and external cues. The individual then becomes maladaptive to the internal or external environment and cannot respond to normal feelings or stimuli from others or other things. In short, the user must walk a tightrope between the benefits of freedom from the chains of anxiety and the adverse effects of medications. Medications for anxiety can ameliorate the incapacitating arousal characteristic of anxiety disorders. Medications for anxiety can also oversedate and dull the individual's reaction to inside and outside influences. In this sense the individual now is paralyzed by an underresponse or interference with normal anxiety. Either case is problematic and causes the individual to be maladaptive.

Anxiety in recovery can be critical. The individual must feel anxiety for motivation for change. The expression "no pain, no gain" is related to the anxiety or discomfort a recovering individual feels while undergoing the process of change to reach a better state. Thus anxiety is important for emotional growth in recovery.

Alcohol and drugs can cause almost any psychiatric symptom or sign or mimic a psychiatric disorder. Therefore, the effects of alcohol and drugs must always be taken into consideration before establishing a dual diagnosis (a psychiatric disorder in association with an addictive disorder) or before treating a case of known dual diagnosis.

Depressants (e.g., alcohol) can produce anxiety during withdrawal, and stimulants (e.g., cocaine) can produce anxiety during intoxication. Because alcoholics and drug addicts are in withdrawal daily (it is impossible to maintain a constant blood level), they experience anxiety from pharmacological withdrawal (dependence) daily. As the alcohol and drug use becomes more chronic, the severity of the anxiety from pharmacological dependence becomes increasingly worse. A period of abstinence (sometimes prolonged—weeks and months) must be established (with confirmation of abstinence with drug testing if necessary) before the anxiety effects of depressants or stimulants can be ruled out. The rule of thumb is that it can take weeks or months for these effects to completely subside, although a matter of a few days to one to two weeks are necessary in most instances in clinical practice (Miller 1991b).

Because anxiety can be a manifestation of conflicts from the addiction, even in recovery, consideration of "real-life" problems must also be included. Treatment of the anxiety disorder is indicated when the anxiety persists and no resolution takes place after sustained participation in a recovery program for addiction. A thorough evaluation to assess whether or not the individual is (1) abstinent, (2) attending self-help meetings, and (3) utilizing other forms of addiction therapy is necessary before a dual diagnosis can be established (Fine and Miller 1993). In this case, treatment of the anxiety disorder is separate from anxiety arising from the addictive disorder.

Medications may be tried, but specific target symptoms for the medications should be kept in mind. Also medications should be tried in time-limited intervals, such as weeks to months. A drug holiday (discontinuation of the medications) should then be attempted to see if the medication remains necessary.

The dual diagnosis patient should be well instructed that the medications will not "cure" the addiction, nor will treatment of the anxiety control the addiction. At the same time, treatment of the addiction will not necessarily ameliorate the anxiety disorder. The addiction must be treated independent of the anxiety disorder and vice versa. The medications may take a week or two to take full effect, but in acute anxiety states some medications may work almost immediately.

Case One

Susan is a thirty-two-year-old schoolteacher who started drinking alcohol in college to "relieve" anxious feelings in social situations. She had noticed over the years increasing feelings of anxiety, especially when she would awaken in the morning. In recent years she has had "tremors" with the anxiety. She had noticed that drinking alcohol in the evening would alleviate the anxiety, and she would take increasing amounts of alcohol over the years. Her psychiatrist had also prescribed Xanax (alprazolam), which she had increased in dosage as well in the past two years.

She now believes she cannot leave the house without Xanax or "get through an evening" without alcohol. Susan was confronted by the principal at the school where she was teaching about her deteriorating performance, and her husband was able to hold an intervention with other family members to convince Susan of the need for addictions treatment. After two years of abstinence, attendance at Alcoholics Anonymous (AA) meetings, and taking the medication imipramine during the first year, Susan no longer suffers from anxiety or agoraphobia. She does notice that when she decreases her AA meeting attendance she becomes more anxious, with feelings of "impending doom" and irritability. A return to her AA program usually results in a resolution of the anxiety symptoms.

DIAGNOSES: (1) Alcohol dependence—treated, (2) Anxiety secondary to addiction and pharmacological dependence on alcohol and alprazolam, and (3) Anxious personality.

Treatment of Depressive Disorders

Depression is also protective and part of normal living and the recovery process from addiction. A grief reaction is a normal process that one usually experiences after a loss. Depression is the essential feeling in the grief reaction. Depression is also a part of the "no pain, no gain" process of recovery from addictive disorders.

Depressant drugs (e.g., alcohol) can produce depression during intoxication, and stimulant drugs (e.g., cocaine) can produce depression during withdrawal. These effects may be prolonged with certain drugs that linger in the body (stored in fat), such as marijuana and benzodiazepines. These drugs can and do produce depression that is indistinguishable from other psychiatric causes of depression. Therefore, use of these drugs must be considered whenever depression is present, and addiction assessed when these drugs are identified. The depression may persist for weeks or months but generally resolves within days in many instances.

Major depression is more likely in older individuals, more likely in females than males, and can be difficult to distinguish from the depression associated with alcohol/drug effects. An assessment of the treatment of addiction and depression from other causes will lead to the proper diagnosis. A reflex attribution of depression to addiction or a neglect of the addiction as a source of depression is not fruitful or therapeutic.

We can institute use of medications if the depression persists beyond a few weeks of alcohol/drug withdrawal or arises in a confirmed recovered alcoholic/drug addict. (Drug testing may be necessary to confirm abstinence.) The risk of suppressing normal depressive processes and the benefit from suppressing those which are abnormal must be weighed, as is the case with anxiety disorders. Generally, it takes a week or two for the therapeutic effect of the medications to take effect.

Case Two

Harry is a fifty-five-year-old newspaper editor. He has been sober in AA for fifteen years. He continues to attend AA meetings two to three times a week, has a sponsor, and sponsors others. He "works the Steps," and his family and AA friends believe he has a "solid" program. However, for the past three months he has felt depressed, with sadness, tearfulness, difficulty sleeping and early morning awakenings, loss of appetite, and thoughts that life is not worth living. He also has lost his enthusiasm for living, and has felt worthless, useless, and hopeless. He recalls that the last time he felt this way was in the last few years of his drinking. He has even tried to increase his attendance at AA meetings, but his mood has not changed much. Finally, he has seriously considered taking his own life. His sponsor suggested that he see a psychiatrist who is knowledgeable about Twelve Step recovery in alcoholics. After a diagnosis of major depression during abstinence from alcohol was made, Harry was started on an antidepressant. Within one month his mood has improved substantially and he has felt more like himself. His enthusiasm, hopefulness, and zest for life have also returned substantially.

DIAGNOSES: (1) Major Depression—single episode, (2) Alcohol addiction—in remission.

Treatment of Manic Disorders

Mania is a condition caused by a biochemical imbalance and is associated with elevated mood, grandiose thoughts, hyperactive behavior, high energy, and poor judgment and insight. The manic will show behaviors of excesses such as spending sprees, sexual promiscuity, little sleep, intrusiveness, and drinking and drug use. The mania may follow or precede or alternate with depressive episodes (manic-depressive illness) (Miller 1991a).

Mania can be produced by stimulants (e.g., cocaine), during intoxication, and during withdrawal from depressants (e.g., alcohol). A period of confirmed abstinence is usually necessary before starting antimanic drugs. Generally it takes a week or two for the antimanic medications to take effect.

Case Three

> Jim is a twenty-five-year-old male who has had a history of marijuana, cocaine, and alcohol addiction since the age of fourteen. Jim recently developed manic attacks during which time he believes he is on a "mission from the Messiah." He realizes the falseness of these thoughts when he is not in the manic phase. He has been prescribed lithium and his manic attacks are controlled when he takes the medication. His manic attacks are distinguishable from his drug use because the attacks are marked by a sustained euphoria, grandiosity, and hyperactivity that do not recede when he ceases alcohol/drug use. He also must attend Narcotics Anonymous (NA) meetings in order to remain abstinent from drugs and alcohol. He will relapse to alcohol and drugs despite taking lithium for the prevention of manic attacks if he stops attending NA meetings.

DIAGNOSES: (1) Multiple Drug and Alcohol Addiction, (2) Bipolar Disorder—Mania.

Treatment of Psychosis (Schizophrenia)

Schizophrenia is also a biochemical disease and is characterized by bizarre thinking and behavior. The hallucinations and delusions are the "positive" symptoms of the psychotic process, as the withdrawal and poverty of emotions are the "negative" symptoms of schizophrenia.

Medications, principally neuroleptics, are most effective against the positive symptoms, or hallucinations and delusions, although not always completely. Behavioral, group, and psychotherapy are more effective against the negative symptoms. Schizophrenia can be a progressive illness that worsens over time (years).

Psychosis can be caused by stimulant drug use during intoxication and depressant drug/alcohol use during withdrawal. A period of weeks or months may be necessary to wait out the effects of drugs of addiction, but as with anxiety/depression/mania, only days are often necessary for the hallucinations and delusions to wane. The antipsychotic medications can be started almost at any time if the psychosis is troublesome enough and a waiting period is not possible. A drug holiday from the medications can be attempted after a few months or sooner if drugs of addiction are clearly implicated as the sole cause of the hallucinations and delusions.

Case Four

Juan is a forty-five year-old male who was diagnosed as schizophrenic when he was eighteen. He started using marijuana and alcohol when he was sixteen and cocaine at age nineteen. He lives with his mother, but he also sometimes lives on the street. He has not been able to hold a steady job at any time in his life. He has not had sustained relationships. His compliance with the mental health clinic is interrupted, but he has periods of abstinence and freedom from hallucinations and major delusions. He has always been "odd" and has had "strange" views of the world, he has had few close friends. He wears "hippie-like" clothes, wears tattoos, and usually appears somewhat disheveled.

Juan does best when he is sober and on medications, but there are times when he will be sober and not comply with medications; and alternately, there are times when he is both taking medications and drinking, although these are fewer in duration and frequency. His case manager is often able to redirect him towards renewed sobriety and compliance with medications. He attends addiction groups at the clinic, sees a psychiatrist, and attends AA meetings. After each relapse, he is accepted back without prejudice and supported in recovery from and treatment of both his addictive and psychiatric disorders. His goals are to have as many sober days as possible with as many compliant medication days as possible. (See Minkoff's chapter in this book.)

DIAGNOSES: (1) Chronic Schizophrenia, (2) Drug and Alcohol Addiction.

The Downside

Medications have minor and major side effects. Some are addictive. The benzodiazepines can be especially addictive to the recovering alcoholic/addict. Antipsychotic and antidepressant medications that have anticholinergic effects are frequently used addictively. These medications also produce anxiety and depression during chronic use (from pharmacological dependence) (table 9.4).

Table 9.4

Antipsychotic Drugs (Antidepressants): Potencies and Side-Effect Profiles

Drug	*Sedative Effects*	*Anticholinergic Effects*	*Hypotensive Effects*	*Extrapyramidal Effects*
Phenothiazines				
Chlorpromazine (Thorazine)	High	Medium	High	Medium
Thioridazine (Mellaril)	High	High	High	Low
Fluphenazine (Prolixin, Permitil)	Medium	Low	Low	High
Perphenazine (Trilafon)	Low	Low	Low	High
Trifluoperazine (Stelazine)	Medium	Low	Low	High
Thioxanthenes				
Thiothixene (Navane)	Low	Low	Low	High
Loxapine (Loxitane, Daxolin)	Medium	Medium	Medium	High
Butyrophenones				
Droperidol (Inapsine—injection only)	Low	Low	Low	High
Haloperidol (Haldol)	Low	Low	Low	High
Indolone				
Molindone (Moban)	Medium	Medium	Low	High
Cyclic agents				
Amitriptyline	High	High	High	Low
Amoxapine	Low	Low	High	Low
Desipramine	Low	Low	Medium	Low
Doxepin	High	Medium	Medium	Low
Imipramine	Medium	Medium	High	Low
Nortriptyline	Low	Low	Medium	Low
Atypical agents				
Alprazolam	High	None	Low	Low
Bupropion	Low	Low	Low	Low
Trazodone	High	Low	Low	Low
Fluoxetine	Low	Low	Low	Low

Antipsychotics and antidepressants can lower blood pressure (hypotension) and even cause light-headedness and syncope in individuals, particularly when they stand up.

Antipsychotic medications produce "extrapyramidal" effects. Acute extrapyramidal effects are dystonia and akathisia. Dystonia is a distorted muscle contraction usually of the face, neck, and upper torso. It can be frightening but not life-threatening. It is treated with anticholinergic drugs such as Benadryl. Akathisia is a subjective feeling of anxiety and tension that makes patients feel compelled to move about restlessly. Chronic effects of antipsychotic medications include "tardive dyskinesia" (TD). TD is abnormal muscle movements that are involuntary and relatively constant. They occur particularly in the face and tongue but also often extend to the upper and lower body. They begin typically after years of chronic use of antipsychotic medications, more often with high-potency types. Interestingly, taking the person off the medication will result in a worsening of the TD. The best approach is preventative—using antipsychotics when needed and at as low an effective dose as possible.

It is important that the recovering alcoholic or addict have as clear a mind and stable a mood (emotions) as possible. Medications have a tendency, sometimes subtly and other times obviously, to dull the sensorium (alertness) and thinking and/or blunt or disrupt the emotional state. Addicts must eventually change and control feelings to remain sober and also to comply with psychiatric management. The addict's ability to use the Twelve Steps and accept the psychiatric advice will depend on clear thinking and emotional balance. In AA, emotional balance is stressed as being central to the recovery process. The use of medications should be accordingly conservative, and the pros and cons of their expected positive and negative effects should be weighed. Few psychiatric medications are totally free of mood-altering properties.

Commonsense Caveats—Never Say Never

Never say never applies to both the addictive and psychiatric disorders. It is as important to avoid excluding any possibility of the use of medications as it is to consider anyone incapable of recovery in a Twelve Step program. Either position of prohibition can potentially result in withholding lifesaving treatments or lowering the quality of ultimate sobriety and remission from the addictive and psychiatric disorders. A belligerent view of never giving benzodiazepines to recovering addicts is just as damaging as always giving them when an addict is anxious.

The key to an optimal therapeutic approach is to understand and be skilled in both addictive and psychiatric disorders. It is best that the staff and setting for the dual diagnosis patients be integrated for diagnosis and treatment. It is no longer useful to argue over turf and ideology while patients continue to suffer and die. Integration will serve as a uniform message to the patient that one disorder is not superior or inferior to the other. The acceptance by staff and patients that addictive and psychiatric disorders are independent but do interact is the cornerstone of integration. Without accepting that addictive disorders are independent and that psychiatric disorders can be independent of addictive disorders, little progress will be made in diagnosis and treatment. (See Minkoff's chapter in this book.)

Conclusions

1. Addiction and psychiatric disorders are independent.
2. Addictive and psychiatric disorders interact with each other.
3. Depressant and stimulant drugs can produce psychiatric symptoms during intoxication and withdrawal.
4. Medications can be a "higher power," as can an AA group.
5. Medications should be used conservatively in the addicted patient, i.e., the pros and cons of their usefulness against their expected side effects should be weighed.

References

Fine, J., and N. S. Miller. 1993. Methodological approach to psychiatric and addictive disorders in drug and alcohol dependence. In *Comorbidity of addictive and psychiatric disorders.* New York: Haworth Press.

Goodwin, D. W., and S. B. Guze. 1984. *Psychiatric diagnoses.* New York: Oxford University Press.

Hyman, S. E., and G. W. Arana. 1987. *Handbook of psychiatric drug therapy.* Boston: Little, Brown and Company.

Miller, N. S. 1991a. Interactions between drugs/alcohol and brain/behavior. In *Comprehensive handbook of drug and alcohol addiction,* edited by N. S. Miller. New York: Marcel Dekker, Inc., 1275-90.

Miller, N. S. 1991b. The psychiatric consequences of alcohol and drugs of abuse and addiction. In *The pharmacology of alcohol and drugs of abuse and addiction.* New York: Springer-Verlag, 77-88.

Miller, N. S., and M. S. Gold. 1989. Identification and treatment of benzodiazepine abuse. *American Family Physician* 40 (4):175-83.

———. 1992. The psychiatrist's role in integrating pharmacological and nonpharmacological treatments for addictive disorders. *Psychiatric Annals* 22(8):436-40.

For persons who experience both addictive and psychiatric illness, therapy means healing and restoring reality. The relationship between therapist and client is where this process begins.

10
Therapy with The Dually Diagnosed Person

Thomas F. McGovern, Ed.D.

RELATIONSHIP IS AT THE HEART OF ANY THERAPY that addresses the needs of persons with dual diagnoses. Addiction and mental illness by their very nature disrupt the lives and stories of those who suffer from them; in combination, the disruptive force of these conditions is magnified. Therapy helps restore relationships with self, with others, and with one's greater world of connectedness. A colleague told me of a woman who came to him for help, saying, "My story is broken. Help me to fix it." "Re-storying" the lives of the broken and suffering who seek restoration of relationship through our therapy is at the core of what we do.

THERAPIES AND DIAGNOSES

For us therapists diagnoses are a means to an end and not an end in themselves. The diagnosis is a framework which facilitates our understanding of the persons we treat. It provides us with a bridge whereby we enter the interior world of the suffering person. Diagnoses, single or multiple, which fail to illuminate and connect us with the person's pain are of little practical or humane value.

Diagnoses are about people and not just impressive descriptions of diseases in their many symptoms. My mischievous side tempts me to ask (tongue in cheek, of course) how many diagnoses can a person sustain without collapsing under their combined weight? And, in a similar vein, how many diagnostic impressions can we therapists absorb in our search for meaningful therapies without meeting a like fate?

Persons with dual diagnosis experience complicated and complicating conditions. Of necessity our therapy need not assume the character of the diseases we treat; somewhere I read about "keeping it simple."

My experiences with persons suffering from a variety of devastating illnesses continue to teach me that simple (yet profound) and helpful responses can always be found. Diagnoses are at their worst when they label and compartmentalize people; conversely, they are at their best when they forge relationships between the suffering person and the therapist. The stories of Joe and Tom will show how the combined insights of mental health and addictions treatment personnel were woven into meaningful recovery for these two persons.

Joe's Story

Joe, in his mid-forties, found his initial sobriety through membership in Alcoholics Anonymous. From the outset he found that his "dark times," which came every nine to twelve months, unraveled his well-being and sobriety. With all the honesty and courage he could muster he sought to practice and live "an honest program"; in fact, sober or drinking, his was an honest program, but to no lasting avail in maintaining ongoing sobriety.

As a true disciple of an earlier AA tradition, he was suspicious of all treatment providers, and especially so of psychiatrists. A health care professional in recovery convinced Joe to seek help for his "dark times." His recurring depression was accurately diagnosed and treated with appropriate medication. His acceptance of medication was based on his regard for the psychiatrist, who was known for his care of persons suffering from addictions; in addition, the psychiatrist directed both a mental health and an alcoholism treatment center with great compassion and insight.

To the end of his life, Joe maintained unbroken sobriety without ever revealing to his AA group that he was taking medication for his depression. In his own words, "I went to AA for my sobriety and to my doctor for my depression." This plan worked for him and for others, too, as his brightly colored van, aptly called the Wobble Wagon, continued to rescue abandoned persons suffering from addiction and mental illness from city streets whence they were conveyed to a place of haven and possible recovery. Joe must have a very interesting existence now in the Heaven of his belief; we wonder what task he has been assigned there. His memory continues to inspire many of us in our earthly pilgrimage.

Tom's Story

Tom's story has a slightly different twist. He came to our mental health unit hotly pursued by the havoc he had caused during a combined mania/drinking phase. A successful broker in his early forties, he had lost everything because of his erratic and out-of-control behavior. Like most persons experiencing bipolar illness, he loved his "high-energy times" and saw alcohol as useful in taking the edge off the highs and lows. At the beginning of his treatment, he was convinced (and almost convincing) that he could manage his problems after a period of rest.

Through the combined efforts of his family and treatment team he was led to an acceptance of losses recurring from his disorder. Armed with a basic understanding of his condition, and following the simple instructions "Don't drink, attend groups, take your medication, stay in contact with us," he left our treatment setting. (He participated in both the mental health and addiction treatment programs.)

Tom was fortunate to have the same psychiatrist as Joe. Under the direction of this wise physician, who understood how the two illnesses came together in Tom's person, Tom made the psychiatrists insight his own; in time, it became a basis of his recovery.

Tom's recovery, now in its fourteenth year, continues to be monitored on an ongoing outpatient basis. He is an outstanding counselor for persons with dual diagnoses: he runs groups, educates, and is a tireless advocate for persons struggling with addiction, mental illness, or both. In addition, his church, at his prompting, sponsors an outreach program to the homeless and

> forgotten, who feel abandoned in their addiction and mental illness.

Joe and Tom are obvious success stories. Their stories and their recovery of meaningful existence show that mental health therapists, together with their counterparts in addiction treatment settings, can successfully combine to treat persons who are dually diagnosed. More decisive, however, in the final outcome were the open attitudes involved, beginning with those of the treatment team. Too often we mental health professionals and those of us in the addiction field are miles apart in our understanding of those who are dually diagnosed. Both fields are capable of developing exquisite diagnoses and equally impressive treatment plans. From such individual perspectives, often accompanied by divisive turf battles, we tend to view the needs of the dually diagnosed from an exclusive, rather than an inclusive, focus. This works to the disadvantage of those who suffer from dual disorders and also to our disadvantage. We lack a united voice that gives the dually diagnosed a clear understanding of their condition. More important, clear and decisive instructions on what to do are often lacking. We need to develop diagnostically sensitive approaches that see dual diagnosis as a condition unified in the person in whom the condition occurs.

We have a credible body of knowledge and experience and know-how in approaching this task. Sadly, we have shared little of our experiences; the silence of the journals reflects our lack of activity.

The Joes and Toms of our experience can teach us practical and effective approaches to treatment. So too can the experience of our struggles with persons who continue to suffer in their illness despite our best efforts. Any time we restore some sense of dignity to the "broken story" of a devastated person, we are exercising the high art and science of our professional callings. I am forcefully reminded of the poignancy of a phrase, shared with me by a colleague, of a person in the late stages of AIDS, who sadly reflected, "There is no one left to stand beside me." Being that someone to "stand beside" persons who struggle with dual disorders is an essential element of our role as therapists.

Our therapy approach is as much an activity of "being" as "doing." In our "being" and "doing," two elements, among others, have special significance: one, we are called to listen to the stories of those who suffer; two, we respond to those stories with humane and helpful therapies. In the telling and in the responding, relationships are established; this is the stuff from which help and meaningful therapy emerge.

Telling the Story: The Sufferer's Perspective

Our stories give life and meaning to the facts and events of our lives. When stories are broken, as happens in the disjointed lives of those suffering from the effects of addiction and mental illness, the re-storying or restoration of such lives is an essential element of a healing process. The psychosocial histories are an important part of our professional work. They help in our understanding of the person we are treating. But they can never replace the real human interaction that occurs when stories are told and human connectedness results.

The Person

Connectedness can happen in an individual or group setting. Such experiences in relationships are an ongoing and rewarding part of our lives as therapists. It is helpful to remind ourselves of this, especially when we are tempted, because of demands on our time and resources, to substitute official responses and histories for the true picture of the persons we treat. "Broken stories" can be truly mangled in the process.

I am reminded of the wisdom of a presenter at a conference I attended many years ago on the relationship between medicine and literature. In the course of a talk, which stressed the importance of real narrative between therapist and the person who is suffering, the presenter (a one-time journal editor, now pediatrician) read a case history from a prestigious medical journal. He underscored the jargon and the professionalese as he spoke with this constant interjection: "What in the name of sanity does this mean?" He reminded us of the ridiculousness of some of our pretentious professional reporting. He recalled for us the sanity which we bring to our daily work in helping us remember what we say to each other at the end of a technical case report. We ask, "What is really going on here?" and in doing so we get precious insightful impressions of what we think is really happening in the lives of those entrusted to our care.

Our gut-level responses, as professional as any others we might give, are critical in caring for severely compromised persons who endure dually diagnosed conditions. These impressions might be part of our record keeping, they are humane remembrances, a kind of "faithful memory" of those whom we treat. To be "memory" for persons whose illnesses causes them to forget and get lost can be a powerful reintegrating activity. Some details from Ed's story, a person suffering from a dual disorder, can illustrate the role of the therapist as faithful memory:

> Ed is a twenty-six-year-old college student who has been seen in an outpatient clinic for a dual disorder condition involving both addiction and a moderately severe borderline personality disorder. With sobriety he is productive and able to maintain a meaningful life and relationships. When he drinks, his life and his relationships become chaotic. He is unable to connect with anything that is meaningful, and in his despair he is often suicidal. Over the years, because of ongoing contact with him, the treatment team has been able to lead him out of the chaotic times by remembering for him the good times experienced in his sobriety. Weaving this type of connectedness across the broken times helps Ed during periods of stabilization.

When we listen attentively to the stories of persons with addiction and mental illness, many meaningful insights emerge. For instance, we learn what the person was like prior to the onset of one or both illnesses. Reclaiming some sense of "original innocence," before the pain and devastation of the illness took over, can often be a revealing and redeeming moment for sufferer and therapist alike. It may offer us a mooring place in the past to which the person's story can be attached. The memory of integrated times in the past can sometimes be a factor in regaining a sense of purpose and dignity in the present. Connecting with lighter and happier times brings relief to any story or condition.

The Story

The suffering of persons who are dually diagnosed can be described in a variety of ways. From the outside it has a clinical description with which we are very familiar. From the inside it has another face—that of a person. To have one's pain validated by another in meaningful sharing is one of life's finest blessings. Countless people tell us that their understanding of themselves and the illnesses they endure began when someone listened to their story. Understanding that persons with dual diagnosis use their drug of choice in search of relief from the darkness, confusion, and isolation that haunts them opens many doors. It is often the beginning of a dialogue about patterns of drug use which provide invaluable clues to the inward chaos people seek to relieve.

A person suffering from a personality borderline condition may use drugs (including alcohol) in a disorganized and chaotic fashion, patterning the illness they seek to treat. Depressed persons sometimes have a more consistent pattern of use, to drown their sorrows, as it were.

It is essential that we appreciate the subjective effects of the drug on the persons whom we treat, keeping in mind the nature of the illnesses they, in turn, are trying to treat. Stories reveal this information and further insights. They relate the person with the dual diagnosis to the therapist in a compassionate dialogue. Out of such a relationship trust is born, a trust that may be a decisive factor in encouraging suffering ones to forsake their treatments and try ours.

Beeder and Millman (1992, p. 677) have written eloquently of this choice. They see persons with dual diagnosis as mistakenly choosing their drugs, which bring freeing relief, escape, and joy (but which result in a worsening of their condition) over our drugs (treatment), which bring little joy, ineffective escape, but better functioning and outcome. In the absence of some basis for trusting the therapist, it is little wonder that dually diagnosed persons choose their own predictable but destructive drug regimens over our unproven (in their perception) but more helpful ones. One must remember, with Miller (1991), that controlled studies do not support the commonly accepted misconception that persons with distressing psychiatric conditions self-medicate with alcohol and other drugs in search of relief.

The need for humane dialogue built on a respect between the therapist and the person who is dually diagnosed is captured in the observation of a recovering dually diagnosed person, Jody N., in the recently published *The Dual Disorders Recovery Book* (1993):

> People who are threatened by our behavior when we're ill, or who cannot or will not understand, won't really matter to our recovery if we choose not to let them. Ultimately, no one can take away our

> dignity. As we become honest with ourselves and gain peace of mind—putting our past actions into perspective and learning to differentiate between our dual disorders and our true selves—others will begin to see us in a different light as well. (p. 100)

Hearing the stories of a dually diagnosed person can confirm that our diagnostic and therapeutic notions of dual diagnosis are, in fact, mirrored in the lives of those who experience such conditions. My suggestion that we be a "faithful memory" for those we treat—a notion I had before the *Dual Disorders Recovery Book* (1993)—was beautifully affirmed in the testimony of Kate S.:

> It is no secret among those of us with a dual disorder that we have what I call a "forgettery." We forget the benefits of sobriety: that without drugs or alcohol, our problems are only "troubles"—which we can manage—and that disasters in our lives can usually be avoided. We forget that after the bad times, there will be better times and that even when the bad times hit, they will not be as bad as they were when we were drinking. Perhaps this is a convenience, but I prefer to think that our illnesses cloud our memories. (p. 69)

My experience convinces me that illnesses dismember the lives of those who experience them; part of therapy must surely be a counterhealing activity of "remembering," of putting memories and lives back together in a meaningful and hopeful context.

Responding to the Story: The Therapist's Perspective

We can approach our task of establishing and maintaining therapeutic relationships with dually diagnosed persons from a number of perspectives. We can identify patterns of treatment on a disease-by-disease basis, looking at the combination of addiction and depression, personality disorders, or the other mental illness on an individual basis. Or, in a more general sense, we can try to isolate elements of treatments common to all of the dual disorders. Both will be encompassed in this section, beginning with some overall observations.

Overall Approach

Therapy for persons who have a dual diagnosis can occur in individual or group settings, in inpatient or outpatient settings. Mental health therapists, as a rule, seem to favor individual therapy because of their fear that certain persons, especially those suffering from severe borderline or psychotic conditions, are unable to tolerate group activity. Addiction therapists, on the other hand, favor group settings because of their belief that the primary focus on abstinence is best maintained in group settings. Whatever the setting or philosophy, the following guidelines have proved helpful in guiding treatment activities. These guidelines are drawn from our experience and from the sources referenced at the end of the chapter.

1. Therapy should be active and directive.
2. Therapy should be aimed at abstinence rather than insight or the resolution of psychological conflict.
3. Therapy should reinforce compliance with treatment recommendations, including medication regimens.
4. Therapy should support and redirect defenses toward the maintenance of sobriety and continuing treatment.
5. Therapy should underscore the failure of self-medication.
6. Therapy should empower patients with responsibility for their own behaviors.
7. Therapy should stress the combined effects of dual disorders on the persons who suffer from them.
8. Therapy should set concrete rules for safe behavior.
9. Therapy should instruct the patient about the working of groups and how to participate in such groups.
10. Therapy should include professionally run support groups.
11. Therapy should recommend and encourage participation in recovery groups and in peer support groups.

These guidelines combine the best insights of the mental health and addiction fields in the overall treatments of persons who are dually diagnosed. These guidelines, of necessity, must be self-explanatory because of page limitations. A brief word on the facilitating of group interaction may be helpful.

Group Activity

Persons with addictions and persons with mental illness can profit from participating in group activities. It seems reasonable to assume that persons suffering from a dual disorder can likewise profit from group participation. Our experience supports the research of Woody et al. (1990) in their assertion that dually diagnosed persons, even those with severe mental illnesses, can be successfully integrated into Twelve Step programs.

Preparation for group participation facilitates such integration. This training is most effectively achieved in professionally directed therapy groups. The opportunity for dually diagnosed persons to participate in ongoing professionally run groups is a decided advantage. Besides facilitating an ability to relate to others, such groups are invaluable in monitoring the mental status of the participants. Early detection of the recurrence of a mental illness with appropriate interventions is invaluable in maintaining the sobriety and well-being of dually diagnosed persons.

Traditionally, we have referred persons with dual disorders to AA or to NA for ongoing support in the maintenance of their sobriety. Timothy H., in recovery from a dual disorder, questions the wisdom of such referrals (*The Dual Disorders Recovery Book,* pp. 221-23). He advocates that dually disordered persons derive the greatest benefit from participating in Dual Recovery Anonymous programs for the following reasons:

1. Dual disordered persons face the stigma and social prejudice associated with mental illness.
2. Dual diagnosed persons often receive misguided advice about the use of medications at traditional AA meetings.
3. The absence of the personal experience of others, together with the absence of emotional acceptance and support, limits the effectiveness of AA and NA meetings for the dually diagnosed.
4. AA is a single purpose—one disease, one recovery—approach.

Whether or not Dual Recovery Anonymous groups confer a greater benefit on dually diagnosed persons remains to be seen. The program seems to be an abstinence-based one, with a focus on both the addiction and the mental illnesses involved in the dual diagnosis. Participation in the newer program in addition to AA would seem to be the wisest course for dually diagnosed persons at this time. A "both-and" approach over an "either-or" approach might be the best suggestion.

Addiction and Anxiety Disorders

Anxiety disorders frequently coexist with addictive disorders. The *DSM-III-R* (1987) lists the following conditions under anxiety disorders: panic disorders, phobic disorders, obsessive-compulsive disorders, posttraumatic stress disorders, and generalized anxiety disorders. Our experience of fifteen years confirms Miller's contention (1991, pp. 1281-82) that possible anxiety disorders identified in active alcohol and drug addiction or in early detoxification may be part of the primary addiction. We have seen symptoms of panic disorders and phobic disorders improve following appropriate detoxification and ongoing treatment for the addictive condition. Likewise, we have seen ongoing anxiety disorders improve in a regimen that includes medication for the anxiety and treatment for the addiction.

Again, it is worth noting that many persons, patients and treaters alike, mistakenly think that alcohol and like sedative compounds alleviate anxiety and promote relaxation (Miller 1991; Daley et al. 1992). This mistaken notion is as old as Hippocrates and as modern as those who support the self-medication hypothesis (Daley et al. 1993).

Agoraphobia is the second most common dual diagnosis among alcoholic women (Daley et al. 1993). This condition needs to be addressed in conjunction with the alcohol addiction if appropriate treatment is to be provided. Issues around the agoraphobia should be an essential focus of the counseling sessions, with specific inquiry about the source of the person's fear.

Whether or not generalized anxiety disorders (GAD) is a distinct diagnosis is a source of controversy. We have seen it coexist with addiction and have successfully treated GAD by considering it another form of depression.

Addiction and Depression

All of the expressions of depression, including major depression, dysthymia, and bipolar disorders, occurring in persons with drug addiction can be treated in traditional addiction treatment programs.

Daley et al. (1993, p. 83) identify the following therapy tasks for persons with a combined addiction/depression disorder:

1. Handling feelings
2. Changing thoughts and beliefs
3. Changing behaviors, relationships, and lifestyle, or developing or improving social skills
4. Participating in self-help (recovery) programs

All of the above tasks are addressed in addiction treatment programs; with the appropriate attention to the medication needs of this population, there is no reason why such persons cannot benefit from addiction treatment interventions.

It is also important to distinguish depression from a grieving process which occurs in response to the many losses resulting from a person's dual disorder. The losses are internal, external, and spiritual, involving the loss of people, places, and things; of ways persons see and value themselves; of cherished values and beliefs. In the active disease process, persons are unable to grieve their losses. They seek relief from their grief, which is a process involving body, mind, and spirit, through their drug of choice. As a result their grief becomes frozen or unresolved; it has many of the features of pathological grief, which in turn resembles depression.

Over the years, I have found that persons with addictions or with dual disorders can be helped in their recovery by the facilitation of grieving process around their losses (McGovern 1986a, 1986b). The dually disordered person can understand and identify the losses he or she had experienced. Seeing the use of drugs as an effort to find relief from the grieving process is enlightening. Building on the grief work of my respected colleague, John Schneider (1989), I have been able to describe the grieving process in addictions and in dual disorders as a process involving phases of holding on, letting go, and awareness. Beyond the awareness stage, there is a transformative stage, which comes later on in recovery.

Individuals try to limit their awareness of any loss through a process of either "holding on" or "letting go." What we have lost either is of ultimate importance or doesn't matter at all. Either way, we cannot face the loss. The dynamics of holding on and letting go have much in common with denial. Helping dually diagnosed persons understand the mental, emotional, and spiritual tug-of-war which precedes their acceptance can be effective. With grief awareness comes a profound awareness of what has been lost and what needs to be faced. Step 1, Step 2, and Step 3 of the Twelve Step programs are a marvelous way of responding to this state (McGovern 1986a).

Schneider (1991) sees the grieving process in terms of three phases of discovery: (1) discovering what is lost, (2) discovering what is left, and (3) discovering what is possible. Exploring these phases with persons who are addicted or addicted with different forms of depression has been very rewarding.

Family members and other persons in relationship with the dually disordered person can find a direction through an understanding of grief/loss involved in their lives too. Seeing how the person who is addicted and how family members view the loss of the drug of choice is illuminating. For the person who is addicted or dually disordered, the loss of the drug, one's relief and solace for years, becomes "good grief" over time. Family members see the removal of the drug as "good riddance" (McGovern 1992).

Persons suffering from depression, dysthymia, or bipolar disorders in addition to an addiction can be effectively treated. The achievement and maintenance of sobriety, coupled with appropriate medication, can restore meaningful existence to such persons. Again, the secret of effective therapy is the attention to both disorders with a sustained focus on the need for sobriety.

Addiction and Personality Disorders

Treating persons with personality disorders, including antisocial and borderline personality disorders, is a difficult task. Forming a therapeutic relationship with addicted persons with antisocial personality disorders is quite a challenge. Unfortunately, we carry many prejudices to this undertaking. Some come from the literature which describes persons in this condition. Beck and colleagues (1990) characterize them as follows:

> I have to look out for myself. People will get me if I don't get them first. Other people are weak and deserve to be taken advantage of.

> What others think of me doesn't matter. I should do whatever I can get away with.

Since we usually see and diagnose persons with this condition when they have been compromised by many years of addiction or mental illnesses and legal troubles, it is little wonder that we see them in such a poor light. The question nags us as to whether we can really help them. The literature again is of little help in suggesting that persons so disordered do not respond to treatment.

A more hopeful picture emerges from the reports of therapists who have enjoyed some modest successes in treating such persons (Nace 1987, p. 233; Daley et al. 1993, p. 51). They recommend individual and group therapy with an emphasis on firm limits, which promotes peer interaction and support. The group setting tends to dissipate some of the conflict involved in treating such persons. Therapists have seen personality development with the maintenance of sobriety. The overwhelming presence in our correctional facilities of persons diagnosed with addiction and antisocial personality disorders must be of concern to us. We cannot arbitrarily dismiss their needs even before we have tried to help them.

Persons with borderline personality disorders in addition to addiction can benefit from a therapeutic relationship which is patient, supportive, and empathic. Somehow the multitude of problems which overwhelm such persons must be kept within a sane perspective. This is no small task for all involved. Recognizing the profound neediness of such persons can tax the resources of the treating staff, sometimes polarizing its members. Open and supportive communication is essential; no one therapist can be a miracle worker.

Addiction in Association and Schizophrenia

Therapy for persons dealing with addiction and schizophrenia involves tailoring the best of addiction and schizophrenia treatment to the needs of such individuals. Our therapeutic approach needs to be highly supportive, low-key, and nonconfrontational. Compliance with medication regimens while maintaining sobriety is essential. The use of existing defenses towards this end can be helpful.

Again, persons with this condition can participate meaningfully in

Twelve Step programs, provided they have been taught how to participate in such activities (Daley et al. 1993, p. 162). Above all, such persons should not be overloaded with information; it is best to share information with them in a piecemeal, supportive fashion.

Conclusion

The focus of this chapter has been on the interaction between dually diagnosed persons and therapists in their mutual efforts to establish and maintain a healing relationship. The spirit of therapy, rather than the practical specifics of clinical work, has been stressed. This, in a way, is a response to the prevailing technological attitude so prevalent in current health care approaches. Our inability to fix people can be frustrating, and our frustration can be compounded by the many interests that clamor for instant results.

We need to remind ourselves that ours is the task to constantly "re-story" people whose narratives are broken by illnesses which, by their very nature, reccur. Ours is a commitment to the long haul in which progress and success are often measured in tiny but meaningful steps. The people we treat are not a collection of diagnoses, symptoms, and dismal prognoses; rather they are people whose dignity and humanity we preserve in our efforts to maintain meaningful relationships with them. The Joes, the Bills, the Eds of our world are not case histories; they are human beings to whom we are connected as other human beings, graced with the art and science of our professional callings. We have every reason to be hopeful in this humane undertaking.

REFERENCES

American Psychiatric Association. 1987. *Diagnostic and statistical manual of mental disorders.* 3d ed, rev. Washington, D.C.: American Psychiatric Association

Beck, A. T. and A. Freeman. 1990. *Cognitive therapy of personality disorders.* Guilford Press: New York.

Beeder, A.B., and R. B. Millman. 1992. Treatment of patients with psychopathology and substance abuse. In *Substance abuse: A comprehensive textbook.* 2d ed. Edited by J. H. Lowinson, P. Ruiz, R. B. Millman, and J. G. Langrod. Baltimore: Williams & Wilkins.

Daley, D. C., H. B. Moss, F. Campbell. 1993. *Dual disorders: Counseling clients with chemical dependency and mental illness.* 2d ed. Center City, Minn.: Hazelden Foundation.

The dual disorders recovery book. 1993. Center City, Minn.: Hazelden Foundation.

Kaufman, E. 1991. The psychotherapy of dually diagnosed patients. In *Comprehensive handbook of drug and alcohol addiction.* Edited by N. S. Miller. New York: Marcel Dekker, Inc.

McGovern, T. F. 1986a. Distinguishing between depression and grief in alcoholism: A pilot study. *Alcoholism Treatment Quarterly* 2 (1): 31-65.

———. 1986b. The effects of comprehensive inpatient alcoholism treatment on measures of loss and grief. *Alcohol* 3: 89-92.

———. 1992. The loss of alcohol in an alcohol dependency relationship: Good grief in good riddance? *Illness, Crisis and Loss* 2 (1): 2-7.

Miller, N. S. 1991. A review of the interactions in psychiatric syndromes and drug and alcohol addiction. In *Comprehensive handbook of drug and alcohol addiction,* edited by N. S. Miller. New York: Marcel Dekker, Inc.

Nace, E. P. 1987. *The treatment of alcoholism.* New York: Brunner/Mazel, Inc.

Schneider, J. 1989. The transformative power of grief. *Noetic Science Review* 12: 26-31.

———. 1994. *Finding my way: Healing and transformation through loss and grief.* Colfax, Wisc.: Seasons Press.

Wallace, J. 1985. Working with the preferred structure of the recovering alcoholic. In *Practical approaches to alcoholism psychotherapy.* 2d ed. Edited by S. Zimber, J. Wallace, and S. Blume. New York: Plenum.

Woody, G. E., A. T. McLellan, C. P. O'Brien, and L. Luborsky. 1990. *Addressing psychiatric comorbidity,* edited by R. W. Pickens and C. R. Schuster. NIDA Research Monograph Series No. 106: Washington, D.C., USDHHS.

Health care professionals can help their dual disorder patients—especially those on psychotropic medicines—in finding and using Twelve Step programs.

11
The Twelve Step Approach

Robert L. DuPont, M.D.

Introduction

DUAL DISORDERS CAN BE DOUBLE TROUBLE for both the patient and the therapist (Miller, in press). Comorbidity, or dual disorders, is especially costly and socially disruptive (Kessler et al., in press).

The most obvious predictor of success for a dual diagnosis patient is participation in one or more of the Twelve Step fellowships. A few dual disorder patients do well without using any of the Twelve Step programs, but in my experience, most dual disorder patients who choose not to use them do not do well. On the other hand, I have not seen any dual disorder patients who have joined one of the Twelve Step fellowships and who have not benefited substantially from their participation. This experience has led me to the conclusion that the best way for dual disorder patients to increase their odds of success is to join one of the Twelve Step fellowships and to participate fully in the program (Chatlos 1989). This means that they are most likely to do well if they attend meetings frequently, work the Steps, have a sponsor, assume leadership roles in their own home meetings, and sponsor newcomers to their fellowships.

Since both addictive and other mental disorders are usually lifelong, the goal of therapy is to help the patients and their families cope as well as possible. A booklet by Daley and Campbell in Hazelden's "Keep It Simple" series, *Coping with Dual Disorders: Chemical Dependency and*

Mental Illness (1989), is useful for patients and families in describing the various mental and addictive disorders and the treatment for both in easily understood language. A useful review of dual disorders was recently published by Miller and Gold (1991).

Denial of the diseases—and futile hopes to be rid of them—is usually part of the problem rather than part of the solution (Fabian 1990). Therapy can help dual disorder patients understand their illnesses and find effective ways to live full, productive, and reasonably healthy lives. *Dual Disorders: Counseling Clients with Chemical Dependency and Mental Illness,* by Daley, Moss, and Campbell (1993) provides useful advice to mental health workers dealing with dual disorder patients. The use of self-help and mutual aid in the treatment of anxiety disorders was recently reviewed (Saylor et al. 1990).

THE PATIENT'S FAMILY

Early in psychotherapy with a dual disorder patient, often at the first session but seldom more than two or three sessions into the process, I meet with the patient's family members. Most often I see the family members with the patient present for at least part of the session so that we can all talk together about each person's concerns. I make clear to the family that their options to help the patient are limited, as are mine and the patient's, as long as the patient continues to use alcohol and other drugs.

To the extent that patients work hard on their own recovery, family members have a great opportunity to support and encourage them. However, if the patient does not do this hard work, for whatever reason, the family is left with two terrible choices. First, they can blame and criticize the patient. This belittles the patient, reducing his or her already low self-esteem. It distorts the love of the family into a hostile caricature. Alternatively, the family can pick up the messes that the patient makes and lower their expectations to match the low levels of performance of dual disorder patients who do not work hard on their own recoveries. In the field of addiction medicine this second approach is called "enabling." It characteristically makes both groups of illnesses, addictive disease and other mental disorders, worse.

For the family members I offer the same basic description of the problems that I give to the patients. I suggest to them that they too are most likely to find help by going to Twelve Step meetings, of which the most accessible for families is Al-Anon. Although Al-Anon is designed specifically to help the families and friends of alcoholics, many Al-Anon groups are helpful to families with a wide variety of problems, including addiction to drugs other than alcohol and to mental health problems. I also suggest that family members contact the National Alliance for the Mentally Ill, 2101 Wilson Boulevard, Suite 302, Arlington, VA 22201 (703) 524-7600, or look up the local chapter in the telephone book. The more that families can break out of the shell of isolation and shame and enter into open and mutually supportive relationships with others suffering similar problems, the better it is for them and for their dually disordered family members. A recent booklet published by Hazelden provides helpful guidance for families coping with dual disorders (Daley and Sinberg 1989).

Finding the Right Twelve Step Program

The first order of business for me in working with dual disorder patients is to get them and their families plugged into the support of a Twelve Step fellowship. The major challenge often is compliance, with the therapist's role being not only to point out the path to recovery, but to help those patients find and follow this path over a long period of time. Table 12.1 and pages 193-196 list the major Twelve Step programs. (Local telephone numbers for each of the major Twelve Step programs can be found in the telephone directory.) Volunteers who answer the phones give information about where and when Twelve Step meetings take place. They also tell which meetings are open (nonmembers of the fellowship are welcome to attend) and which are closed (meetings are limited to people who themselves suffer from the problem being addressed in that fellowship).

Emotions Anonymous (EA) is a useful fellowship that deals with mental disorders of all kinds. (Addiction is seen as a separate issue.) EA tends to focus on emotional or mental problems in general rather than on specific mental disorders and uses the Twelve Steps of AA to help the mentally ill lead better lives. In contrast, Dual Recovery Anonymous (DRA) allows each member to be specific about the particular coexisting mental disorder.

Alcoholics Anonymous is the oldest and largest Twelve Step

fellowship. Many people start with the programs with which they most easily identify, but as they become more involved in the Twelve Step process, some people gravitate toward AA, which has numerous as well as more sophisticated and varied meetings. This evolution to AA is especially common for people who start with Narcotics Anonymous (NA) and become deeply involved with the program. It is less likely to occur in people who enter the Twelve Step fellowships through EA or Overeaters Anonymous (OA). In any event, AA's commitment to singleness of purpose—the fundamental focus on loss of control over alcohol use—makes some AA members unfriendly to this more generic use of the AA program.

I suggest to my patients that they find someone who is a Twelve Step fellowship member and go to meetings with that person until they are comfortable with the meetings and the program. Alternatively, I refer them to one of my patients who has volunteered to be a temporary sponsor to get newcomers started with the program. Another way to handle the initial referral is to call the local central number of one of the Twelve Step programs and ask about meetings that are particularly good for newcomers. Patients can then be referred to these meetings to get started.

I also suggest to patients that they find people at meetings who are most like them and ask them where they can find other good meetings. Newcomers often need to repeat this sorting process several times to find meetings in which they are comfortable. Patients then can make one weekly Twelve Step meeting their home meeting, although they should go to a different meeting every day to get started in the process. For more disorganized patients, it is helpful for their parents or other caregivers to go with them to meetings, especially at first.

Some Twelve Step fellowships now have dual disorder meetings. Although there are few and, in some areas, no meetings of AA and NA which focus explicitly on dual disorders, there are few Twelve Step fellowships anywhere that do not have any members who are suffering from mental disorders other than addiction. It is wise for the newcomer who suffers from a mental illness as well as from addiction to state that fact directly during the meeting. In general, others at the meetings will accept that information. Those with similar problems are likely to make a point of speaking to the newcomer with the dual disorder after the meeting. Whether to speak out in meetings about the use of psychotropic medicines is less clear-cut. Some meetings are supportive of appropriate use of psychotropic medicines, while others are not. It is useful to refer to AA's official statement on this issue of medicines in the publication, *A.A. Member: Medications and Other Drugs* (1984).

The most likely place to find Twelve Step meetings that explicitly reach out to the dual disorder patient is through inpatient and outpatient mental health programs dealing with dual disorder patients. Many of these programs encourage dual disorder Twelve Step meetings, which are open to anyone in the community and not restricted to current or former patients in these treatment programs. Dual disorder treatment programs can often provide the time and location of such meetings.

Dual disorder patients should be encouraged to get a temporary sponsor within the first week of meetings so that they can relate directly to someone who knows how the fellowship works. Patients also need to be encouraged to say a few words at each meeting and to get a copy of the "Big Book" of Alcoholics Anonymous at their first meeting so that they can begin to work the program systematically. At the start it is hard for many patients to work the program, so a good starting point is simply to show up at the meeting. The common adage of the Twelve Step fellowships is "Bring the body, and the heart and the mind will follow."

In my experience, it is difficult for health care professionals to make good referrals to Twelve Step programs if they have not attended several meetings themselves. Without this personal experience they do not understand what the fellowships are and what they can do. Without such personal experience it is difficult for therapists to help patients and their families overcome their resistance to the Twelve Step fellowships. My advice to all readers of this chapter is to go to Twelve Step meetings yourself. Attend at least half a dozen different meetings spread over several fellowships, including at least AA and Al-Anon, so that you will know what goes on and can see for yourself how the fellowships work.

One way to get started is to find a friend, relative, or colleague who is active in a Twelve Step program and go to some meetings with that person. Then go to a few open meetings by yourself. Before the meeting introduce yourself by your first name and say that you are there to learn about addiction. As you become more comfortable at meetings, it will be easier to describe why you are there and what help you need. You will be surprised by the respectful way you will be treated, not because you are a doctor or other professional person, but simply because you are open in your admission that you do not have all the answers and that you are coming to learn from some people who have found successful ways to live good lives despite their addictions and other problems (including other mental disorders). You are doing this so that you can better help your patients. You may also find, as I have, help in living your own life at those Twelve Step meetings.

Patients Who Are Active Addicts

Typically, the diagnosis of a mental disorder in a patient who is actively using alcohol and other drugs reflects the toxic effects of drug use. These effects include the primary effects of intoxication and withdrawal and the secondary effects of the life of addiction, including anxiety, depression, and psychosis, as well as unemployment, ruptured interpersonal relationships, crime, and accidents.

The biggest challenge for therapists working with dual disorder patients who are actively using alcohol and other drugs, or who have stopped using recently but are not in a Twelve Step fellowship, is to get them active in one of the Twelve Step programs. The easiest way to achieve this goal is to get the patient into a formal addiction treatment program based on the Twelve Steps. The alternative is to help the patients and their families to access meetings directly and to engage fully in the fellowship process. Such a direct approach is possible, but it often requires active support from the therapist. It takes time, persistence, and patience.

My first order of business in therapy with dual disorder patients is to shrink the task of psychotherapy by focusing first on addiction. I put it to my patients this way: "We cannot figure out what mental problem, if any, you have until you have been clean and sober for at least three months." For actively addicted patients there is no better approach than the old advice of going to ninety Twelve Step meetings in ninety days: the "90-90 solution."

For many active addicts, the Twelve Step fellowships are not accessible until the patients have participated in an organized addiction treatment program that weaves the Twelve Step programs into the fabric of mental health care. These programs can be either inpatient or outpatient. They help stabilize the addicted patients and get them enough clean time so that the toxic brain effects of alcohol and other drugs are reduced. Then these short-term treatment programs introduce the patients to lifelong membership in one of the Twelve Step fellowships.

Many of my dual disorder patients already have been to some Twelve Step meetings by the time I first see them, so I talk with them about what they found there and about the problems they had that kept them from attending meetings. Sometimes these problems are common to many addicted people; namely, they have not had enough alcohol and other drugs to come to the conclusion that the only stable and healthy number for them, when it comes to chemical use, is zero. They bargain with themselves and think about cutting down on or eliminating one or the other specific drug, but they want to hold on to "safe" drugs, most often alcohol and marijuana. Or, if they have had problems with alcohol, they think about cutting down on the quantity they drink or limiting the times or settings in which they drink.

I label this process of trying to run their own program while continuing to use alcohol and/or other drugs as "personal research" on addictive disease. I tell my patients that, based on my experience over many years, I have a good idea of how this research will turn out, but that I respect their need to conduct their own studies. The research usually ends when the pain produced by the continued use of alcohol and other drugs is so great that it cannot be tolerated any longer. At that point, and not before, the patient is open to the suggestion to join a Twelve Step fellowship. This is called "hitting bottom."

Resistance to Twelve Step Programs

It is helpful for therapists working with dual disorder patients to understand the common sources of resistance to Twelve Step programs and to be able to work through them with the patient (Weiss and Mirin 1989). For example, perceptions that the programs are "religious" and feeling that the admission of "powerlessness" is a sign of weakness need to be resolved by most people before they can participate actively in a

Twelve Step program. The dual disorder patient may also reject a Twelve Step program because of other members' concern about his or her use of psychotropic medications. Many of the most common resistances to wide use of the Twelve Step programs, including ethnic and cultural concerns, have been recently reviewed in an excellent article by David Smith and his colleagues (1993).

Most often the distrust of any medications is based on one or more of four important and solvable concerns. First, some physicians and other therapists mistakenly think that the Twelve Step fellowships generally and categorically oppose the use of psychotropic medicines. Contrary to this common expectation, my own experience with many dual disorder patients is that the Twelve Step fellowships unambivalently accept and even encourage the use of psychiatric medicines that do not have abuse potential in the treatment of well-defined mental disorders.

Second, the Twelve Step fellowships are not sympathetic to the use of medicines to treat addiction itself. Thus, methadone, naltrexone, and Antabuse are generally discouraged as primary approaches to addiction treatment. Unlike the first concern, this can be a real problem. I have found that the Twelve Step programs are on solid ground here because of their long experience in the treatment of addiction. They believe, with ample reason, that the best approach to overcoming addiction itself is the Twelve Step approach. For this reason psychotherapy as a treatment for addiction is frowned upon by the Twelve Step fellowships, just as is the use of medicines to treat addiction. Medicines and psychotherapy are not discouraged per se; in fact, the opposite is true for many fellowship members who are dual-disordered. Medicines and psychotherapy are encouraged, but not for the primary treatment of addiction.

Third, the use of controlled substances by recovering people is generally discouraged within the Twelve Step fellowships because of the risk of relapse to active abuse of alcohol and other drugs. The definition of a controlled substance is abuse potential; thus the controlled substance designation is an important danger signal to physicians treating recovering people.

Fourth, there is a deep skepticism within the Twelve Step fellowships about the use of psychotropic medicines to treat the symptoms of mental disorders among patients who are still actively using alcohol and other drugs because of the high probability that the symptoms of the mental disorder will be reduced or even eliminated once the patient is in a stable recovery.

These four specific concerns are not difficult to understand. But they seldom if ever, conflict with sound management of dual disorder patients once they are clearly understood by therapists and patients.

Feeling alienated at the first few Twelve Step meetings because of the coexistence of other mental disorders can be a problem also. This process of feeling alienated after the first few Twelve Step meetings is called "affiliating out." It is a common experience for many addicted people when they first go to Twelve Step meetings. Many newcomers quickly, and wrongly, conclude that the other people in the meeting are not "like them." This perception rationalizes their quitting the fellowship and continuing to use alcohol and/or other drugs. I have found that if the dual disorder patients will speak up about their mental health problems at the first few meetings they attend, they are virtually certain to find others there with similar problems, much to the patients' surprise and relief.

For patients with social phobia and schizophrenia (both usually associated with fear of being close to other people), meetings can themselves be a special problem. It helps to focus in the psychotherapy on the meetings as opportunities to do what is hard but what is helpful to the patients' own long-term self-interest, in the sense that the meetings are relatively safe and predictable "practice" opportunities to overcome painful feelings around other people.

It is useful to ask the dual disorder patients to go to some Twelve Step meetings "as an experiment" and then to talk over what happened at the meetings and what the patient thought about the experience. This exploration and subsequent discussion integrate the Twelve Step meetings into the psychotherapy process. When therapists themselves have been to enough Twelve Step meetings to understand how the Twelve Step programs work, they are better able to understand that the patients' objections and fears are common but potentially crippling distortions of the Twelve Step fellowship experience. The therapist can help dual disorder patients find meetings and temporary sponsors to ease the entry into the Twelve Step fellowships. Therapists can also help by meeting with the patient and his or her sponsor to talk over problems the patient is having in making fuller use of the Twelve Step program and concerns that may arise about the use of medicines in the patient's treatment.

Patients Who Are in Recovery

Dually diagnosed patients who are in stable recovery are fortunate. They have experienced the joy of recovery, they have a working support system, and they have a program that provides them with solid guidelines for living a good life. Unfortunately, this does not protect them from suffering from other mental illnesses at about the rate that the general population does. Although it is unlikely that addictive disease causes or increases the risk of other mental disorders once the addiction is controlled, it is also not realistic to think that addictive disease (or recovery from it) protects people from any other diseases, physical or mental.

Patients in recovery—that is, people who are active in a Twelve Step fellowship and who are not using alcohol and other drugs—who suffer from other physical or mental diseases often worry that they are not working their recovery programs correctly because they assume, unrealistically, that they would not suffer from another disorder if they were following the Twelve Step program correctly. It is helpful to reassure dual disorder patients on this point in psychotherapy and to help them learn how to cope as well as possible with the other illnesses from which they suffer in addition to addiction. Often the Twelve Step fellowships can be helpful in this process, especially the patient's sponsor, who can help to develop an action plan and relieve any inappropriate guilt or shame the patient may feel.

I have seen many anxious or depressed patients in recovery who have fallen away from regular attendance at Twelve Step meetings and who are no longer "working the program." They usually need only the encouragement of their therapists to go back to their sponsors and to their Twelve Step work for their symptoms of anxiety or depression to abate. On the other hand, I have seen active Twelve Step program participants who continue to suffer from the symptoms of mental disorders despite their full and active participation in Twelve Step programs. For this group of patients, it is important to help them use psychotherapy and/or appropriate medicine to achieve fuller, happier lives.

Dual disorder patients in Twelve Step programs need the same types of mental health care, both pharmacological and nonpharmacological, as other patients, except that the use of controlled substances in outpatient settings is generally unwise for people with addictive illnesses. Practically speaking, this mostly means the use of narcotic analgesics and benzodiazepines. In my experience, dual disorder outpatients who are actively using alcohol and other drugs should virtually never use controlled substances. On the other hand, some addicted people in recovery appear to respond to the use of controlled substances in the treatment of various illnesses as nonaddicted people do.

This simple-seeming advice needs to be tempered by an appreciation for what the Big Book calls "the cunning, baffling, and powerful" disease of addiction. Denial is not willful misconduct on the part of the addicted patient. When the disease of addiction becomes active, denial and dishonesty regain control of the addicted person's thoughts and behaviors. The subtlety of addictive disease makes it elusive, especially in the early stages of a relapse, for the patient, the family, and the physician. Most patients active in Twelve Step programs not only do not want to use controlled substances, they actively fear exposure to them.

Physicians considering the use of a controlled substance in outpatient settings for recovering addicted people should attend some Twelve Step meetings to listen to the stories about the sometimes well-meaning but misguided physicians who play a role in their patients' relapse to active addiction. As a practical matter it is seldom, if ever, necessary to use controlled substances for the treatment of any mental disorder in a dual disorder patient, including panic, insomnia, and anxiety, because there now are many pharmacological options available that are not controlled substances. Many mental disorders can be managed effectively with nonpharmacological treatments.

Dealing with Conflict and Confrontation In Twelve Step Programs

Many mental health professionals are concerned that their dual disorder patients will be misunderstood and even mistreated in Twelve Step programs because of their use of psychotropic medicines or even their use of psychotherapy or other mental health programs.

If dual disorder patients use controlled substances—most often a benzodiazepine to treat manifestations of anxiety or methadone to treat heroin addiction—they are likely to be confronted in the Twelve Step programs. The problem lies in the fact that these patients are pursuing approaches to addictive disease that conflict with the experiences and beliefs of the Twelve Step program. Dual disorder patients are, in my experience, never blackballed from the fellowships, but they are confronted about their behaviors. They need to be prepared to defend (or change) their conflict-generating behaviors if they are to continue in the Twelve Step program. It is usually possible to work through any conflicts that arise by talking honestly and directly with the patient and the patient's sponsor.

In other conflict situations, the patient often is compelled to attend Twelve Step meetings by parole or some other agency and is actively (but surreptitiously) using alcohol and other drugs while going through the motions of participation in the Twelve Step program. It has been my experience that in such situations of conflict over the use of controlled substances, the prescribing physician is seldom familiar with the treatment of addictive disease or the Twelve Step programs.

Worry about this conflict tends to be more common than the problems themselves. Often all that is needed to solve such conflicts, if they do arise, is the support, understanding, and encouragement of the patient by the health care professional, since, as mentioned earlier, most of the use of medicines and therapy for dual disorder patients is officially accepted and even encouraged within the Twelve Step programs. The continuing use of controlled substances, however, including benzodiazepines and methadone, by dual diagnosis patients is an area of conflict with the Twelve Step programs generally.

Despite the official acceptance of psychotropic medications in Twelve Step groups, many individual fellowship members, and many meetings as a whole, remain hostile to the use of such medications by recovering addicts, even when they have clear-cut, coexisting mental disorders. These conflicts are real and can be serious barriers for dual diagnosis patients. These conflicts seem to be best handled by a close collaboration between the patient, the treating physician, the Twelve Step sponsor, and the patient's family. If this network is open with each other, I have found that most problems about medicine use that arise can be resolved. In some cases, it is necessary for the dual diagnosis patient to change meetings and to remain silent about the use of psychotropic medicines in order to find full benefit from the Twelve Step fellowships.

Fortunately, the old mutual hostility between the Twelve Step programs and medical (and psychiatric) care is disappearing. Increasingly, Twelve Step programs encourage mental health care, including the appropriate use of medicines. Also increasingly, physicians and other health care professionals are encouraging the use of Twelve Step programs for dual disorder patients. Most of what resistance persists today regarding the use of psychotropic medicines is based on unfamiliarity and fear, not recent experience.

Again, direct, honest, and open approaches usually solve any problems that appear. For example, patients who are concerned about Twelve Step hostility to their mental health care can bring in their sponsors and other leaders of their Twelve Step fellowships to talk with their physicians and other therapists. Alternatively, their physicians and other therapists can go with the patients to some of their Twelve Step meetings and discuss these issues there. Such direct encounters are likely to resolve quickly whatever conflicts exist. If they do not, efforts can be made to find local experts with sympathies on both sides of the conflicts who can help find solutions.

One of the best ways to find help in this sort of brokering between Twelve Step programs and health care professionals is to find physicians who specialize in addiction medicine and who also routinely use the Twelve Step programs in their work. Twelve Step addiction treatment programs and/or the American Society of Addiction Medicine (ASAM) at 5225 Wisconsin Avenue, N.W., Suite 409, Washington, D.C. 20015 (202) 244-8948 are also good places to start.

With respect to dual disorder patients who are doing well on methadone or other controlled substances, it is seldom necessary for the patients to bring up their use in large Twelve Step meetings, where such use may be misunderstood and even lead to embarrassment and disapproval. On the other hand, patients' families and Twelve Step program sponsors must be fully and honestly informed about their use of medicines. Physicians need to be fully informed about their patients' addiction histories.

The other side of the resistance problem is the resistance of some health care professionals to the use of Twelve Step programs in the treatment of addicted people, including those with dual disorders. I have found that the best solution to this problem is to encourage health care workers to attend half a dozen or so open meetings. Most health care professionals who have learned about the Twelve Step programs have done so when they have been "sponsored" by their own addicted patients; that is, the addicted patients have leveled with their doctors about their addictions and about how they have gotten well. Often this means telling their physicians that in the past their addiction has been misdiagnosed and perhaps even perpetuated if the physicians prescribed controlled substances or aided in their patients' denial.

Physicians often resist understanding addiction and the Twelve Step programs, but when their own patients describe their experiences in direct and honest ways, physicians are likely, sooner or later, to get the message. This is how I learned about the Twelve Step programs and what led to my interest in attending meetings to see for myself what was going on. I now go to meetings often. I have never been to a Twelve Step meeting where I did not learn much of value to me both personally and professionally.

SUMMARY

Dual disorders are double trouble, but the unique and powerful Twelve Step programs of recovery provide road maps to living lives not only free of alcohol and other drugs but based on honesty and sound values. The support available in these programs includes not only immediate access to a caring person twenty-four hours a day, 365 days a year, but also a workable plan for living. No other therapeutic experience comes close on either score.

Nor do mental health patients who are not addicted to alcohol or other drugs lack a ticket into the Twelve Step community. They can go to Emotions Anonymous (EA), the Twelve Step program to meet the needs of the nonaddicted mentally ill. Those people who are members of families dominated by addiction are eligible for Al-Anon. Finally, addicted patients whose lives are disorganized and made more painful by the coexistence of another mental health disorder are especially likely to benefit from the organizing and supportive nature of Twelve Step programs.

Physicians and other mental health workers need to understand Twelve Step programs and encourage their dual disorder patients, and their dual disorder patients' families, to use these programs. Mental health professionals can also encourage the development of more Twelve Step fellowships to deal with the specific needs of dual disorder patients, including the new Dual Recovery Anonymous program. They also need to help patients find appropriate Twelve Step programs and to help them overcome the common sources of resistance to using these programs. When physicians and other professionals enlist the power of the community of recovery found in these programs, the odds of success for dual disorder patients are substantially improved.

Making an effective referral of a dual disorder patient to a Twelve Step fellowship is seldom easy. It requires experience, skill, and patience wrapped up in the therapeutic alliance during the course of therapy.

Bibliotherapy

Several books are helpful for dual diagnosis patients in terms of their use of the Twelve Step programs. Two books recently published are especially useful for all people seeking help from Twelve Step fellowships: *The Recovery Book,* by Al J. Mooney, M.D., Arlene Eisenberg, and Howard Eisenberg (New York: Workman Publishing, 1992) and *The Twelve-Step Facilitation Handbook: A Systematic Approach to Early Recovery from Alcoholism and Addiction,* by Joseph Nowinski and Stuart Baker (New York: Lexington Books, 1992).

With my coauthor, John P. McGovern, I have written a book called *A Bridge to Recovery: An Introduction to 12-Step Programs* (Washington, D.C.: American Psychiatric Press, 1994). This book focuses on building bridges to link major social institutions (such as health care, education, criminal justice, and religion) to the Twelve Step fellowships.

Especially useful for dual disorder patients is a book published by Hazelden in 1993, *The Dual Disorders Recovery Book: A Twelve Step Program for Those of Us with Addiction and an Emotional or Psychiatric Illness.*

For those interested in research studies of the Twelve Step programs, I recommend "Recent Research in 12-Step Programs," by Robert L. DuPont and Sarah Shiraki, soon to be published by the American Society of Addiction Medicine as a chapter in *Principles of Addiction Medicine.*

Excellent material on the individual Twelve Step fellowships, including information dealing with mental health professionals and psychotropic medicines, is available free of charge from each of the major Twelve Step programs listed on pages 193-196. Especially useful for the dual disorder patient on medication is the pamphlet *A.A. Member: Medications and Other Drugs* (A.A. World Services, 1984).

TABLE 12.1
TWELVE STEP FELLOWSHIP GUIDE

Name	*Abbreviation*	*Orientation*	*Number of Groups*
Alcoholics Anonymous	AA	Personal Alcoholism	94,000
Narcotics Anonymous	NA	Personal drug addiction	22,000
Cocaine Anonymous	CA	Personal cocaine addiction	1,500
Al-Anon Family Groups	Al-Anon	Family alcoholism	32,000
Alateen		Young Al-Anon members	4,100
Adult Children of Alcoholics	ACOA/ACA	Adult children from alcoholic families	1,800
Dual Disorders Anonymous		People with mental disorder and addiction	25
Dual Recovery Anonymous	DRA	People with mental disorder and addiction	50
Emotions Anonymous	EA	Nonaddicted people with mental health problems	1,200

Twelve Step Fellowship Resources

Al-Anon Family Groups—International organization based on the Twelve Steps and Twelve Traditions adapted from AA. Founded in 1951 as a mutual-aid program of recovery for family and friends of alcoholics. More than 32,000 groups.

Al-Anon Family Group Headquarters
P.O. Box 862
Midtown Station
New York, NY 10018-6106
(212) 302-7240
(800) 344-2666 (meeting information)
(800) 356-9996 (general)

Alateen—An international fellowship that is part of Al-Anon Family Groups. Founded in 1957 for teenagers and young adults affected by someone else's drinking. Adult member of Al-Anon serves as group sponsor. More than 4,100 groups.

Alateen
Al-Anon Family Group Headquarters
P.O. Box 862
Midtown Station
New York, NY 10018-0862
(212) 302-7240
(800) 344-2666 (meeting information)
(800) 356-9996 (general)

Alcoholics Anonymous—International organization of men and women devoted to helping themselves and others overcome alcoholism by following Twelve Step program to recovery. Founded in 1935. More than 94,000 groups.

Alcoholics Anonymous World Services, Inc.
General Service Office
P.O. Box 459
Grand Central Station
New York, NY 10163
(212) 870-3400

Adult Children of Alcoholics—International organization founded in 1976 and based on the Twelve Steps of AA. Mutual-aid group for adults who grew up with alcoholic parents. More than 1,800 groups.

Adult Children of Alcoholics World Service Organization
P.O. Box 3216
Torrance, CA 90510
(310) 534-1815

Cocaine Anonymous—International mutual-aid organization of men and women helping themselves and others achieve recovery from cocaine addiction. Founded in 1982. More than 1,500 groups.

Cocaine Anonymous World Services, Inc.
3740 Overland Avenue, Suite H
Los Angeles, CA 90034
(310) 559-5833 (business office)
(800) 347-8998 (meeting information)

Co-Dependents Anonymous—National organization of men and women who grew up in dysfunctional families. About 3,500 groups. Founded in 1986.

Co-Dependents Anonymous
P.O. Box 33577
Phoenix, AZ 85067-3577
(602) 277-7991

Dual Disorders Anonymous—Illinois model program for men and women suffering from both mental disorder and addiction to alcohol or other drugs. Founded in 1982. About 25 chapters.

Dual Disorders Anonymous
P.O. Box 4045
Des Plaines, IL 60016
(708) 462-3380

Dual Recovery Anonymous—A new organization for people who suffer from both a mental disorder and addiction based on the Twelve Step format. About 50 groups.

Dual Recovery Anonymous
Central Service Office
P.O. Box 8107
Prairie Village, KS 66208
(913) 676-7226

Emotions Anonymous—A national organization using the Twelve Step program to gain better emotional health. Founded in 1971. About 1,200 chapters.

Emotions Anonymous
P.O. Box 4245
St. Paul, MN 55104
(612) 647-9712

Families Anonymous—International organization of family and friends of individuals with substance abuse or behavioral problems. Based on the Twelve Steps of Alcoholics Anonymous. Founded in 1971. About 500 groups.

Families Anonymous
P.O. Box 528
Van Nuys, CA 91408
(818) 989-7841
(800) 736-9805

International Doctors in Alcoholics Anonymous—Organization whose members are mostly medical doctors who are alcoholic. Founded in 1949.

International Doctors in Alcoholics Anonymous
P.O. Box 199
Augusta, MO 63332
(312) 781-1317

Nar-Anon—International organization based on the Twelve Steps of AA. Founded in 1967 for families and friends of drug addicts.

Nar-Anon Family Group Headquarters
P.O. Box 2562
Palos Verdes, CA 90274-0119
(213) 547-5800

Narcotics Anonymous—International organization based on the Twelve Steps of AA. Founded in 1953. Men and women meet together in community meetings to support one another in recovery from drug addiction. More than 22,000 groups.

Narcotics Anonymous World Services, Inc.
P.O. Box 9999
Van Nuys, CA 91409
(818) 780-3951

Pill Addicts Anonymous—International organization for recovery from addiction to prescribed and over-the-counter mood-changing pills and drugs. Founded in 1979.

General Service Board of Pill Addicts Anonymous
P.O. Box 278
Reading, PA 19603
(215) 372-1128

References

Alcoholics Anonymous. 1984. *A.A. member: Medications and other drugs.* New York: Alcoholics Anonymous World Services, Inc.

———. 1976. *Alcoholics Anonymous.* 3d ed. New York: Alcoholics Anonymous World Services, Inc.

Chatlos, J. C. 1989. Adolescent dual diagnosis: A Twelve Step transformational model. *Journal of Psychoactive Drugs* 21:189-201.

Daley, D. C., and F. Campbell. 1989. *Coping with dual disorders: Chemical dependency and mental illness* ("Keep It Simple" Series). Center City, Minn.: Hazelden Educational Materials.

Daley, D. C., H. B. Moss, and F. Campbell. 1993. *Dual disorders: Counseling clients with chemical dependency and mental illness.* 2d ed. Center City, Minn.: Hazelden Educational Materials.

Daley, D. C., and S. Sinberg. 1989. *Taking care of yourself: When a family member has dual disorders.* Center City, Minn.: Hazelden Educational Materials.

Fabian, C. A. 1990. The "dual diagnosis" patient. *Directions in Psychiatry* 10 (Lesson 17), edited by F. F. Flach. New York: Hatherleigh Co. Ltd.

Kessler, R. C., K. A. McGonagle, K. B. Carnelley, C. B. Nelson, M. E. Farmer, and D. A. Regier. In press. Comorbidity of mental disorders and substance use disorders: A review and agenda for future research. In *Research in Community and Mental Health,* edited by P. Leaf. Greenwich, Conn.: JAI Press.

Miller, N. S., ed. In press. *Comorbidity of addictive and psychiatric disorders: diagnosis and treatment.* New York: The Haworth Press, Inc.

Miller, N. S., and M. S. Gold. 1991. Dual diagnoses: Psychiatric syndromes in alcoholism and drug addiction. *American Family Physician* (June): 2071-76.

Saylor, K. E., R. L. DuPont, and M. Brouillard. 1990. Self-help treatment of anxiety disorders. In *Handbook of anxiety 4: The treatment of anxiety,* edited by R. Noyes, M. Roth, and G. D. Burrows. Amsterdam, The Netherlands: Elsevier Science Publishers B.V., 483-96.

Smith, D. E., M. E. Buxton, R. Bilal, and R. B. Seymour. 1993. Cultural points of resistance to the 12-step recovery process. *Journal of Psychoactive Drugs* 25:97-108.

Weiss, R. D., and S. M. Mirin. 1989. The dual diagnosis alcoholic: Evaluation and treatment. *Psychiatric Annals* 19:261-65.

A Minnesota model addiction treatment program can be adapted in several ways to provide relapse prevention treatment for a dual diagnosis patient. Adaptations include the admission, education, medication, psychotherapy, and participation in Twelve Step programs.

12
Relapse Prevention

John N. Chappel, M.D.

> *The failure of the client to remain both clean and sober and psychiatrically stable has several negative consequences. Clients, families, and providers can become pessimistic and burned out. Options can disappear as resources become exhausted. Clients and families often use up their insurance, and public sector providers sometimes refuse services in an attempt to conserve limited funding for cases more likely to respond. Finally, the client faces distress, disability, and even death.*
>
> *—(Evans and Sullivan 1990, p. 142)*

RELAPSE, ESPECIALLY WHEN PROLONGED AND SERIOUS, is the bane of the addiction professional's existence. When it occurs in too high a proportion of our clients/patients, we can easily feel both incompetent and hopeless. These reactions lead to the pessimism and burnout described above. The antidote to this difficult problem, in our opinion, is a multidisciplinary treatment team, including a clinical psychologist and a psychiatrist, that has strong links to the recovering fellowships of Alcoholics Anonymous and Narcotics Anonymous.

As has been well documented elsewhere in this book, it is impossible to work with addicted clients/patients without encountering dual diagnosis problems. Kofoed and his colleagues (1986) described one of the pioneering programs that attempted to treat addicted patients with chronic mental illness. Despite an intensive program that used psychotherapy and disulfiram in addition to education, groups, and a variety of approaches designed to establish a relationship within which treatment and recovery could occur, there were major problems with noncompliance and relapse. Only seven (22 percent) of the thirty-two dual diagnosis patients who started treatment continued for at least a year.

In a more recent study, Wolpe et al. (1993) studied forty-eight inpatients with dual diagnosis. All were expected to continue in aftercare to work on their recovery. Compliance was defined as at least three visits to aftercare, a truly subminimal amount. They found that the presence of depression decreased compliance. The same was true for cocaine addiction.

Relapse Prevention

How can we prevent this recurring problem of noncompliance and relapse? Our approach begins with educating the patient upon entering treatment.

Case History

R. P., a forty-seven-year-old man, was admitted to the inpatient addiction program with the following diagnoses:

Axis I	Benzodiazepine dependence
	Heroin and alcohol dependence in apparent remission
	Major depression, with grief over multiple losses
	Two prior suicide attempts
Axis II	Antisocial personality disorder (ASPD)

Drug use had begun at age eleven with paregoric. The patient quickly graduated to heroin, which he continued to use for the next sixteen years, except when in prison. There were multiple juvenile arrests, followed by several terms in reform school.

At age eighteen he was convicted of armed robbery and spent several years in prison. Following his release he moved to the East

Coast and pursued a career as a musician, playing saxophone and flute. At age thirty he experienced grief over the overdose deaths of his friends Coltrane and Culpepper.

At age thirty-two his wife divorced him. This was followed by a suicide attempt and psychiatric hospitalization in southern California. Later that year he entered an addiction treatment program and stopped using heroin. At age thirty-six he was convicted of armed robbery and incarcerated in San Quentin. While in prison he began work as a butcher. A quarter of beef fell on him, fracturing two cervical vertebrae and initiating a seizure disorder. He had two neck surgeries and was put on clonazepam (Klonopin) and carbamazepine (Tegretol).

Following release from prison, R. P.'s use of clonazepam slowly escalated. He was unable to work and at age forty-three was put on social security disability. Depression and troubled relationships continued. At age forty-six he made another suicide attempt with a gun and was admitted to a psychiatric hospital. Here he was diagnosed as having bipolar disorder, and imipramine (Tofranil) was added to the other medications.

Admission to our program occurred after he had been turned down by the state psychiatric hospital because he had obtained extra prescriptions of clonazepam from the staff. He was also turned down by an addiction treatment program because he was on psychiatric medications. At the time of admission he was taking carbamazepine (Tegretol), 200 mg three times a day; imipramine (Tofranil), 100 mg at bedtime; clonazepam (Klonopin), 2 mg twenty to twenty-five daily; and any other benzodiazepines he could get.

R. P. illustrates some of the worst problems for potential noncompliance and relapse. His long history of drug addiction, his antisocial personality disorder, and the depression with two suicide attempts combined to give our treatment team a hopeless feeling about his prognosis.

R. P. was on the inpatient unit for nineteen days. During this time the clonazepam was gradually reduced, with some phenobarbital substitution. At the time of discharge and transfer to aftercare, which the treatment team felt was premature, he was on

> clonazepam 0.25 mg each evening for four days and phenobarbital 60 mg twice a day for seven days, then one daily for four days. One year later, R. P.'s comment was that, "Klonopin (clonazepam) was ten times worse than heroin to kick."

For the inpatient program, which is similar to but more intense than outpatient or aftercare, our relapse prevention activity included the following modifications of our regular treatment program in four areas: education, support systems, medication, and alternative activities.

Education

- *The disease of addiction and its effect on the brain.* This is the core of the education component and is described by the American Society of Addiction Medicine (ASAM) (Morse and Flavin 1992). This education occurs in group settings with discussion. R. P. was prepared for the recurrence of addictive thoughts and impulses, which may be triggered by any sensory input or by memories and dreams. For the dual diagnosis patient who has relapsed, this conditioned reflex cue recognition requires particular emphasis. R. P. was encouraged to learn and remember the "cunning, baffling, and powerful" way in which his own addiction kept surfacing.
- *Education about R. P.'s mental disorders.* This was done on a more individual basis. Early recognition of signs and symptoms was emphasized. R. P. was encouraged to explore and describe the ways his depression and impulses led to alcohol and other drug use. The importance of treatment was emphasized and he was urged to continue in psychotherapy after discharge.
- *The goal of abstinence from any addicting drugs or medications.* This was part of R. P.'s basic education. We tried to link the pain he had experienced during his relapse with his use of addicting drugs and medication. Although they provided temporary relief, the end result was worse for him. This was particularly true of his medical and psychiatric problems. He was told many times that continued use of addicting drugs would, at best, slow or delay his response to medical or psychiatric treatment and would likely make things worse.

- *R. P.'s responsibility for his recovery despite repeated relapse was strongly emphasized.* We explained that he was not responsible or to blame for being an addict, being depressed, being self-centered and impulsive, or having a seizure disorder. He was and is responsible for recognizing that these conditions exist and for actively seeking treatment and working toward recovery. This is a tough message for many patients to hear, especially if they are on a pension and/or have a sense of entitlement that the world should fix them.

A Recovery Support System

- *This begins with the treatment team.* R. P. was encouraged to talk to each person on the team and learn all he could from them. We realized that his ASPD made trust in any relationship difficult. Fortunately the pain of his depression was such that he developed a relationship with one of our recovering counselors.
- *Group, individual, and family therapy.* These were used to illustrate the importance of supportive relationships in recovery. We emphasized that these are models of real relationships and safe places to work out new relational skills. R. P. was also informed of the research indicating that the greater the severity of his psychiatric problems, the more likely he was to benefit from psychotherapy (McLellan et al. 1986).
- *Introduction to, and immersion in, the Twelve Step programs of AA and NA.* This important but difficult aspect of relapse prevention begins during detoxification. R. P. had not been successfully bonded to a Twelve Step program in any of his previous treatments. Literature was given to him and he was expected to attend open meetings of AA and NA held in the hospital. Recovering alumni of the treatment program frequently visited. Temporary contacts took him to meetings in the community. The process of choosing a sponsor and a home group was begun. He was encouraged to develop and use a phone list. The first three Steps were worked during his inpatient stay. His life graph was prepared and presented to the group in preparation for doing Steps Four and Five with his sponsor after discharge. R. P. surprised us. He was initially given NA literature and

encouraged to attend NA because of his history of heroin addiction and his prolonged exposure to prison. But he very quickly gravitated to AA. Although he was very resistant to these programs while an inpatient, he returned thirty-seven days after discharge and asked his counselor to help him find a sponsor. The man he chose just happened to walk onto the unit a short time after this and agreed to become his sponsor. R. P. experienced this as a powerful, good omen.

Medication

- *Education about the importance of psychiatric medication in preventing relapse.* This starts after detoxification. R. P. was referred to the pamphlet *A.A. Member: Medications and Other Drugs* (1984). It was explained to him that taking medication for his mental disorder does not break or interrupt his sobriety. In fact, the medications make it possible for him to work a Twelve Step program of recovery, which will help both his mental disorder and his addiction. R. P. was prepared by our staff for the well-intentioned AA/NA members who would tell him to stop taking carbamazepine and imipramine. R. P.'s difficult withdrawal and other experiences had sensitized him to the hazards of benzodiazepines and likelihood of relapse. By the time of discharge he was ready to educate any physician who tried to prescribe benzodiazepines or other controlled medications and to refuse the prescriptions if they were given.
- *Preparation for acute pain episodes.* R. P. was informed that he might have an accident or need surgery that would require CNS depressant and/or opioid medication. If and when this occurred he was urged to prevent relapse by following these procedures, which we use in teaching prescribing practices to physicians (Chappel 1991):
  - Be aware of the danger of relapse due to his response to any addicting medication and inform every prescribing physician involved in his treatment.
  - Notify his recovery support system about the drugs he will be getting. This includes family, friends, sponsor, home group, and people on his phone list.

  - Request permission from his attending physician for AA/NA visitors and for meetings in his hospital room.
  - Request rapid withdrawal from all addicting medication, before discharge if possible.
  - Expect craving and drug-seeking behavior, which are normal responses of an addicted brain when reexposed to addicting drugs. These reactions should be recognized, described, and treated with good humor. There is no need for guilt, anger, or depression, especially if the impulses are not acted upon. Zweben and Smith (1989) cite an example of a recovering patient who was prescribed benzodiazepines for panic attacks. The above approach was used successfully without triggering a relapse.

Develop Alternative Activities Which Produce Benefits Similar To Those of the Patient's Addicting Drugs

- Vaillant (1983) found alternative activities to be an important factor for those alcoholics who achieved stable sobriety. He also pointed out how useful AA was in accomplishing this task. We told R. P. that it was imperative that he find some nonchemical ways (alternative activities) to change his brain chemistry. It was emphasized that the most effective activities, such as aerobic exercise and sharing in relationships, took time and practice to develop. He was warned against using potentially addicting behaviors, such as sex, gambling, eating, spending, etc., because they change brain chemistry rapidly and require little practice. We encouraged him to talk to people at AA/NA meetings to find out what they did to deal with craving, anxiety, depression, anger, frustration, and other states that carry a high risk of relapse.

These modifications to our regular inpatient treatment program for the purpose of relapse prevention are not always effective. Too many of our dual diagnosis patients still relapse. Additional suggestions and ideas can be found in Evans and Sullivan (1990, ch. 9), Gorski (1989), and Marlatt and Gordon (1985).

R. P.'s Response to Relapse Prevention

Fortunately, R. P. has not relapsed in the year since his discharge from the inpatient unit. He is now off all medications and is engaged to be married. Because his admission followed several previous treatments and he had been refused admission by one of the places which had treated him before, the episode described above can be considered a way of dealing with relapse in a dual diagnosis patient.

Our emphasis in dealing with any relapse is to review the episode and its antecedent events, thoughts, and behaviors in great detail. Galanter (1992) describes a similar approach, which revealed forgotten antecedents in an alcoholic woman who relapsed during an anxiety-producing episode after six years of sobriety. The questions used by Evans and Sullivan (1990, p. 150) illustrate this approach:

1. What triggered your relapse?
2. What happened when you relapsed?
3. How did you fail to be responsible for your own behavior?
4. What could you have done differently?
5. What will you do differently next time?
6. Why do you think you should forgive yourself for relapsing?
7. How do you plan to avoid future relapses?

These and other questions are designed to relieve guilt, counteract hopelessness, and stimulate learning. Any relapse should be viewed as a learning experience, a window of opportunity.

The issue of whether to admit R. P. in the first place was a controversial one. When I first entered the field of addiction medicine in 1968, working with chronic alcoholics at the Woodlawn Mental Health Center and heroin addicts in the Illinois Drug Abuse Program, we had heated debates over how long a relapsed individual should have to wait before being readmitted to treatment. Many of our units set thirty-, sixty-, or ninety-day intervals from the last treatment before they would agree to readmit someone who had relapsed. These decisions were troublesome, especially when some of the former patients died while awaiting admission. The problem with this thinking is that it puts all the responsibility for change on the patient and none on the treatment team. The difficulty in avoiding this kind of thinking is reflected in the program Kofoed and his colleagues (1986) set up in the early eighties.

Patients who did not comply with program requirements, such as taking disulfiram and attending AA/NA meetings, were discharged.

R. P. is convinced that if we had refused admission or discharged him for noncompliance he would probably be dead now. During his nineteen days as an inpatient he got very angry and struck out at the staff in a critical, belligerent way. He developed paranoid ideas about the staff and other patients, and he was very depressed. As he looks back on this experience, from the perspective of one year in recovery and aftercare, two things stand out for him:

1. The staff were understanding. He did not understand what was happening to him and did not like the experience. The staff accepted him, interpreted his behavior to him as being the result of his dual disorders, and told him to stay. Of interest in this regard, and reflecting the humility physicians need to have as members of the treatment team, R. P. has no memory of my participation in his treatment!
2. The emphasis on going to AA. R. P. refers to this now as "force-feeding." The misery R. P. experienced in the month after discharge helped motivate him to try working a Twelve Step program of recovery. In addition to a weekly aftercare meeting, he goes to several AA meetings each week. In particular, he enjoys his "Get grateful" meeting every Sunday at the public addiction treatment program, which refused him admission before he came to us. R. P. sits among the people who are smelly and in pajamas and remembers "where he was." He says he'd "like to be able to contribute to these people." He finds himself practicing Step Three every day, which involves turning things over to his higher power. He reflects, "During my whole life, my self-esteem has been real low; I set high goals and couldn't reach them." He has now applied to Vocational Rehabilitation and is considering the possibility of getting off disability.

R. P. is not totally symptom-free. He still experiences mood swings. Occasionally he has a "crying jag," and says, "I don't know why, because life has been so good recently." He hastened to assure me that he was not suicidal and didn't need medication.

R. P.'s response to a Twelve Step program of recovery, after initially rejecting it, illustrates the importance of our persisting in educating and helping our patients overcome their resistance to a proven source of help. This help from AA/NA is not only for their addictions, but also for the promotion of normal growth and development. The research by Walsh and her colleagues (1991) demonstrates the value of treatment programs in helping alcoholic patients make use of AA. Those who went through treatment were significantly more likely to be abstinent and involved in AA at follow-up then those who were sent directly to AA once their alcoholism was identified.

We believe that managing a relapse requires teamwork between the relapsing dual diagnosis patient and the health care professional, including the whole treatment team. Every relapse calls for a change in treatment. That change should be directed at the cause(s) of the relapse, without relinquishing what we know to be the fundamentals of recovery from both addictive and mental disorders.

We also believe that physicians need to be educated about their role in relapse prevention with recovering alcoholics and other addicts. We like the agreement that Evans and Sullivan (1990, p. 33) get from physicians who work with their dual diagnosis patients:

- No use of addictive (controlled) medications after detox without prior approval of the medical director (or a staff meeting).
- Require attendance at AA/NA meetings during treatment and after discharge.
- Order psychological evaluations on all patients to insure a comprehensive assessment.
- Require patient attendance in family therapy.
- No discharge until written aftercare plans are complete.
- Follow all rules regarding urine drug screens, passes, visitation, etc.

This agreement recognizes that most health care professionals have had little or no education in the treatment of addictive disorders and often act as trained enablers. Evans and Sullivan (1990) emphasize the need for physicians, especially psychiatrists, "who believe that both the disease of addiction and the mental illness require comprehensive, simultaneous care."

Discussion

Relapse is a poorly understood but common phenomenon. External and internal events may trigger relapses. In R. P.'s case, uninformed prescribing shifted his addiction from heroin and alcohol to benzodiazepines. Traditional addiction treatment did not prevent relapse. Traditional mental health treatment did not prevent relapse. Yet a combination of the two has resulted in a full year of recovery without relapse. Why?

We believe one important factor is the establishment of a therapeutic relationship with someone on the treatment team. In R. P.'s case the relationship was with a recovering counselor, and to some extent with the team and the institution. This relationship helped him endure the distress of a prolonged detoxification and a slowly resolving depression. He was then able to ask for help and to direct his efforts to working a program of recovery.

Associated with the therapeutic relationship, but not caused by it, is a change which takes place within the individual. This change contains components of decision and desire, but appears to be beyond our current research capability to define or measure. R. P.'s comment was that he had never had the desire to recover before: "I wanted an easier, softer way and thought I could drink and use and still function."

The role of the Twelve Step programs often appears to be central to the process of helping this change in brain state to occur. There is growing scientific support for the efficacy of the Twelve Step programs in maintaining abstinence and in promoting growth and development. Unfortunately, no professional training provides the knowledge and skill necessary to help dual diagnosis patients utilize AA/NA in working a Twelve Step program of recovery (Chappel 1992). In most cases this knowledge and skill is acquired through the process of personal recovery by the professional or by serendipity, as in my own case.

The apparent resolution of R. P.'s depression and seizure disorder is difficult to understand. The Twelve Step programs have one single purpose: to help the suffering person recover from alcoholism or other addictive disease. They do not treat psychiatric or medical disorders. The fact that some of these disorders resolve with sobriety and working a Twelve Step program of recovery suggests that the alcohol and other drug use either caused or sustained those problems. The evidence from AA's triennial surveys is that recovering alcoholics do experience mental disorders. The percentage of AA members who have sought professional help after sobering up has risen from 40 percent in 1980 to 60 percent in 1989 (Chappel 1993). These figures are just a little lower than the percentages for those who received professional help while actively alcoholic. My personal experience is that psychiatric treatment is much more effective when a patient is also working a program of recovery. AA and NA are fully compatible with mental health and medical treatment. These programs want to be our friends and are very cooperative.

Research involving members of AA/NA will help us understand better how these programs work in helping dual diagnosis patients like R. P. The change in his ASPD has been remarkable. Similar changes are rarely, if ever, seen after a year of psychiatric treatment. As I talk to R. P. and observe him in the community, I am coming to believe that only his tattoos remain as evidence of his former criminal lifestyle. Other evidence makes this apparent transformation easier to believe. At open-speaker meetings of AA/NA I have often heard accounts of similar changes in personality and recovery from severe mental illness. These changes are confirmed by people who know the individuals. Twenty-five years of psychiatric practice has convinced me that we need all the help we can get in treating these serious disorders. The Twelve Step programs provide a resource that we need and cannot afford to overlook.

Wallen and Weiner (1989) have clearly described the barriers that exist in and between the mental health system and the addiction treatment system. A major barrier is the combination of ignorance and negative attitudes that exist in both systems with regard to the other.

Dual diagnosis patients are found in both treatment systems. Their presence challenges us to find more effective ways to provide concomitant treatment both within and between mental health and addiction programs. While we are meeting this challenge we need to begin training professionals during postgraduate and continuing education. Since supervised clinical experience is the most effective way to train professionals, we need to place students with competent, experienced clinician teachers who are comfortable working in multidisciplinary treatment teams with dual diagnosis patients. These clinician teachers are most likely to be found among the members of the American Society of Addiction Medicine (ASAM) and the American Academy of Psychiatrists in Alcoholism and the Addictions (AAPAA).

> *Dual diagnosis patients will always need a little extra. We have found that by providing the extra care in the beginning, long-term success with this population is more likely.*
>
> —*(Evans and Sullivan, 1990, p.153)*

References

Alcoholics Anonymous. 1984. *A.A. member: medications and other drugs.* New York: AA World Services, Inc.

Chappel, J. N. 1991. Educational approaches to prescribing practices and substance abuse. *Journal of Psychoactive Drugs* 23 (4):359-63.

———. 1992. Effective use of Alcoholics Anonymous and Narcotics Anonymous in treating patients. *Psychiatric Annals* 22 (8):409-18.

———. 1993. Long term recovery from alcoholism. *Psychiatric Clinics of North America* 16 (1):177-87.

Evans, K., and J. M. Sullivan. 1990. *Dual diagnosis: Counseling the mentally ill substance abuser.* New York: The Guilford Press.

Galanter, M. 1992. Office management of the substance abuser: The use of learning theory and social networks. In *Substance abuse: A comprehensive textbook,* edited by J. D. Lowinson and R. B. Millman. Baltimore: Williams & Wilkins.

Gorski, T. T. 1989. *Passages through recovery: An action plan for preventing relapse.* New York: Harper & Row.

Kofoed, L., J. Kania, T. Walsh, and R. M. Atkinson. 1986. Outpatient treatment of patients with substance abuse and coexisting disorders. *American Journal of Psychiatry* 143:867-72.

Marlatt, G. A., and J. K. Gordon, eds. 1985. *Relapse prevention: Maintenance strategies in the treatment of addictive behaviors.* New York: Guilford Press.

McLellan, A. T., L. Luborsky, and C. P. O'Brien. 1986. Alcohol and drug abuse treatment in three different populations: Is there improvement and is it predictable? *American Journal of Drug and Alcohol Abuse* 12:101-20. (See also *Psychiatric Clinics of North America* 9:547-62, 1986.)

Morse, R. M., and D. K. Flavin. 1992. The definition of alcoholism. *JAMA* 268 (8):1012-14.

Vaillant, G. E. 1983. *The natural history of alcoholism.* Cambridge, Mass.: Harvard University Press.

Wallen, M. C., and H. D. Weiner. 1989. Impediments to effective treatment of the dually diagnosed patient. *Journal of Psychoactive Drugs* 21 (2):161-68.

Walsh, E. C., R. W. Higson, D. M. Merrigan, et al. 1991. A randomized trial of treatment options for alcohol abusing workers. *New England Journal of Medicine* 325 (11):775-82.

Wolpe, P. R., G. Gorton, R. Serota, and B. Sanford. 1993. Predicting compliance of dual diagnosis inpatients with aftercare treatment. *Hospital and Community Psychiatry* 44 (1):45-49.

Zweben, J. E., and D. E. Smith. 1989. Considerations in using psychotropic medication with dual diagnosis patients in recovery. *Journal of Psychoactive Drugs* 21 (2):221-28.

The family goes through its own typical phases of recovery when one of its members has a dual disorder. Treatment providers will benefit from having (a) conceptual and practical tools for working with the family as it initiates and sustains recovery; (b) guidelines for the family when a member is severely disturbed.

13
Working with the Family

Joan Ellen Zweben, Ph.D.

Introduction

WORKING WITH THE FAMILY OFFERS US AS CLINICIANS unparalleled opportunities to strengthen the support structure for recovery from addiction and to ameliorate the psychiatric disorder. When intact, the family is an enduring residential support system; hence efforts directed at improving its functioning have far-reaching consequences. The term *family* in this chapter is used broadly to encompass the wide variety of constellations we see today. It includes gay or lesbian partners, household members who may have no legal ties, and members of the extended family who are influential though they do not live in the household. It may also include concerned employers, friends, and neighbors. For practical purposes, the clinician should consider including any member of the patient's life who collaborates in the addiction or is likely to play a significant role in the patient's recovery.

At the outset, the clinician must assess the forces in the family which enhance or undermine potential for recovery. This involves an assessment of active substance abuse in other family members, coping patterns which perpetuate addiction, and covert investment in the user's addiction in order to express or obscure other elements of family dysfunction. In the latter case, the addiction may serve as a means of deflecting or masking other family conflicts, avoiding intimacy, or achieving synthetic cohesion around coping with the negative behaviors of the user.

The clinician should also assess the extent of family maladaptation and suffering which results from the user's behavior. Washton (1989) offers a family questionnaire to evaluate this and other dimensions. Family members can be queried about how the substance use affects their emotional state, marital satisfaction, sexuality, financial status, social life, and relationships with others inside and outside the family. They can be asked to describe how they have tried to handle the problem, and what has and has not worked. The clinician should also explore how they view addiction: as a psychological problem, an illness, a sign of a character defect, the result of a poor choice of friends, etc. Clarification of these issues allows the treatment provider to engage the family in treatment and more effectively address their concerns. Swiftly providing practical assistance on a key source of confusion and distress will generate a lot of momentum for the family's ongoing participation in recovery efforts. Usually, such an opportunity will become available while the clinician is reviewing the family's previous efforts to cope with their situation.

> The Stone family arrived in a state of uneasy truce to discuss the alarming behavior of their thirty-two-year-old son James, who had refused to attend. Clara, the divorced mother, had been in recovery herself for three years, and viewed her former husband George's behavior as enabling. George and his girlfriend Pam had allowed James to live in their in-law apartment, but were frightened by recent developments. Smoking marijuana together had been a family ritual for many years, but James was now smoking cocaine and using a wide array of other drugs. His behavior deteriorated markedly during the last year. He was unable to hold a job, had several recent episodes of violent behavior, and heard voices telling him that Pam was bad and that he needed a weapon. He had recently decided that he and George should make a movie. He was firmly convinced that if he only had something meaningful to do with his time, he could clean up without entering a program.
>
> The family therapist confirmed that there were indeed reasons to be concerned about safety and focused the family on how to set firm limits about using or dealing drugs while James lived in the apartment. The therapist outlined the possibility that James's behavior was not solely a function of drug use, and also identified

a residential program capable of handling dual diagnosis patients should he become willing to participate in treatment. The family was assisted in cooperating together to apply their leverage to bring James into treatment. The therapist offered guidelines for appropriate resources for the family to supply and helped the family to set appropriate limits. The therapist addressed the unresolved tensions between the divorced parents only so far as was necessary to maintain their teamwork in this difficult situation.

An important dimension of assessment is to describe the nature and extent of enabling and codependent behavior. *Enabling* refers to behaviors which perpetuate the development and maintenance of addictive behavior; it can take the form of avoiding, shielding, minimizing, attempting to control the addict's behavior, taking over responsibilities, colluding, and rescuing. *Codependency* refers to unhealthy adjustments made by others in relation to the abuser; their attention shifts from their own lives, and they become preoccupied with the activities of the addict. In this way, family functioning comes to be organized around the behavior of the addict as the individuals gradually abandon their own interests and needs. It is the task of the family therapist to restore a healthier equilibrium.

Family members are often confused about what constitutes a desirable balance of engagement and detachment. They may label appropriate forms of support as negative. Unfortunately, the concepts of enabling and codependency are now frequently applied as epithets to any behavior of a significant other when someone else disapproves or are used in a context which discourages appropriate forms of helping. The treatment outcome literature repeatedly confirms the importance of supportive family members; thus our task is to cultivate desirable forms of assistance, not discourage family members from nurturing. This is done through education and work with family dynamics.

Forms of Family Work

Intervention

Intervention is a carefully planned, professionally facilitated, structured confrontation by family members and/or significant others (such as employers and friends) that aims to break through the denial of the user and secure a commitment to a treatment effort. Betty Ford and Governor Ann Richards of Texas are well-known recipients of an intervention. Generally, the intervention counselor works with family members to obtain a clear description of how the behavior of the alcoholic/addict affected them negatively, and helps them communicate that in a loving but firm manner which includes specifying consequences if the problem is not addressed. The immediate goal is to precipitate a commitment to treatment. Chemical dependency programs often provide intervention (often called "pretreatment counseling") as part of their intake services, but intervention can be done by staff of outpatient programs, EAPs, or private practitioners. It is extremely important that interventionists have proper training, as the benefits can be great but the risks may also be high. It is especially important to assess the recipient's potential for suicide or violence, as intervention can temporarily heighten these dangers.

Less systematic forms of intervention are also common. Family members in treatment for their own issues often gain insight about collusive behaviors, particularly if the therapist is informed about addiction. Therapy often results in an unfolding process, in which a significant other gradually discontinues behaviors which support addiction. The addicted family member increasingly experiences negative consequences and eventually seeks help. This frequently occurs when spouses or partners are in treatment and begin to make changes which expose the user to more consequences of his or her addiction.

Family Education

Despite the fact that families may have acquired considerable life experience with addiction, it is usually beneficial to expose them to relatively systematic information, as this clarifies issues, gives them direction, and forms part of the foundation for treatment. Such education should cover alcohol and drug effects in intoxication and withdrawal, long-term effects, and health hazards. It should describe the process of addiction, including a presentation of the disease model, as a way of removing shame and stigma and orienting the family towards constructive action. It should also elaborate on the stages of the recovery process and describe its tasks, with the aim of creating realistic expectations for progress and providing guidelines for appropriate participation.

Family education has also been found to be useful in addressing psychiatric disorders, though it is done more often in family meetings with the treatment provider and less often in group formats. Topics to cover include myths that need to be dispelled; theories about etiology of the relevant disorder; identifying symptoms, especially those of the prodromal period; medication issues (compliance, side effects); relapse warning signs; handling stress in the family; getting appropriate help; and developing a survival plan. These will need to be followed up with process work to help the family apply the information and work through the difficulties encountered.

In educational sessions, as well as throughout treatment, clinicians need to remind family members that those with dual disorders are likely to have a more difficult time establishing abstinence and may have a more tumultuous and discouraging relapse pattern. Unrealistic expectations need to be modified according to what is known about the pattern of chronicity of the psychiatric disorder. Frequently, a relapse in one area is accompanied by a relapse in the other. It is more appropriate to seek to build on the gains of the good periods and reduce the destructive impact of relapses rather than to measure success by an enduring achievement.

Those with a primary identification with the addiction field may have more difficulty with the concept of a chronic relapsing disorder, despite the fact that major mental health disorders and addictive disorders both share that characteristic.

Family Therapy

These sessions provide families with an arena to apply new concepts within their own family and explore how to make changes. Family therapy goes beyond family education to examine unique family functioning, especially the obstacles to change. Typically, improvement in addictive behavior unmasks other issues which need to be addressed. These may be long-term dysfunctional consequences of an addictive disorder (e.g., husband treated as another child in the family because of his inability to take a leadership role due to his drinking) or consequences relatively independent of the addiction but affected by it (such as a wife unable to communicate her needs due to her experiences in her family of origin.) Families may remain in treatment only so long as necessary to obtain a comfortable change in the behavior of the addicted family member, or they may remain to explore the many issues which surface as recovery progresses.

Multifamily Groups

Though not widely available, multifamily groups provide an arena for family members to compare experiences and explore solutions. They differ from Al-Anon groups in that they provide an arena for interaction and discussion between participants. They may exclude addicted family members in order to permit more freedom in venting of feelings without concern for the negative impact on a vulnerable family member.

Recovery-Oriented Family Therapy

Family work requires certain tasks according to the stages the identified patient is moving through in recovery. Each stage brings new issues, benefits, and challenges. As therapists, we need to make our activity flexible and offer a range of skills to shift accordingly (Zweben 1986, 1989). In this model, the addictive behavior of the identified patient needs to be addressed in its own right, and the family issues handled concurrently. A firm grounding in addiction is needed, because the family may be ready to tackle issues the recovering person is too vulnerable to face, or the recovering person may outpace the family's ability to adapt. A keen sense of timing is necessary to facilitate a transition that adequately meets the needs of all participants. A variety of family therapy approaches have been found to be useful, provided they are flexible and pragmatic in addressing recovery tasks.

A systemic approach which defines presenting problems solely in terms of family dynamics will be of very limited use when addressing the complex problems of the dual diagnosis patient and family. Similarly, approaches which dictate that all family members must always be seen together will reduce options at crucial junctures.

Families with a schizophrenic family member need to be advised that the emotional climate in the family can exert a strong influence on the stability of the patient. Patients returning to families that have a high level of stress and tension (referred to as "high-expressed emotion") have significantly higher relapse rates than those in which the emotional environment is more tolerant and supportive. Severely disturbed patients are even less able than others to tolerate critical and intrusive behavior, demandingness, confrontation, and challenge. Low levels of environmental stimulation, mild-mannered friendliness, and calm are important qualities to cultivate. Time-outs are useful. This does not mean that communication should be shut down; indeed, remoteness or disinterest are also undesirable. Communication patterns emphasizing active listening, acknowledging positive behavior, making positive requests, and expressing negative feelings in a calm and matter-of-fact manner are areas in which the family therapist can provide skill development. Many of these principles are useful for the patient in early recovery (Lieberman et al. 1987; Leff 1989).

Working with the Family of a Patient Who Is Actively Using

It is quite common for family members of dual diagnosis patients to contact treatment facilities in despair about their ability to engage the user in treatment. Psychiatric problems enormously complicate the task of finding an appropriate treatment program and eliciting a commitment on the part of the patient. Assuming a viable treatment option has been identified, the family therapist can help the family handle its own stress and can also work to increase the leverage applied to bringing the addicted member into treatment. Family members are often confused about what constitutes appropriate forms of pressure, having repeatedly heard that the addict "must want to do it for himself." They need to be reminded that alcohol and drug users have impaired judgment and frequently cannot make good decisions for themselves, and that psychiatric disturbances compound the problem. The more severely disturbed can be especially difficult because of an impaired ability to process information that results from their thought or mood disorder. Coordinated efforts between family members, social services, and/or the criminal justice system may be of value in precipitating a treatment attempt.

The family therapist can assist in distinguishing between appropriate forms of pressure and excessive attempts to control (alas, there is no simple formula for this) and can provide support during what may be an extended process. Dual diagnosis patients may be very difficult to engage; it is useful to remember that it may take considerable time between recognition of a problem and mobilizing to address it, even if addiction is the only issue. Appropriate expectations help lighten frustration and despair.

Entering Treatment and Establishing Abstinence

Once the patient has agreed to enter treatment, it is crucial that we engage the family as rapidly as possible. Including them immediately in the intake process is highly desirable; if they conclude that the treatment providers will take the problem off their hands, the therapist's ability to engage them is markedly reduced. Family participation from the outset is preferable, as it has been shown to influence retention in treatment significantly—a key factor in producing a positive outcome.

Patients can be informed that the agency routinely includes family members as part of the intake process in order to get a fuller perspective on the patient and to clarify how the family can be of help (as well as to help the family reduce its own stress). Even defiant patients may feel guilty about subjecting their loved ones to distress and are often relieved at the prospect of someone offering help to them. If the patient appears to have difficulty recruiting family members, the therapist should move quickly to make the contacts directly, as it is usually unproductive to leave the patient in a conflict position between the agency and the family.

Family members can be asked to come to an interview to give their perspective, particularly if we stress the need to have their help in understanding the patient and his or her needs. Many welcome the chance to vent their frustration and anger and may initially be less willing to provide other kinds of help. The therapist can present himself or herself as a coach who can help the family avoid certain errors families often make in their efforts to cope with a difficult situation. In many cases, it is preferable to postpone confronting the family with their own dysfunction, as this often results in their feeling blamed and refusing to participate further. The concept that each family member has his or her own recovery to address is something that families often appreciate more once work is partially underway. Instead, the therapist can look for a way to supply practical assistance or relief from a key issue of distress and establish a therapeutic alliance by doing something beneficial for the family.

Janice came for consultation with the therapist about her thirty-year-old daughter Sally, who had a drinking problem. She was concerned about Sally's well-being, and also about her ability to care for her two young children. Janice described several relatives as alcoholic. In the interview with Sally, it emerged that she had a ten-year history of panic attacks, for which a physician had given her Valium. She thought that much of her current anxiety problems were due to the fact that her husband, who worked nights, had begun staying out all night. She says he does not drink, and she is sure there is no other woman. He says he stays with friends, but does not call, and she has no idea how to reach him.

Sally refused to let the therapist contact the physician who was prescribing the Valium and was very sensitive to her mother's encroachment on her autonomy. She had begun attending initiated Twelve Step meetings, felt they were useful, and pleaded to be allowed to address her problem in that way. The therapist suggested the family give her some room, but act on signs of trouble. They were encouraged to support treatment efforts and Twelve Step meeting attendance (e.g., by taking care of their grandchildren during this time) and to avoid responding to Sally's emotional upset by trying to control her.

All went well for a while, but the family returned two years later. It emerged that the husband was now using both heroin and cocaine; his behavior had totally deteriorated. Sally's drinking had escalated, and again there was reason to be concerned about her ability to care for her two children. Sally had left her husband and moved to her parents' house with both children, thoroughly disrupting Janice's efforts to complete her professional degree. Sally sought treatment but refused to allow her parents to participate. At this point the therapist recommended clear contracting around household responsibilities and treatment activities. Inasmuch as the grandparents were providing food, shelter, and care for Sally and the children, it was appropriate for them to be included in the treatment plan. Sally retained her ability to participate in many treatment activities alone, but there were also regular family sessions. The chemical dependency program was informed about her prescription for Valium, and appropriate collaboration began between these treatment providers.

The initial treatment contract should describe the involvement and commitments from the significant others, and releases of information should be obtained to permit all relevant parties to communicate with each other. We need to prepare family members for what to expect through the withdrawal stage and early abstinence period. They need to appreciate that the behaviors at this stage may be very similar to the period while the addict was using: irritability, sleep disturbance, difficulty fulfilling responsibilities, keeping specific time commitments, etc. Urinalysis can provide a means of documenting that the patient is indeed staying clean and can protect him or her from the discouraging experience of being doubted by family members while in fact the patient is struggling successfully. If this is desirable, patients sign appropriate releases of information to notify family members in the event of a positive screen, and can then use urinalysis to demonstrate their success and restore their credibility. Such objective measures often provide enormous relief in a situation where trust is a highly charged issue.

We also need to coach family members so they do not underestimate the vulnerability of the newly abstinent member. Once the patient has been abstinent more than a month, he or she may appear dramatically better, and family members may expect a level of responsibility that is premature or try to approach conflict areas the patient is not ready to handle. During this time, the therapist can provide an alternate safety valve for family members to express feelings, as the patient may not be able to respond constructively. In general, serious efforts at conflict resolution need to be postponed until abstinence is well consolidated. Conflictual topics will be raised at all stages, but when the patient is newly abstinent, the therapist needs to find ways to help the family express or contain the feelings without exacerbating stress to the degree that is overwhelming. Abstinence is the foundation of much therapeutic progress, and the family therapist must gauge what the addict can tolerate without giving undue emphasis to any one person's needs.

A perspective on the time frame needed to build a solid recovery is also important. Family members may resent the extensive time commitment required by Twelve Step program attendance in the early stages of recovery. They are often distressed by the absence of the addicted family member over the years and expect recovery to restore much-needed participation in family activities. Some express bitter disappointment; first they lost the person to drug and alcohol use; then they lose to the Twelve Step programs. As family therapists we can provide support, direction, and encouragement; we can explain the benefits of a solid recovery to the family in the long run and give them a realistic view of the time investment needed to achieve this.

An understanding of the need for the patient to abstain from all intoxicants is essential for family members, who might otherwise undermine recovery through their naivete. For example, it is still common for families of cocaine users to fail to understand the importance of eliminating alcohol. "But he never had a drinking problem before he found cocaine," they protest. For many, abstinence would be conspicuous and uncomfortable at occasions such as family celebrations. We need to inform family members carefully that there are at least two problems with trying to abstain from one drug while continuing to use others. First, there is a heightened possibility of substituting one drug for another—if not relatively quickly, then perhaps over a period of several years. Second, and much more common, is the repeatedly observed phenomenon that use of another intoxicant often precedes relapse to the primary drug of abuse. This may not occur immediately; it may be delayed several months. For example, the recovering cocaine user who has a glass of wine at a party, then another three weeks later, may find himself using cocaine again six weeks after that. Because of the time intervals, the connection may be missed. Addicts and family members need to be informed that the use of another intoxicant greatly increases the risk of relapse (as studies increasingly confirm). It is not necessary for the patient or family members to endorse the disease model in order to accept this; cooperation can be secured on the grounds that systematic observation suggests that the success formula is abstinence from all drugs. For dual diagnosis patients on medication, it is important to clarify the difference between psychoactive drugs and medication, and also to clarify that compliance with medication regimens is quite compatible with Twelve Step program participation (Alcoholics Anonymous 1984).

For the dual diagnosis patient, there is the additional factor that even small amounts of alcohol or illicit drugs can worsen the psychiatric disorder. In addition, there is a great possibility that these drugs will interfere with the action of the medications given for the primary disorder. Family members need to be sensitized to the fact that even recreational use of small amounts of alcohol or drugs can have adverse effects and thus must be taken seriously. For example, marijuana is often an attractive drug to schizophrenics, who report that smoking it makes them feel better. However, close observation (and some empirical studies) indicate that the patient tends to decompensate over the next day or two, and greater frequency of crises and rehospitalization has been reported in the group that smokes marijuana. The self-medication question is complex; we need to educate family members to look for consequences which develop over time so they do not minimize the importance of what they see as relatively casual drug use. Studies of chronically mentally ill patients indicate that those who abused drugs and alcohol were less able to maintain good community adjustment (regular meals, adequate finances, stable housing, regular activities); showed greater hostility, suicidality and speech disorganization; and had poorer medication compliance. Needless to say, they were much more likely to be rehospitalized (Zweben 1992).

The presence of alcohol (or other intoxicants) in the home is another issue which usually generates considerable feeling. Family members often argue that alcohol is legal and readily obtainable; hence there is little reason to ask for it to be removed from the home. The family therapist may wish to take a different position: Everyone needs a safe place, and if that place is not your home, where is it? When dealing with addiction, introducing a delay can make all the difference between getting through a difficult moment without using drugs and initiating a major relapse. It is also quite enlightening for family members to accompany the addict on the journey by also abstaining from alcohol and drugs. Many eventually conclude this is a profoundly symbolic form of support that is not always obvious at first glance. It sensitizes them to the degree to which alcohol use, at least, is embedded in our culture; it is common for family members who do not meet criteria for addiction to notice the loss when they abstain. It also protects the alcoholic/addict from the behavioral cues, smells, etc., of someone else who is drinking.

It is important for the therapist not to lock into a power struggle over this issue, as it will have considerable value as a catalyst even if compliance takes a long time to secure. It is difficult for family members to maintain the position that they are not alcoholics or addicts if they cannot eliminate intoxicants from their lifestyle for a period of time. Resistance is often based on complex issues which discussion can bring into sharp relief; a clinical stance that promotes exploration is more valuable than rigid rule-setting.

Ongoing Recovery Issues

Many issues emerge as recovery progresses, and families differ widely in the time frame within which they are able to address important issues productively. In early recovery, the nonaddicted spouse often needs to be encouraged to disengage and attend to his or her own needs. Emphasis is often on boundaries and differentiation, with the focus on achieving a comfortable "holding pattern" rather than working on relationship issues. Once some stability has been achieved, the couple may be ready to work on negotiation skills regarding issues that are relatively simple and not loaded. This is often the beginning of a transition in roles, as the addicted family member is able to take a more mature role in the family. As recovery progresses, we can focus on reintegrating the couple in increasingly important ways.

Conflict management is a major area in which the therapist's skill and timing are crucial. The family needs to tolerate unresolved conflict without falling back on previous coping patterns, such as using or drinking. They need to learn skills such as disconnecting from anger rather than escalating it, particularly if domestic violence has been a part of the alcohol/drug use picture. The therapist should never assume that abstinence alone will eliminate the potential for domestic violence, but rather should presume that this behavior may have a momentum of its own and assess it carefully (Gorney 1989). Strategies are similar in principle to those used with addiction: learn early warning signs and address them, develop a strategy for de-escalation, be clear about when it is necessary to call for help, and identify sources of help. Later in recovery it may become possible to deal with anger from the past and come to a position which makes it possible to move on.

It is typical for families to need considerable time before they are ready to address issues of intimacy. When alcohol and drugs played a key role in a couple's sexual relationship, difficulties which arise once they are abstinent will have to be addressed. Childhood sexual abuse may add an additional dimension to this difficulty. Mates may also be inhibited about expressing affection when they can't rely on intoxicants. In general, as family therapists we must try to assure that key benefits of the active use period are incorporated into the abstinence phase when possible.

Discussing what would be constructive in the event of relapse is another topic for family sessions. It is important that they understand that addiction, like many psychiatric disorders, is typically a chronic, relapsing condition and that if it does occur, it is important they neither minimize nor overreact. They need to be prepared for the possibility, without covertly giving permission to the addict. In periods of calm, it can be helpful for family members to ask the addict what would be useful should they notice signs of alarm. Family members are frequently attuned to early warning signs but are confused about how to communicate their concern. Discussing what kinds of responses would be useful, and what would be offensive, can build a sense of teamwork around the recovery process without inviting a return to the codependent behaviors which did not prove useful in the past. In the event relapse does occur, family members may be bitterly disappointed, because in the course of treatment their hopes had risen beyond what they had previously thought possible. In such cases, the therapist may consider meeting with them for a few sessions without the addict present in order to maximize freedom of expression while restoring a healthy perspective.

Al-Anon

Al-Anon provides an arena for family members to do ongoing work on extricating themselves from unhealthy adaptations to the addict and attending to their own emotional, physical, and spiritual needs. The three Cs provide an orientation: You didn't cause your loved one's addiction, you can't control it, and you can't cure it. Exploring these themes provides an understanding of how to detach with love. It also supplies an opportunity for developing a support system. It is important to appreciate that although Al-Anon is a major resource for families, its "separate but equal" strategy does not provide an arena to work on family dynamics or family system issues. Although engagement in Al-Anon may produce a highly successful family outcome, this is not its focus or goal; thus the addition of family therapy may accelerate improvement in family functioning as a whole.

Other Considerations

Many practical obstacles need to be addressed in dealing with families. Providing child care goes a long way towards reducing obstacles to participation in treatment, particularly for women. Federal guidelines increasingly permit funds to be used for child care, and in some cases even extend the opportunity for women to bring their children with them into residential treatment. As a result, access to treatment has been improved for those who have historically been underserved. Encouraging other kinds of family support is also important. It is especially necessary for single parents to strengthen their network, which programs should help facilitate when possible. Some innovative programs do an assessment of the children, spouses, and partners of those in treatment and attempt to provide some help to them through a variety of activities and services. These efforts not only improve quality of life, but reduce the intergenerational transmission of addiction.

Conclusion

There are a multitude of ways in which the fields of addiction treatment and mental health need to integrate family work into treatment. From the point of recognizing the problem through the many stages of addressing it, family members have an ability to enhance or undermine all other efforts. Shaping their influence can immensely improve the efficacy of our own endeavors. It is to be hoped that future training of professionals, particularly family therapists skilled at addressing addiction, will supply increasing resources to meet these needs.

References

Alcoholics Anonymous. 1984. *A.A. member: Medications and other drugs.* New York: Alcoholics Anonymous World Services, Inc.

Gorney, B. 1989. Domestic violence and substance abuse. *Journal of Psychoactive Drugs* 21 (2):229-38.

Leff, J. 1989. Family factors in schizophrenia. *Psychiatric Annals* 19 (10):542-47.

Lieberman, R. P., V. Cardin, C. W. McGill, I. R. H. Falloon, and C. D. Evans. 1987. Behavioral family management of schizophrenia: Clinical outcome and costs. *Psychiatric Annals* 17 (9):610-19.

Washton, A. 1989. *Cocaine addiction: Treatment, recovery, and relapse prevention.* New York: W. W. Norton.

Zweben, J. E. 1986. Recovery-oriented psychotherapy. *Journal of Substance Abuse Treatment* 3 (4):255-62. Revised February 28, 1993.

———. 1989. Recovery-oriented psychotherapy: Patient resistances and therapist dilemmas. *The Journal of Substance Abuse Treatment* 6 (2):123-32.

———. 1992. Issues in the treatment of the dual diagnosis patient. In *The chemically dependent: Phases of treatment and recovery,* edited by B. Wallace. New York: Brunner/Mazel.

Delivery

Case management is an essential component of care for the individual with a dual diagnosis. It allows the treatment provider to focus on practical interventions in the client's environment.

14
Case Management

Douglas L. Noordsy, M.D.
Robert E. Drake, M.D., Ph.D.

CASE MANAGEMENT HAS BECOME THE DOMINANT FORM of practice for the community care of individuals with severe mental disorders and is now also used in the care of individuals with addictions. Because models of case management differ widely (Harris and Bergman 1993), we need to be specific about the model. In this chapter we will present guidelines for case management in the Continuous Treatment Team (CTT) model (Drake et al. 1990). CTT was developed specifically for persons with a dual diagnosis of severe mental disorder and substance use disorder. Initial research indicates that the CTT approach enables most individuals with chronic mental illness to achieve stable remission from addiction (Drake, McHugo, et al. 1993).

THE CONTINUOUS TREATMENT TEAM (CTT) APPROACH

New Hampshire's CTTs combine the principles of intensive case management from the Training in Community Living model (Test 1992) with emerging concepts of dual diagnosis treatment (Carey 1989; Drake, Bartels, et al. 1993; Minkoff and Drake 1991; Osher and Kofoed 1989). Rather than putting the burden of integrating systems and interventions on the client, CTTs ensure the continuity of mental health and addiction treatments across services and over time. Case managers integrate addiction interventions into an array of direct services that include crisis intervention, housing support, skills training, vocational rehabilitation, supportive psychotherapy, medication monitoring, and family psychoeducation.

CTTs provide active outreach and community-based services. The client's home, as well as restaurants, public parks, and community centers, becomes a clinical site. Meetings often occur while assisting the client with practical tasks, such as transportation to appointments. Meeting in natural surroundings emphasizes the client's strengths, abilities, and functional roles rather than sick roles. Working with clients in these settings enhances the case manager's awareness of their life circumstances, facilitates involving social network members, increases the ability to tailor treatment to client-specific needs, and reduces concerns about the transfer of skills from the clinic to the community.

The team shares responsibility for each client and serves as a fixed point of responsibility for a relatively small set of clients. Caseload should be inversely proportional to the acuity and severity of the client's needs. On a typical CTT, four to six clinicians, including a half-time psychiatrist, work with approximately fifty clients.

A team leader coordinates scheduling, but treatment planning, case reviews, and supervision are done as a team. Frequent team meetings allow team members to coordinate interventions and to support each other. The team approach has numerous advantages (Boyer and Bond 1992). Through shared responsibility, each clinician's areas of expertise can be brought to bear on a particular client. Clinicians can cover for each other during vacations or illnesses and work in pairs when appropriate. They share the stress of demanding clients and unexpected crises. Using a shared-caseload approach reduces burnout among clinicians. Clients rapidly learn that they can contact any team member rather than one individual and appreciate the opportunity for greater access. Difficult relationships between a particular clinician and a particular client can be mitigated by the flexibility to shift and share responsibility. In practice, about one-third of the clients continue to relate to several clinicians over time, while others develop a stronger relationship with one clinician but continue to receive some services from others.

Working as a team also facilitates the development of dual diagnosis expertise among all team members. Learning occurs through regular team supervision, sharing perspectives and literature in team meetings, cross-training among team members, and the daily experience of struggling as an interdisciplinary staff with a recurrent set of problems. For example, case managers use the team to discuss clinical dilemmas such as balancing support with avoidance of enabling.

Case managers in CTT come from a variety of backgrounds: addictions counselor, social worker, psychologist, rehabilitation counselor, or mental health specialist. Case managers typically have a bachelor's or master's degree in a human services field. CTTs are specifically designed to be interdisciplinary and to allow for cross-training through teamwork. Each team generally includes a psychiatrist, a nurse, one or more addictions specialists, and one or more individuals with a mental health background.

Stages of Addiction Treatment

Integrated treatment for people with dual disorders is a process that takes place over years rather than weeks or months (Drake, Bartels, et al. 1993). Over time many periods of substance use, abstinence, compliance with treatment, and noncompliance occur. These fluctuations are expected when treating chronic, relapsing illnesses. The case manager uses them as shared opportunities to discuss addiction and recovery. The CTT represents a long-term commitment to providing continuity and facilitating recovery over years. For clients who have histories of many failures and difficulty engaging in treatment, this approach may be particularly effective. Once clients are engaged, the consistency and continuity of case management support them through other stages of substance abuse and mental health treatments.

Addiction treatment for persons with severe mental disorders has been conceptualized as occurring in four stages: engagement, persuasion, active treatment, and relapse prevention (Drake, Bartels, et al. 1993; Osher and Kofoed 1989). These stages refer to developing a trusting relationship (engagement), helping the client to perceive and accept the problem of substance abuse (persuasion), achieving stable abstinence (active treatment), and maintaining abstinence (relapse prevention). In practice, progress is highly individual and variable.

Engagement usually begins with helping a client to meet an immediate need such as finding food or shelter. A small client loan fund facilitates the process before work or benefits begin and serves as a powerful engagement tool. As soon as a relationship is established, the case manager can assess needs and strengths and develop a treatment plan.

Persuasion is a motivational stage for clients who are not yet ready for active treatment. The case manager poses questions that encourage clients to consider their use of alcohol and other drugs, the discrepancies between their goals and current behaviors, and their treatment alternatives. If they do not feel judged, most clients will soon share their ambivalence about substance use with the case manager. During engagement and persuasion, we access resources appropriate to the client's needs and abilities without excessive concern about enabling. We assume that hopelessness and boredom are reinforcers of addictive behaviors, while work and supported housing limit the client's ability to use alcohol and other drugs. Many clients respond to improvements in their circumstances with optimism, hope, and a willingness to work toward new goals. Groups are also strongly encouraged during this stage.

When the client is motivated for active treatment, case managers in CTT provide behavioral therapy (Monti et al. 1989), community reinforcement (Higgins et al. 1993), and supportive counseling to help clients develop the skills necessary to attain and maintain abstinence. They also link clients to self-help groups by preparing them for the experience, attending meetings with them, and discussing the experience afterwards (Noordsy et al., under review). The case management relationship is always used to reinforce goals behaviorally. Taking clients out for a treat when they achieve success can reinforce appropriate behaviors and help clients learn to celebrate without using substances. Keeping contacts brief and businesslike when a client presents intoxicated avoids irrational conversations, erratic behavior, and inadvertent reinforcement of use. The case manager also offers to review the episode when the client is sober and able to benefit from the discussion.

In relapse prevention, the case manager and client focus on risk factors for return to addictive behaviors. Clients learn to recognize early warning signs of relapse and to use medication, social support, and clinician contact to prevent further progression. Stress management techniques may also be useful in this process.

Individual Counseling

Behavioral approaches to counseling, which are demonstrably effective with clients who have severe mental disorders, are less stimulating and confrontational than other approaches to addiction treatment. They address the development of skills that dually diagnosed clients often lack. Case managers train clients in assertiveness, drink or drug refusal skills, and managing thoughts about alcohol or other drug use. For example, the client learns to use social contact, music, or exercise as substitutes for alcohol or drug use. The client also learns to use mental imaging to get beyond cravings for substances and to change positive images of alcohol or drug effects into images of hangovers, withdrawal, psychotic symptom exacerbation, and other negative consequences.

Supportive counseling includes help in labeling and managing emotional experiences that may have been buried by addiction. Many clients need help with concrete situations, such as learning how to set limits on substance-abusing friends or managing relationships with family members or significant others. The case manager can help clients to develop strategies to resolve loneliness or sexual indiscretion. As clients are guided through recovery, they can be helped to appreciate the gradual improvements in their mental health and stability that come with sobriety and to gain a greater sense of responsibility for managing their illnesses.

Case One

Don was a twenty-year-old man with diagnoses of bipolar disorder and alcoholism. He suffered severe symptoms of mania and psychosis throughout his adolescence. He was referred to the CTT after an extended hospitalization. In the early stages of skills training, he learned to manage his mental illness with medications and support. Meanwhile, individual counseling focused on the consequences he had suffered from alcoholism. Since Don reported using alcohol to facilitate social contact, he was trained to develop social skills for friendship and dating. During this time Don achieved full-time employment and established an intimate relationship with a nondrinking woman. The individual counseling addressed the development of social skills for an effective relationship and for parenting his girlfriend's children. His alcohol use decreased dramatically.

Following a series of stressors, however, Don left his girlfriend, quit his job, and began using alcohol heavily again. He rapidly relapsed to active mania, medication noncompliance, and rehospitalization. During the hospitalization the team visited him regularly. Manic symptoms led to variable commitment to his relationship and rapidly changing plans for the future. Don was advised to delay major decisions until his thoughts were clearer, and one of the team members met regularly with Don's girlfriend to help her understand the symptoms of his illness and his erratic statements.

As Don's mania remitted, the team assisted him in returning to the community and regaining employment. The individual counseling focused on the relationship with his girlfriend as well as maintaining abstinence and medication compliance. Couples counseling was used to solidify his relationship with his girlfriend and to further her ability to support his abstinence and treatment compliance.

Crisis Intervention

Response to crises is often part of building trust and engagement. Crises are also the time when carefully developed treatment plans fall apart. We find that it is most effective, and generally less work in the long run, for a team member to drop everything whenever possible and promptly see the client who is in crisis. Rapid response usually leads to a resolution that is consistent with the treatment plan. Emergency coverage at all hours is provided by an extended treatment team that is familiar with each client's treatment plan. A CTT member is always available to consult with the coverage team and to make direct emergency contact when necessary. Clients who receive CTT soon stabilize and have few unanticipated crises.

Case Two

Larry was a thirty-three-year-old man with schizophrenia and polysubstance addiction. He was bothered by loneliness at night and on weekends, and frequently called the emergency coverage system with an urgent request to speak to a CTT member. During these episodes, he was usually intoxicated, rambling, and irrational. At other times, he typically declined contact, saying he no longer needed it. The team affirmed a strategy of keeping contacts brief if he called intoxicated, but being generous with time and encouragement if he called before using substances. The team explained to Larry this plan to support his attempts toward sobriety.

Within a month of instituting this plan, Larry began to call the emergency systems at local hospitals and to request admission for suicidal ideation. The inpatient teams soon became frustrated with his frequent calls, admissions, and demands to be discharged within a few days. The CTT met with Larry and the inpatient teams at each hospital to discuss coordination of admissions in conjunction with the treatment plan. The hospital teams were enlisted in responding to Larry in a manner consistent with the CTT approach. Over a period of six months, Larry's addictive behaviors decreased and he formed a relationship with a woman. He continued to report urges to seek hospitalization, but now found that he was able to resolve these on his own or with his girlfriend's support.

Working with Families

Case managers reach out to families to educate them about addiction, chronic mental illness, negative symptoms, medications, and rehabilitation. Families have frequently felt frustrated and confused as they have attempted to help their loved ones, but they can serve as powerful reinforcers of treatment goals if enlisted to participate as part of the treatment team (Higgins et al. 1993). Regular family meetings, usually in the home with the client present, are routine practice for CTTs, and some CTTs also organize multiple-family groups to discuss common issues (McFarlane 1990).

Case Three

Jerry was a thirty-five-year-old man with schizophrenia and alcoholism. He was well engaged, but had little interest in changing his drinking despite years of effort at persuasion. Jerry showed little concern that his drinking was leading to significant medical consequences. He reported feeling criticized by his family for his failure to make anything of himself, while his family reported frustration over his drinking. The CTT was concerned that some family routines may have been inadvertently reinforcing his drinking.

A family meeting was held at Jerry's parents' home. After a discussion of each person's concerns, the team presented a plan to use contingent daily contact with team or family members to support Jerry's movement toward sobriety. Each person agreed to spend a half-hour or more with Jerry on an assigned day, depending on his sobriety at the scheduled time and his report of sobriety over the previous day. If Jerry was not sober, the person expressed hope that they could meet the following week, mentioned possible activities, and left. Activities involved recreation, social outings, and community events. After several months, Jerry's drinking decreased, and his family now expresses relief at having something they can do that is helpful.

Group Interventions

CTTs provide addiction treatment groups that are tailored to the needs of the individual with severe mental illness (Noordsy and Fox 1991). The groups are co-led by two team members, including at least one case manager. Case managers encourage resistant clients to attend by including groups in treatment plans, providing transportation, or holding the group in nearby community settings. They sometimes arrange compulsory attendance as a condition of hospital discharge, probation, or parole.

Group sessions often begin with a review of each member's use of alcohol and other drugs over the previous week. As a member discusses a recent period of intoxication, the rest of the group helps to identify antecedents and consequences of use. This discussion must be nonjudgmental so that members feel safe in reporting their use honestly. Leaders start the discussion and encourage all members to contribute to this process but attempt to get members to assume responsibility for the group over time.

Group leaders field questions and provide brief educational vignettes on addiction, the effects of various substances on physical and mental health, and the interactions between drugs and medications. Dual-diagnosis groups are not confrontational. They assume instead that genuine acknowledgment of a problem occurs over time in the context of peer-group support and education. Therefore, group leaders limit the level of affect, monitor psychotic behaviors, facilitate peer interactions and feedback about substance use, and maintain the group's focus on alcohol and other drugs.

Behavioral principles of addiction treatment (Monti et al. 1989) are used in treatment groups as well. The group setting is ideally suited for the development and practice of social skills (Liberman 1992). When a client reports a recent problem that led to craving or substance use, the group works to identify coping skills which could have helped the situation. The leaders suggest coping strategies and responses and set up role-playing exercises to solidify skill acquisition. Many repetitions may be required for individuals with substantial skill deficits.

Case Four

Cheryl, a thirty-three-year-old with schizoaffective disorder and polysubstance addiction who had been abstinent for two months, complained in group that she no longer had any friends. She spoke longingly of past sexual activity when intoxicated and complained of her current inability to meet people. Her complaints of being disliked by others seemed to stem in part from hallucinatory experiences. Bill and Jeff, who were also in group that day, offered that they felt able to make friends. The leaders acknowledged their expertise by exploring where they met people and how they made friends.

A role-play exercise was organized to practice meeting new people. First, a leader played a stranger, while Bill demonstrated his skill at introducing himself and striking up a conversation. The leaders praised specific aspects of his successful outreach, and the group discussed other skills for starting and maintaining conversations. Next, Cheryl practiced these skills with a leader and then with Jeff. After each attempt Cheryl was praised for her successful use of particular skills and given pointers for developing further skills.

Boundary Limitations

Case management frequently crosses boundaries that traditional forms of therapy or counseling would not, such as meeting in the client's home, accepting a cup of tea, giving clients a ride, meeting their children, or talking with their employers. Clients with severe mental disorders may require training in basic functions such as washing their hair, shopping, or managing their money. Case management emphasizes attention to practical life issues, recognition of reinforcers and inhibitors of behaviors, and awareness of risk factors and warning signs of relapse. Once established, the case management relationship often carries powerful persuasive influence. However, just as boundaries were created to avoid abuses in therapeutic relationships, the clinician practicing case management must be particularly careful to avoid such abuses while developing a close working alliance.

Case management practice is so flexible that drafting a set of rigid regulations would be difficult. Perhaps the most important principle is that the goals of the relationship be kept in mind at all times. Case management uses a human relationship to help someone with a disability to maximize his or her adjustment in life. The relationship is built on trust. The case manager should never do anything that violates that trust. When the case manager participates in something with which the client disagrees, such as petitioning for involuntary hospitalization or guardianship, the action should be thoroughly explained to the client in a manner that communicates respect, caring, and concern. The client may disagree with an action at the moment but come to trust the case manager's judgment and vigilance.

Case management includes many gray areas, such as nonsexual touching and revealing details of the clinician's personal life. These activities should occur only when they will benefit the client and should not be driven by the clinician's needs. For example, teaching clients grooming skills without touching them may be difficult, yet touching to resolve the clinician's need to feel close may be overwhelming for the client. Boundary decisions will vary by client diagnosis and characteristics; the socially withdrawn individual with schizophrenia will require different boundaries from the gregarious individual with bipolar disorder and past sexual abuse.

Some behaviors are clearly outside of appropriate boundaries for case managers and harmful to clients. These include sexual contact, taking or using a client's money or property for personal gain, employing a client for personal gain, and using a client for emotional support. These activities are clearly to be avoided. Case managers who find themselves in more ambiguous areas should use the treatment team for assessment and guidance as to appropriate behaviors. Often other team members can clarify issues by adding another perspective.

Case Five

Joan was a twenty-nine-year-old woman with diagnoses of schizophrenia, alcoholism, and amphetamine addiction. She was frequently noncompliant with prescribed antipsychotic medication. She consistently denied current drug and alcohol use, while reporting it in the recent past. She presented to the mental health center receptionist one day complaining that her payee was stealing her money. When her case manager and a teammate came to see her, she was agitated and paranoid. As they attempted to reassure her, the client struck both case managers. The case managers protected themselves but did not strike back or attempt to restrain her as she fled the building.

The team met and agreed that the client should experience the natural consequences of her actions, so assault charges were filed with the local police. Primary responsibility for her day-to-day care was shifted to another team member to reduce the affective intensity and to give the assaulted case managers a break. She was ultimately found guilty of assault and ordered to perform fifty hours of community service.

Joan began to complain of her irritability to the team psychiatrist and agreed to have her antipsychotic dose increased for the first time in years. She soon began to explore with the case manager and psychiatrist the consequences of her alcohol and drug use. She rapidly developed an abstinence goal and made several attempts to achieve it over the next month before finally succeeding. She maintained medication compliance and reported abstinence from drugs and alcohol for several months. She became quite pleasant to work with, apologized to her former case manager, and started to develop vocational goals as a result of her community service experience.

Conclusions

Case management in the CTT model permits clinicians to share in the daily practical struggles of the individual with dual disorders, to demonstrate compassion and understanding, and to help the person work toward his or her goals. The case manager-client relationship provides the person with co-occurring addiction and mental illness a unique opportunity to develop hope, motivation for abstinence, and the skills and supports needed to attain and sustain an abstinent lifestyle.

References

Boyer S. L., and G. R. Bond. 1992. A comparison of assertive community treatment and traditional case management on burnout and job satisfaction. *Outlook* (July-August-September).

Carey, K. B. 1989. Emerging treatment guidelines for mentally ill chemical abusers. *Hospital and Community Psychiatry* 40:341-42.

Drake, R. E., S. J. Bartels, G. B. Teague, D. L. Noordsy, and R. E. Clark. 1993. Treatment of substance abuse in severely mentally ill patients. *Journal of Nervous and Mental Disease* 181:606-11.

Drake, R. E., G. H. McHugo, and D. L. Noordsy. 1993. Treatment of alcoholism among schizophrenic outpatients: 4-year outcomes. *American Journal of Psychiatry* 150:328-29.

Drake, R. E., G. B. Teague, and S. R. Warren. 1990. New Hampshire's program for people dually diagnosed with severe mental illness and substance use disorder. *Addiction and Recovery* 10:35-39.

Harris, M., and H. Bergman, eds. 1993. *Case management for mentally ill patients: Theory and practice.* Langhorne, Pa.: Harwood Academic Publishers.

Higgins, S. T., A. J. Budney, W. K. Bickel, J. R. Hughes, F. Foerg, and G. Badger. 1993. Achieving cocaine abstinence with a behavioral approach. *American Journal of Psychiatry* 150:763-69.

Liberman, R. P., ed. 1992. *Handbook of psychiatric rehabilitation.* Boston: Allyn & Bacon.

McFarlane, W. R. 1990. Multiple family groups and the treatment of schizophrenia. In *Handbook of schizophrenia,* edited by H. Nasrallah. Amsterdam: Elsevier Science Publishers.

Minkoff, K., and R. E. Drake, eds. 1991. *Dual diagnosis of major mental illness and substance disorder.* San Francisco: Jossey-Bass.

Monti, P. M., D. B. Abrams, R. M. Dadden, and N. L. Cooney. 1989. *Treating alcohol dependence: A coping skills training guide.* New York: The Guilford Press.

Noordsy, D. L., and L. Fox. 1991. Group intervention techniques for people with dual disorders. *Psychosocial Rehabilitation Journal* 15:67-78.

Noordsy, D. L., B. Schwab, L. Fox, and R. E. Drake. Under review. The role of self-help programs in the rehabilitation of persons with mental illness and substance use disorders. *Community Mental Health Journal.*

Osher, F. C., and L. L. Kofoed. 1989. Treatment of patients with psychiatric and psychoactive substance abuse disorders. *Hospital and Community Psychiatry* 40:1025-30.

Test, M. A. 1992. The training in community living model: Delivering treatment and rehabilitation through a CTT. In *Handbook of psychiatric rehabilitation*, edited by R. Liberman. New York: Pergamon Press.

A comprehensive and integrated treatment team is crucial to working successfully with dual disorder patients.

15
The Treatment Team

Michael S. Levy, Ph.D.

THE TREATMENT OF THE CHRONICALLY MENTALLY ILL is a difficult enterprise. The same can be said for the treatment of patients afflicted with chemical addiction problems. When mentally ill individuals also experience an addictive disorder, treatment can be even more difficult and confused. For a number of reasons, appropriate treatment of the dual diagnosis patient requires the effort of a comprehensive treatment team. In this chapter, I will outline why an integrated treatment team is needed to successfully treat this difficult and often treatment-resistant patient population. I will then briefly discuss the necessary components of such a treatment team and demonstrate how our team worked together to better serve dual diagnosis patients.

THE NEED FOR A TREATMENT TEAM

Patients Require a Specialized Clinical Approach

Dual diagnosis patients require a specialized clinical approach in which both their emotional difficulties and their addiction to chemicals are treated simultaneously. There are a number of relationships between substance abuse and psychopathology (see Meyer 1986) that need to be understood to treat these patients effectively. In addition, the mind-altering properties of various substances can interact with a patient's baseline psychopathology in various ways, causing new problems and considerable diagnostic confusion. How to integrate this knowledge into one's clinical work to work successfully with these patients is a special skill that must be developed through training and experience.

All too often, dual diagnosis patients present at mental health centers or inpatient psychiatric facilities and are treated by providers who are not skilled in the treatment of addictive disorders. Such patients might also arrive at alcohol/drug treatment programs and obtain treatment from providers who lack knowledge about the care of psychiatric patients. Either scenario results in the dual diagnosis patient's receiving less than adequate care.

Dual diagnosis patients require a specialized psychotherapeutic intervention. Psychotherapy must concurrently attend to patients' psychological pain, their addiction to chemicals, and the many interrelationships between these two problems. Psychopharmacological intervention must also be sensitive to patients' addictive disorders, as some medications that are typically used may be unsuitable for such patients. It can never be forgotten that dual diagnosis patients habitually use chemicals to alter their consciousness and that such use, if not made a focus of treatment, will render successful treatment unlikely. At the same time, their psychiatric difficulties cannot be dismissed and must be treated as well. It is erroneous to think that the addiction can get treated in one agency and the emotional difficulties in another. While there are two (or more) problems, there is only one patient, and the entire patient must be treated holistically.

In summary, dual diagnosis patients are different from both primary psychiatric patients and addicts. Furthermore, a specialized form of treatment is indicated for these patients. If one agrees with this model, it then becomes obvious that any agency attempting to treat such patients must have staff who are knowledgeable about the unique treatment needs of dual diagnosis patients. A community which has both well-established and extensive mental health and addiction services still needs to develop a comprehensive dual diagnosis treatment team to meet the needs of these patients effectively. In fact, dual diagnosis patients have a number of unique features that make the development of a treatment team even more important, which I will now discuss.

Patients Are High Utilizers of Different Services

Dual diagnosis patients typically present themselves through a number of different treatment services. For example, some may frequently find themselves in a psychiatric emergency room because they feel out of control and in need of help. In fact, the psychiatric emergency room can become the main source of comfort and treatment for some patients. Other patients, after evaluation, may need to be hospitalized for stabilization due to their psychiatric fragilities. Others' route of entry into the mental health system will be through outpatient community mental health centers. Still other patients may find themselves in some kind of legal difficulty and will eventually find their way into some type of mental health treatment program through the court system. Fischer (1990) has shown that dual diagnosis patients have greater problems and receive more services than other subgroups of patients. Due to the varied presentations and needs of these patients, an entire system of treatment services must be available to meet the treatment requirements.

Dual diagnosis patients are also commonly resistant to treatment and do not want to follow providers' treatment recommendations. Quite commonly, patients admitted to our inpatient program quickly wanted to leave as soon as they began to feel better. This resulted in less than adequate discharge planning, and within a short time, they decompensated and presented to some other treatment service in need of help. Prior to discharge, we would routinely call the emergency room and other relevent treatment providers in our system to inform them of the status of such patients and to offer them our treatment recommendations. If the patient arrived there, providers would already know about the patient, which would help with disposition.

Dual diagnosis patients are frequent service utilizers. For example, substance abuse contributes to one-half of psychiatric emergencies in emergency rooms (Atkinson 1973; Trier and Levy 1969). As a result, these patients commonly come into contact with a number of different treatment programs. It is essential that expertise be available in all treatment agencies that could interact with these patients—from inpatient programs to every outpost in the community.

Diagnostic Dilemmas

Patients with emotional difficulties who also drink excessively or abuse other chemicals are difficult to diagnose. For example, a patient may present with paranoid delusions of a persecutory nature. This could be a manifestation of paranoid schizophrenia or a cocaine-induced psychosis. In a similar vein, a patient may experience marked depressive symptomatology, which could reflect a true depressive disorder. On the other hand, such feelings may be secondary to traumas to the self that can be caused by a lifestyle centered around drinking and chemical abuse. Loss of significant relationships, disruptions in living situations, and legal entanglements that frequently result from substance abuse problems can cause considerable depression as well. How the patient's coexisting psychopathology is understood has important treatment implications.

While thorough clinical interviewing and history taking—as well as allowing enough time for the patient's system to clear from the effects of ingested drugs—can help to ascertain a proper diagnosis, a true diagnosis can still be a challenge with these patients. Quite often, such patients are paranoid, do not trust treatment providers, and are hesitant to reveal themselves to others. Denial of substance use, which is quite common among substance abusers in general, can be further intensified in these patients because of their paranoia and mistrust of others. Such patients are frequently poor historians and are out of touch with their feelings, as in conditions like alexithymia (Krystal 1988).

In addition, the psychiatric conditions of patients with major mental illness frequently fluctuate. At times, patients are lucid, well oriented, and able to focus quite clearly. Other times, however, they become less organized, more internally preoccupied, and appear decompensated. While such a fluctuating clinical presentation can occur in mentally ill patients, the use of chemicals in and of themselves can be responsible for these patients' mood changes. In addition, chemical use can further exacerbate and react with these normal mood changes. In fact, in fragile individuals, even small amounts of mood-altering substances can greatly affect their mental state. As a result, it is hard to know a person's true baseline level of functioning and what treatment is needed.

To combat this problem, we established weekly treatment team meetings for the staff who work in the various programs in our system.

In these meetings, the staff discussed their confusion and different perspectives regarding patients and developed a comprehensive strategy to understand and treat patients. By learning from each other and working together, a greater understanding of the patient frequently emerged, along with a clearer diagnostic impression.

I am reminded of a schizophrenic and alcoholic man I worked with for four years who eventually was able to achieve sobriety. However, for the next two years I worked with him, he continued to have periods of extreme agitation and paranoia, which I could not understand. After numerous treatment team meetings that sensitized all staff to my confusion and what was occurring with this patient, the patient finally revealed to his community case manager, and eventually to me, that he had started using amphetamines during this period. This was responsible for all his decompensations.

Treatment Engagement Difficulties

Dual diagnosis patients can be difficult to engage in treatment. Psychiatric problems and problems with substance use are commonly denied, as is the overall need for treatment. As already mentioned, even when hospitalized such patients request premature discharges, which prevents them from engaging with inpatient staff. When these patients are seen as outpatients, frequent no-shows or cancellations are common because of substance use, psychiatric impairment, or both. Continued substance use will inevitably take control of their lives; following through with treatment contracts simply is not a priority.

While these situations are bad enough in and of themselves, treatment noncompliance and resistance may cause subtle (and sometimes not so subtle) negative feelings among staff, which will add to the difficulty in engaging such patients. For example, staff can become disenchanted with this patient population and not work as hard to foster working alliances with them. Staff can get angry with these patients, view them as being unmotivated for treatment, and give up on them. In a parallel way, the staff may feel out of control, resonating with the patient's own disorganized life. Early on in my training, I was once told by a supervisor that the biggest problem in the treatment of addicts—and dual diagnosis patients in particular—was countertransference. These patients can elicit powerful feelings, and, unless attended to, these feelings can destroy any effective treatment attempts. This was important advice and something that all treatment providers who work with these patients should heed.

Finally, the patient may have no interest in the treatment goal of abstinence, and thus treatment will not be offered unless the patient agrees to strive for abstinence. I think that denying treatment to patients because they are not ready to be abstinent does not make sense. Such patients must first discover a compelling reason to get sober before they can ever be expected to strive for abstinence. Treatment can be extremely useful despite a patient's continued use of substances (Kofoed et al. 1986; Levy 1993).

As a result of these patients' resistance to treatment and the countertransferential feelings that can arise towards them, it is important to have a range of programs available to meet their needs. Some patients may connect better to staff on an inpatient unit. Others may find an outpatient treatment relationship more comfortable. Even others may find solace in a less structured drop-in center and begin to form an important relationship with a staff member there. And because these patients can elicit such powerful negative feelings in treatment providers, it is important to have different agencies available to them. While staff in one program may be burned-out on a particular patient, staff in another program may be better able to effectively develop a working relationship with the individual. Over time, patients will enter and engage into treatment through many different channels. Consequently, having a full range of programs with expertise to treat these patients will help to counter the treatment engagement difficulties.

Different Levels of Care Are Required

Both psychiatric patients and patients who experience chemical addiction difficulties require different levels of care based upon their presenting symptomatology and what is required to help them reach their optimal level of functioning. Generally, levels of care for both populations range from inpatient treatment facilities, to day or evening treatment programs, to outpatient counseling, where individual, family, and group therapy are available. Less structured programs such as social clubs and drop-in centers may also be available for psychiatrically ill patients, as are case management services in which staff develop advocacy/counseling relationships with patients who require this additional support. Finally, for both of these patient populations, a range of residential services exists, from halfway house settings with a fair amount of structure to less structured rooming houses or apartment programs.

Dual diagnosis patients also require a range of services to meet their varied needs. Some will need to be hospitalized in order to be properly assessed and to determine the need for psychotropic medication. Others will require hospitalization because they become suicidal or homicidal under the influence. Still other patients will need the structure of a hospital to attain abstinence. After discharge or for other patients living in the community, involvement in day treatment programs and other outpatient facilities will be necessary to support their sobriety and psychiatric fragilities. Various types of residential programs will be necessary as well.

While it is tempting simply to use existing psychiatric and chemical dependency programs for these patients, these patients require a specialized psychotherapeutic intervention, as stated in the beginning of this chapter, in which their psychiatric difficulties and their addiction to chemicals are simultaneously addressed. In order to treat them appropriately, either new programs must be developed to meet their special needs or staff with such expertise can be hired in existing programs to develop new programs within particular agencies. However programming for this patient population occurs, a range of services must be available. In addition, treatment providers who work with these patients must work together as a team as these patients move back, forth, and between these different levels of care.

Dealing with the Unmotivated Patient

Before discussing how a treatment team for dual diagnosis patients works together, we must say a few words about working with the patient who continues to use substances or who is unmotivated for treatment. Certainly, among both the chemically dependent and the mentally ill, denial of problems (or of illness in general) is extremely common. Quite often, dual diagnosis patients do not want to become sober. They may also refuse to acknowledge that they have psychiatric difficulties.

While the overall treatment of noncompliant dual diagnosis

patients is beyond the scope of this chapter, an issue that needs to be addressed is how to provide for dual diagnosis patients who continue to use chemicals and, as a result, are homeless. Estimates suggest that from 10 to 20 percent of homeless persons are dually diagnosed (Tessler and Dennis 1989). Dual diagnosis patients are more apt to lose their residences because of substance abuse, disruptive behavior, and overall noncompliance with treatment (Belcher 1989; Benda and Dattalo 1988). Because of these patients' psychiatric fragilities, homelessness can be a particularly dangerous scenario. Homelessness can also result in patients "falling through the cracks" and never getting the treatment they so badly need.

While controversial, one approach to the patient who is, or becomes, homeless because of active substance abuse is the development of a "wet" shelter. This is a program where addicts and dual diagnosis patients can live if other housing options are unavailable because they are actively abusing alcohol or other drugs. Staff at our wet shelter are trained to work with dual diagnosis patients, and access to medical or psychiatric services is readily available. Patients are accepted as they are, but staff is present to encourage them to get involved in treatment to address their specific needs and refer them to appropriate treatment organizations if and when they are ready. Our wet shelter serves as a transitional environment where patients unable to tolerate either treatment or sobriety can be held loosely, yet tightly enough to protect them from the worst consequences of their behavior (Levy and Mann 1988). Thus, while patients may not formally be in treatment, they are informally, as they constantly interact with staff who are members of an overall treatment team. As Drake, Osher, and Wallach (1991) have noted, low-demand settings, such as a wet shelter, may at least reduce morbidity and allow the development of trusting relationships so that residents can be persuaded to participate in treatment and to strive for abstinence.

We once worked with a patient who repeatedly came to our attention through the court system (because of stealing or disturbing the peace). He typically presented as guarded, mistrustful, and internally preoccupied. Our task was to assess his competency to stand trial and/or criminal responsibility. While he acknowledged that he used some chemicals (he carried the diagnoses of alcohol dependence, cocaine abuse, marijuana dependence, and paranoid schizophrenia), he greatly minimized this and denied that his chemical use was a problem. He would quickly recompensate with neuroleptic medication and would then be returned to the court with treatment recommendations. Because his charges were not particularly serious, he was never sent to jail, nor was treatment strictly enforced. Within a short time, he would return to his pattern of using drugs and living on the streets.

During one hospitalization, it was decided that two staff members of our wet shelter would attempt to establish a relationship with the patient. Our hope was that the patient would at least connect with these individuals so that after discharge he might feel comfortable living at the shelter, which might make it easier for him to get involved in treatment. Over the next several years, the patient eventually became a "resident" of the shelter. Shelter staff accepted him as he was but also helped him understand how stopping chemical use could benefit him in the long run. While his use of alcohol and other drugs continued, it was considerably less than it had been, and the patient was able to maintain some limited periods of sobriety. His legal entanglements lessened, his hospitalizations became less frequent, and overall he was more socially connected.

The Treatment Team

As is probably now evident, in order for treatment providers to meet the needs of the dual diagnosis patient effectively, competence in conducting clinical work with this patient population must exist in all treatment programs where such a patient may be found. Programs specifically for dual diagnosis patients must be established, or programs for dual diagnosis patients must be developed within existing programs. Expertise in working with dual diagnosis patients must exist in psychiatric emergency rooms, inpatient facilities, community residences (such as halfway houses and apartment programs), partial hospitalization and day treatment programs, and outpatient mental health centers offering psychotherapy services. Social clubs and drop-in centers should also have staff with such proficiency, as should case management programs. In fact, in our system we had a separate case management team specifically designed to work with our dual diagnosis patients. Finally, to complete this network, a wet shelter should be developed to provide a holding umbrella for unmotivated patients.

As patients will inevitably move back and forth and between different programs, staff must work together to share their insights and concerns about particular patients. As previously noted, we held weekly staff meetings with all relevant treatment providers. Meetings were used to help clarify diagnosis, to aid in treatment planning, or to assist with discharge planning.

We once worked with a patient who had been attending a psychiatric day treatment program but who had been doing quite poorly. He was taking a variety of medications, was strongly suspected of compulsive drinking, and frequently expressed suicidal thoughts and complained of intense anxiety. Whenever he was hospitalized, he quickly recompensated and wanted to be discharged. This prevented us from finding out both what truly ailed him and how to help him. As an outgrowth of one treatment team meeting, staff at his day treatment program convinced the patient that he should remain at the hospital. While he was hospitalized, his medications could be tapered so that his psychiatric diagnosis could be ascertained and the true extent of his problem with alcohol thoroughly assessed. As a result of this hospitalization, we discovered (as did the patient) that the patient did have a serious problem with alcohol and that although he was schizophrenic and required some medication (thioridazine), he needed less than he had been taking. He was eventually discharged to a psychiatric halfway house where an important component of his treatment was to maintain his sobriety. His entire treatment team is now aware of the importance of attending to his addiction to alcohol in addition to his psychiatric difficulties. Without the coordinated effort of his treatment team, the patient never would have stayed in the hospital long enough to receive the help he needed.

Summary

Dual diagnosis patients are challenging, confusing, and frequently resistant to treatment. They require specialized care which is different from that of psychiatric patients and nonpsychiatrically impaired addicts. Treatment of the dual diagnosis patient requires the effort of an integrated treatment team who are knowledgeable about the special needs of such patients, who are skilled in conducting clinical work with them, and who are available in all treatment settings where dual diagnosis patients might be seen. Staff must work together, learn from each other, and support one another in order to treat this difficult patient population effectively.

References

Atkinson, R. M. 1973. Importance of alcohol and drug abuse in psychiatric emergencies. *California Medicine* 118:1-4.

Belcher, J. R. 1989. On becoming homeless: A study of chronically mentally ill persons. *Journal of Community Psychology* 17:173-85.

Benda, B. B., and P. Dattalo. 1988. Homelessness: Consequence of a crisis or a long-term process? *Hospital and Community Psychiatry* 39:884-86.

Drake, R. E., F. C. Osher, and M. A. Wallach. 1991. Homelessness and dual diagnosis. *American Psychologist* 46:1149-58.

Fischer, P. J. 1990. *Alcohol and drug abuse and mental health problems among homeless persons: A review of the literature, 1980-1990.* Rockville, MD: National Institute on Alcohol Abuse and Alcoholism and National Institute of Mental Health.

Kofoed, L., J. Kania, T. Walsh, and R. M. Atkinson. 1986. Outpatient treatment of patients with substance abuse and coexisting psychiatric disorders. *American Journal of Psychiatry* 143:867-72.

Krystal, H. 1988. *Integration and self-healing: Affect, trauma, alexithymia.* Hillsdale, N.J.: The Analytic Press.

Levy, M. 1993. Psychotherapy with dual diagnosis patients: Working with denial. *Journal of Substance Abuse Treatment* 10:499-504.

Levy, M. S., and D. W. Mann. 1988. The special treatment team: An inpatient approach to the mentally ill alcoholic patient. *Journal of Substance Abuse Treatment* 5:219-27.

Meyer, R. E. 1986. *Psychopathology and addictive disorders.* New York: The Guilford Press.

Tessler, R. C., and D. L. Dennis. 1989. *A synthesis of NIMH-funded research concerning persons who are homeless and mentally ill.* Rockville, MD: National Institute of Mental Health, Division of Education and Service System Liaison.

Trier, T. R., and R. J. Levy. 1969. Emergent, urgent, and elective admissions: Studies in a general hospital psychiatric emergency service. *Archives of General Psychiatry* 21:423-30.

Building on concepts of individualized treatment, clinicians, and programs can "retool" to cope with managed care and still maintain high-quality dual diagnosis treatment.

16
Managed Care and Dual Diagnosis

David Mee-Lee, M.D.

WITH THE HEALTH CARE INFLATION RATE RISING at two to three times the general inflation rate and the number of employees enrolled in managed care doubling over the past four years, treatment providers who hoped managed care would fade away are in for continuing disappointment. Cost containment, utilization management, accountability, and scrutiny of treatment will be increasing whether one works in the public or private sector.

Many health insurance companies, employers, and government funding agencies find addiction and mental illness difficult to understand and expensive to treat. As a result, they "unbundle" addiction and mental health benefits from other health benefits and contract with managed care organizations (MCOs) to ensure appropriate treatment and contain costs. For the therapist struggling to cope with the clinical complexities of dual diagnosis patients—who span the addiction and mental illness systems—herein lies an opportunity. Now, it may be difficult to imagine how anything to do with managed care could be an "opportunity," when the first generation, at least, of managed care has felt like the "just say no" generation of MCOs—no, you can't admit the patient into the hospital; no, you can't keep them there longer; no, we won't pay for any more therapy; and on and on. Nevertheless, the opportunity that managed care offers is better coordination of patients' addiction and mental health treatment. In traditional addiction and psychiatric programs, dual diagnosis patients frequently have their acute detoxification or psychiatric crisis addressed and reimbursed separately, with little coordination between the addiction and mental health treatment. But MCOs that are interested in quality (not just cost-containment) and working with treatment providers with an equal interest in cost-conscious quality care can reduce the human and financial cost associated with poor continuity and coordination of care through careful case management. Even the most conscientious therapist committed to close teamwork between the addiction and mental health providers invariably cannot track and monitor every dual diagnosis patient's addiction or mental health crisis. It may be some days or even weeks before the therapist catches up with the whereabouts of the dual diagnosis patient who has once again bounced around different mental health or addiction treatment providers.

What managed care can do is function as early-warning radar and alert the therapist of new crises or hospitalizations. This promotes continuity of care through proactive coordination of addiction and mental health services rather than reactive "catch-up" contact between the therapist and other treatment providers. Patients deserve proactive, holistic dual diagnosis treatment. The place to start is with a behavioral health biopsychosocial perspective endorsed by both the therapist and the managed care case manager.

Behavioral Health Biopsychosocial Perspective

The focus and attention on dual diagnosis as a term and as a separate group of patients who often fall through the gaps have been necessary and beneficial. Yet, viewed from another perspective, there is nothing unique about dual diagnosis patients if we see addiction as a biopsychosocial disorder in etiology, expression, and clinical presentation and treatment (Mee-Lee 1992).

In other words, comprehensive biopsychosocial assessment and holistic behavioral health treatment considers patients with both addiction and psychiatric problems (i.e., "dual diagnosis") just another subtype of addiction and mental health patients. This is not to undo or deny the increasing attention, knowledge, and expertise resulting in better care for dual diagnosis patients, but a behavioral health biopsychosocial perspective closes the gaps between addiction and mental health treatment. It reduces the polarization and separation of the two fields and places dual diagnosis patients under the one umbrella of holistic, integrated, comprehensive care. Now, instead of dual diagnosis patients being seen as not quite fitting into the addictions field or the mental health field, they fall fully within the behavioral health continuum of care.

MCOs, with their tight case management of this behavioral health biopsychosocial system, have the potential for facilitating well-monitored, nonfragmented dual diagnosis treatment. But addiction treatment providers are often frustrated. Why don't MCOs understand that our patients need more time, not less? Why do utilization managers want us to transfer the patient to a psychiatric unit if there is a psychiatric diagnosis involved when we feel we can treat dual diagnosis patients too?

Knowing that managed care is not going away anytime soon, we need to develop a better working relationship to preserve the therapist's time, energy, and sanity, as well as to protect the dual diagnosis patient's access to treatment. The first step is to know what managed care is and wants.

What Managed Care Is Looking For

Managed care is a system that integrates both how care is provided and how it is paid for. This is achieved by a variety of methods: (1) health maintenance organizations (HMOs) and preferred provider organizations (PPOs), which save money by choosing only a limited number of providers and giving incentives to ensure that patients see only those providers in this limited network; (2) utilization review and quality controls, which influence the treatment decisions of clinicians and patients; and (3) various payment systems, such as capitation and diagnosis-related groups (DRGs) payment, which expect the treatment provider to take on some financial risk (Iglehart 1992). To get a better understanding of why treatment providers have often experienced endless battles with managed care, comparing what "they" want us to give with what "we" have traditionally given can be quite illuminating.

TABLE 16.1

MANAGED CARE VS. TRADITIONAL TREATMENT: A COMPARISON

Managed care	*Traditional treatment providers*
1. Least intensive level of treatment appropriate to patient's severity of illness, within a continuum of care	1. Inpatient care predominates; other levels of care to match patient's severity of illness less developed
2. Clinically driven treatment	2. Program-driven treatment
3. Flexible lengths of stay	3. Fixed length of stay and/or little use of flexible levels of care
4. Individualized treatment plans	4. Standardized, sometimes even preprinted, plans
5. Good outcome data	5. Minimal outcome studies or appeals to a tradition of care and caring

While it is true that many treatment providers have moved beyond the right-hand column of table 16.1, there are still many who, in practice and in their hearts, are not at all convinced that they need to change. The spiraling health care inflation rate and burgeoning national deficit, along with the increasingly loud cries for health care reform, make further change inevitable.

COPING WITH MANAGED CARE: INDIVIDUALIZED TREATMENT FOR DUAL DIAGNOSIS PATIENTS

For many treatment providers, coping with managed care has meant playing games with the utilization reviewers: adding psychiatric diagnoses to increase the severity of the patient; embellishing suicidal or other severe aspects of the history—even if not a current concern—to eke out a few more days of care; and using certain trigger words known to elicit authorization of more care.

In love and war it may seem fair to use whatever information you have to gain an advantage, and often it has felt like a war. However, this kind of coping is temporary and demoralizing. This is especially so when individualized treatment has too often meant essentially doing what the MCO tells you to do—discharge the patient now, or keep the patient but don't expect any further payment.

If treatment providers are truly to cope with managed care and regain the initiative of the clinician to determine treatment, we must first be convinced that changing is the right thing to do. We cannot view ourselves as helpless victims compromising all we've ever believed in. For too long, treatment providers have behaved like a wealthy supermarket shopper or credit card user for whom money was no object—selecting from the shelves whatever seemed desirable, approaching the checkout counter without the slightest concern for the amount rung up, and paying with a card, not knowing what it cost or even where the money came from.

Health insurance coverage or Medicaid/Medicare funding has lulled therapists into the same lack of awareness and concern for costs as the shopper at the checkout counter—ordering tests, perpetuating program-driven treatment, and lengthening days or units of service without knowing what tests cost or how the health care bill was being paid for. Until therapists consider costs and manage them as conscientiously as if we were paying the bill ourselves, we will continue to struggle with managed care and react like some spoiled rich kid who has suddenly lost the use of his or her credit card.

When we begin to practice individualized care as carefully as cost-conscious supermarket shoppers, our energies can blossom into creative treatments instead of getting bogged down in reactive conflicts with MCOs. Our goal should be to design treatment with the same concern we would have if a patient had mortgaged his house and entrusted us with his last $5,000 for care. Then we will have begun the attitude changes necessary to cope productively with managed care.

So what are the steps we can take to protect access to quality care for our dual diagnosis patients? How can treatment providers design and decide treatment instead of abdicating the authority and authorization of care to a utilization reviewer at the end of a telephone line?

By combining our knowledge of what managed care is looking for with a heightened awareness that we need to be efficient and effective, treatment providers can regain the initiative in dual diagnosis treatment. Clinically driven treatment, not cost- or program-driven treatment, is the path to coping with managed care. Careful assessment is the next step down that path towards cost-conscious, individualized treatment.

Multidimensional Assessment

In the not-too-distant past, diagnosis alone defined treatment. If a patient met criteria for alcohol or some other drug addiction, there was basically one treatment model—twenty-eight days of inpatient, Twelve Step-based program treatment. Likewise, if a patient carried a psychiatric diagnosis, he or she was admitted to the psychiatric unit, placed on medication and, if fortunate, involved in a therapeutic milieu. The mental health issues were minimized or ignored in the addiction program and the addiction issues were minimized or ignored in the psychiatric program.

But to protect access to quality treatment and conserve health care resources, providers and payers must increasingly focus on matching patients to levels of care and treatment modalities. Matching dual diagnosis patients to the most efficient intensity of service all starts with assessment of the severity of the addiction and psychiatric problems in addition to the verification of the diagnosis.

Cost-conscious individualized treatment involves placement in a level of care, movement through a continuum (as seamless as possible), and specific matching to a variety of treatment modalities in all the levels of care. The ongoing process starts with careful assessment of the severity of illness (SI) and a plan whose progress is continually reassessed. Modification of the problems and treatment plan are made as necessary. (See figure 16.1.)

COST-CONSCIOUS INDIVIDUALIZED TREATMENT

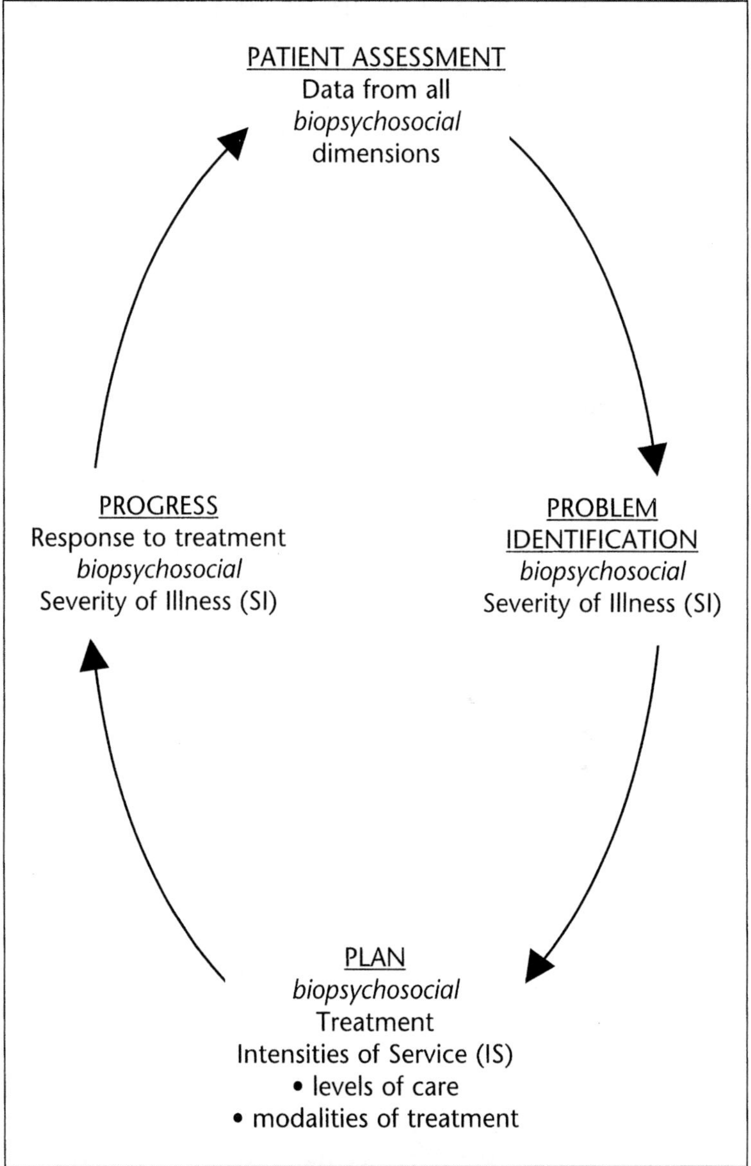

FIGURE 16.1

A behavioral health biopsychosocial perspective of addiction and mental disorders allows for a single multidimensional assessment. This assessment encompasses all of the clinically relevant issues that can ensure comprehensive treatment while at the same time ensuring direct, efficient care. While not everyone agrees on what dimensions should be assessed and how to identify and measure them, four approaches represent similar efforts to produce a useful multidimensional assessment. Table 16.2 lists the assessment dimensions of the Addiction Severity Index (ASI) (McLellan et al. 1980); the Recovery Attitude and Treatment Evaluator (RAATE) (Mee-Lee 1988); the Drug Use Screening Inventory (DUSI) (Tarter 1990); and the Patient Placement Criteria for Psychoactive Substance Use Disorders—American Society of Addiction Medicine (ASAM) (Hoffmann et al. 1991).

By assessing the severity of problems in each area of a multidimensional assessment, the therapist can develop a severity profile that can guide not only what level of care in which to place a patient, but also focus the treatment plan on specific modalities of treatment to match the patient's type and severity of problems.

Levels of Care and Modalities of Treatment

To be able to move away from what the traditional treatment provider offers toward what managed care and cost-conscious, individualized treatment requires, we must take another step: namely, to define the behavioral health biopsychosocial treatment to which the patient's SI will be matched. This requires a comprehensive system of levels of care or settings and a range of treatment modalities within those levels and continuum of care.

An Institute of Medicine report defines four levels in the continuum of care: inpatient, residential, intermediate and outpatient (Institute of Medicine 1990, pp. 72-73). The ASAM Patient Placement Criteria also describe four levels of care but named them to be more descriptive of the intensity of service (IS) provided: Level I—Outpatient Treatment; Level II—Intensive Outpatient/Partial Hospitalization; Level III—Medically Monitored Intensive Inpatient Treatment; Level IV—Medically Managed Intensive Inpatient Treatment (Hoffmann et al. 1991, p. 11).

Table 16.2

Four Approaches to Multidimensional Assessment

ASI	*RAATE*
1. Medical Status 2. Employment/Support Status 3. Drug/Alcohol Use 4. Legal Status 5. Family/Social Relationships 6. Psychological Status	1. Resistance to Treatment 2. Resistance to Continuing Care 3. Acuity of Biomedical Problems 4. Acuity of Psychiatric Problems 5. Extent to Which Social/Family Problems Unsupportive to Recovery
DUSI	***ASAM***
1. Substance Abuse 2. Psychiatric Disorder 3. Behavior Patterns 4. Family System 5. School Adjustment 6. Work 7. Social Competence 8. Peer Relationships 9. Health 10. Recreation and Pastimes	1. Acute Intoxication and/or Withdrawal Potential 2. Biomedical Conditions and Complications 3. Emotional/Behavioral Conditions and Complications 4. Treatment Acceptance/Resistance 5. Relapse Potential 6. Recovery Environment

While these levels of care describe addiction treatment, the same continuum of care could describe a behavioral health system of care that would serve dual diagnosis patients well. In fact, if we are truly to provide individualized treatment in as efficient a way as possible, the "program" will increasingly take on the characteristics of a single system of addiction and mental health care combined under one behavioral health administration and treatment team. The dual diagnosis patient then accesses whatever levels of care are needed and is matched with a variety of modalities of treatment, groups, and other treatment experiences.

The range of treatment modalities depends on the variety of theoretical models integrated in the behavioral health continuum of care. The Institute of Medicine report describes modalities as "the specific activities that are used to relieve symptoms or to induce behavior change" and notes that "the content of treatment is usually referred to as the technique, method, procedure, or modality" (Institute of Medicine 1990, p. 73).

Biomedical modalities focus on improved detoxification regimens, anticraving medication, antagonist medication, methadone treatment, and psychotropic medication for the coexisting psychiatric diagnosis. Psychological treatments span the range from addictions counseling to psychodynamic and cognitive-behavioral treatment modalities, including insight-oriented psychotherapy, skill-building, and behavioral self-control training.

In the sociocultural dimension, treatment modalities include vocational assistance and support, family therapy and education, therapeutic communities, and various crisis outreach and emergency services. In fact, many modalities span more than one dimension, such as social skills training, relapse prevention techniques, and self-help, or mutual-help, programs.

Matching patients to treatment means matching SI with IS. For example, a twenty-two-year-old single mother who was addicted to methamphetamine ("ice") and who was depressed with suicidal thoughts presented for evaluation. She was living with a drug-using drug dealer and depended on him for both emotional and addiction needs.

Her withdrawal and biomedical severity did not need medical

detoxification and hospital level of care. But her psychiatric severity, relapse potential, and toxic recovery environment all warranted placement in a medically monitored, intensive inpatient (residential) program. This patient's multidimensional, biopsychosocial assessment highlighted high-severity assessment areas that helped determine correct placement in a level of care and also directed a comprehensive specific treatment plan.

Her individualized problem list and treatment plan addressed her emotional dependency needs, her relapse potential if she continued living with the drug dealer, and practical steps to move into a safer environment. This patient was unlikely to stay sober simply by not using and going to Alcoholics Anonymous meetings. Managed care, along with other influences, is pushing us to sharpen the focus of our treatment.

Implications for Clinicians, Programs, Payers, and Policy

In the era of managed care, providing cost-conscious dual diagnosis treatment requires a "retooling" of the addiction and mental health systems. The clinician competent to provide dual diagnosis treatment will be well trained in addiction and psychiatric theories, modalities of treatment, and assessment and diagnostic skills. He or she will be sufficiently confident professionally so that interdisciplinary teamwork will be assertive, respectful, and routine. His or her treatment plans will be individualized, not rote or "rubber-stamped," and case management will be expeditious and continuous.

Cost-conscious behavioral health dual diagnosis treatment programs will structure broad continuums of overlapping levels of addiction and psychiatric care. Within these levels of care, patients will stay for only the length of time their severity and progress warrant. Programs will provide a wider variety of modalities of treatment from all addiction and psychiatric schools of thought and develop expanded services to fill in gaps in current services. Innovative program structures such as "residential outpatient" will piece together services and settings to give patients only the intensity of service they individually need.

Savvy administrators and payers of care will recognize the wisdom of funding all levels of care to allow continuity and efficiency of care. With increased incentives for less costly care and thorough case management, patients will have access to a wider variety of addiction, mental health, and social services. Because dual diagnosis patients so frequently cross back and forth over the public-private sector line, administrators will see the need for better integration of services in a patient-focused spectrum of care.

Clinicians, payers, programs, and policymakers will continuously seek to prevent duplication of services, develop common clinically based criteria and guidelines, and improve services based on outcomes research and quality-improvement activities.

Managed care, rightly used, can help make the future a current reality. MCOs have the ability to use case management for better tracking of patients and integration of treatment services and to flex reimbursement and fund alternative settings and services. By combining the creativity of cost-conscious treatment providers with the individual case management techniques of managed care, we have an opportunity to improve dual diagnosis treatment.

Conclusion

The addiction and mental health treatment systems have for too long been polarized, allowing dual diagnosis patients to fall through the gaps. The expansion of managed care and our negative reactions to that expansion can add another dimension to the polarization that already exists. But patients will only suffer more again.

Dual diagnosis patients need no more turf battles and intersystem fragmentation. What they do need are for therapists and utilization management professionals, administrators and clinicians, bureaucracies and grass-roots advocates, to work together. By preserving all that is good in treatment—while innovating to combine this with all that is good in managed care—we can and should create better care for dual diagnosis patients. The cost of continued polarization, in human and financial terms, can only be unmanageable.

References

Hoffmann, N. G., J. A. Halikas, D. Mee-Lee, and R. D. Weedman. 1991. *Patient placement criteria for the treatment of psychoactive substance use disorders.* Washington, D.C.: American Society of Addiction Medicine.

Iglehart, J. K. 1992. Health policy report: The American health care system—Managed care. *New England Journal of Medicine* 327:742-47.

Institute of Medicine. 1990. *Broadening the base of treatment for alcohol problems.* Washington, D.C.: National Academy Press.

McLellan, A. T., L. Luborksy, G. E. Woody, and C. P. O'Brien. 1980. An improved evaluation instrument for substance abuse patients: The addiction severity index. *Journal of Nervous and Mental Disease* 168:26-33.

Mee-Lee, D. 1988. An instrument for treatment progress and matching: The Recovery Attitude and Treatment Evaluator (RAATE). *Journal of Substance Abuse Treatment* 5:183-86.

Mee-Lee, D. 1992 (March/April). Dual diagnosis and the ASAM patient placement criteria. *The Counselor,* 14-17.

Tarter, R. 1990. Evaluation and treatment of adolescent substance abuse: A decision tree method. *American Journal of Drug and Alcohol Abuse* 16:1-46.

Index

Other titles of professional interest...

Ethics for Addiction Professionals

by LeClair Bissell, M.D., N.C.A.C. II, and James E. Royce, S.J., Ph.D.

The first two recipients of the Marty Mann award combine practical expertise, common sense, and careful analysis of the world of addiction professionals and their clients in this revised version of the classic ethics guide. The new edition includes a close look at the ethical questions posed by the current crisis in health care costs, dually diagnosed clients, and sexual abuse of clients. Bibliographies and references have been updated.
Order No. 5028

Dual Disorders

Counseling Clients with Chemical Dependency and Mental Illness

by Dennis C. Daley, M.S.W., Howard Moss, M.D., and Frances Campbell, M.S.N., C.S.

A practical, must-read resource for mental health and chemical dependency counselors. *Dual Disorders* focuses on educational, cognitive, and behavioral interventions for clients and families affected by both psychiatric illness and chemical addiction. A comprehensive overview for the working counselor.
Order No. 5023
